MW01518357

Wisdom of THE ALL

A step-by-step guide into Love

Laura Saltman

SAVAAH
MEDIA

Published by Savaah Media
Boca Raton, FL
USA
www.laurasaltman.com
Contact publisher for bulk orders and permission requests.

Cover and interior book design & formatting by
Leesa Ellis of 3 ferns books ⚜⟶ *www.3fernsbooks.com*
Cover illustration by Almir Gusić

The information and opinions expressed here are believed to be accurate based on the best judgement available to the author. This book is intended to be educational, as a means to guide you on your spiritual journey. The author of this book does not dispense medical advice or prescribe the use of any technique as a form of treatment for physical, emotional or medical problems without the advice of a physician or medical professional. In the event you use any of the information in this book for yourself, the author and the publisher assume no responsibility for your actions.

Printed in the United States of America.

ISBN: 978-1-948443-07-4
eISBN: 978-1-948443-08-1

TABLE OF CONTENTS

To Brenner

The One who taught me unconditional love.

What is salvation? I do not know. Tell me that I may understand.

Salvation is recognizing within you the power to transform and heal thoughts which do not serve the soul. Any thought emanating from pain and upheaval. Attack thoughts and unkind words. These are falsities and illusions of self. You are soul and only soul.

What is a body for then, dear All?

To learn to think with the mind of Love.

And how long does that take dear All?

All of your life and lifetimes.

Foreword by Laura

Follow the 'rules' and you follow the ego.
Follow the Love and you follow truth.

− The All

hy am I writing my own foreword? Because I can. Because I no longer follow the rules that society has set in place for the "right" way to do something. I quit following ego and started following Love implicitly, living life on my own terms. I let my soul guide me and not my human self with all its limitations and false beliefs.

Even though this book has my name on it, the words were a gift to me. As much as I am its writer, I am more a translator of information. The contents came from a separate part of me; a divine part that lives inside of all of us. Getting to the discovery of who you truly are and what lives inside you is a quest we each take individually. Everyone has their own set of endless twists and turns for finding ultimate truth.

What is truth? You are Love. It's simple, yet complex. Love is our true being. It is not romantic or platonic or familial love. It is essence. An essence inside all which calls to you as you go about each day - to be. To be is to love everyone, enjoy everything, share and care for yourself and everyone else.

Love has many names. Words used to describe being such as God, Source, Universe, Divine Mind, Allah, Elohim, Consciousness, Elevated Soul or Oneness. The list is quite long and every One (another name we use) decides on their version of it. Here in this book, we are using the term 'The All' or just 'All', as it had been part of my soul contract to create this; a life blueprint set long before "Laura" came to be.

So now you know truth, but putting it into practice and finding belief, unwavering all out belief is a journey, an ongoing quest to enlightenment; the most difficult adventure you take. It doesn't stop just because you read a book, found spirituality, meditate daily or know Law of Attraction. It's an undoing process where you find out who you are every single day through endless opportunities for expansion. Choice is the gift we have each been given on Earth to discover ourselves. Every day you make a choice between love or fear (ego) and follow the path that choice leads you on.

When you actually begin to consciously pay attention to the world around you through the eyes of the soul or cocreation with All, you will find clues everywhere. Books, memes, poetry, animal messengers, signs and symbols. Love is all around us, guiding us, if only would we notice it. Fear keeps it hidden (although it's always available to see) and love makes it known.

To say my own personal journey to recognition of Love's presence has been an uphill battle would be an understatement. It's been a brutal climb that has brought me to the brink of pain, but also to the highest of joy. Unraveling the mystery of life and uncovering the "amnesia of the soul," which keeps us stuck in our falsities, was an arduous process that I fought long and hard through for many years until one day it finally clicked; or so I thought. Because even when I believed I had reached the top of the mountain (salvation), I realized there was infinitely more to discover and learn. It's the process of expansion each and every one of us is moving through here on Earth. Always be evolving. Growth is our goal.

You will find during the reading (or listening) of this book that I wavered many, many times from my path of belief. Even as the words flowed in with the most eloquent explanations of divinity, I still found myself like a wild stallion, bucking back and forth from love into fear. Just when I felt confident that I had this whole 'Universe thing' figured out and knew what it meant to be Love (Divine), something or someone would trip me back into fear. Even writing with 'The All' as my coauthor didn't keep me convinced that I was being given the ultimate guide to life and how we could be living it.

The ego's job is to keep you stuck and questioning all of your life. Like a nagging voice you can't quite get rid of, each day reminding you of failure and falsity. Because my personal life stalled and nothing was changing in my career goals, I was beyond frustrated even as I wrote sometimes. I often wanted to give up, stop listening, writing and asking questions but something always called me back to these pages. You may find your journey very similar to mine. The ups and downs, the heavy shadow of fear and disappointment which follows you everywhere you go as you hold on to your pain, frustration and disbelief with a tight grasp.

The process of awakening to Love is like peeling an onion; the closer you get to the center, the more truth is discovered and accepted within you. What you read or write is based upon your level in the shedding of limited thinking. Though I call myself a channel, I have simply peeled away the layers of my self (metaphorically) to allow an instant connection to my Spirit self. You are no different than me. In fact, we are One mind experiencing itself deliberately differently. What I have chosen to uncover is different than what someone else does. So where we are in our remembering of who we are is our own onion to peel.

My voyage to awakening began (or so I thought) around age 21, just after college. I was someone who believed in an afterlife, and I began to experience sensations and feelings of those who had crossed over. I gave very little time or attention to it, though; too busy in my Hollywood career goals to care until I started realizing, somewhere in my late thirties, that I had a sixth sense that most others seemed to not have. I could sense energy and spirits, and began to hear a voice in my head different than my own. It was my first clue I might be psychic or a medium. It was not the discovery of Love just yet, but mere clues to a life beyond here.

It wasn't until my brother, Jason, died of cancer in 2013, that I found myself not just questioning life, but ready to go seeking answers to it and to what my "gift" really was. I began working with mediums and psychics, taking courses on how to unlock my intuition. Then, after my dad died from suicide in the summer of 2015, I began hearing that voice inside of me loud and clear. There was something inside beckoning to remind me of who I truly was.

What brought me out of my spiritual slumber was my dad's and brother's shocking deaths. I was by far at the darkest point of my entire life, and so I went looking for help. For most of us, weathering the worst storms, the harshest hills and the saddest losses are when we finally go seeking light. I had hit rock bottom and was ready to peel my onion to find what ticked within, to find connection in some way to a source beyond myself, to ask why and to find the help I needed.

First, I tried grief counseling, which didn't seem to ease my sorrow. Because of my sixth sense, and knowing there was more to this life (and the afterlife), being in my grief group with attendees who didn't hold that same belief left me feeling lonely and confused. So that's when I decided to become a student of the Divine. I read books, listened to audio recordings, worked with a spiritual life coach, learned how to meditate (and became an instructor), devoured content on energy healing and, most importantly, began to write my books, which started out as personal journals and became what they are today, *Wisdom of The All*.

What I unearthed through the reading and writing of my first three *The All* books (*The All of Everything, The All of The All, The All That Is*) is that we are always guided throughout life whether we know or sense it or not. Our Spirit teams, made up of guides, angels (hierarchal souls) and our own soul, offers us signs, messages, guided thoughts and inspiration throughout our entire existence. Whether we notice these divine moments or not had been chosen before we decided to jump in to a particular life. Most people are living unconsciously in a way chosen by them, for them. My choice (as soul) was to awaken through a torrential storm and rise from the ashes an accomplished writer and speaker. With limited foresight (as the human part of me did most of my thinking) it took me a while to 'get over myself' and become aware of truth.

> 66 *You can't awaken those who do not wish to be awoken.* 99
>
> – The All of Everything

After I wrote and published my first book, *The All of Everything, a Spiritual Guide to Inner World Domination*, I felt as if I was on top of the world and nothing could bring me down. I thought the whole world was going to join me on my discovery of the Universe and all its mysteries and complexities. I thought I had something so magical, unique and different; important information that very few people knew about, and that I was going to be a messiah leading those who are suffering through the dark forest and into the light. So I worked overtime to awaken others believing I was enlightened. (Hint – I wasn't).

As I posted content online, wrote blogs and dedicated myself to sharing my books, I found an audience of very few, and even the ones who did follow me were not that intent on becoming enlightened, which only frustrated me more. I was angry, confused and sad that I couldn't shake the world awake. Ego had me trapped, big time, while my soul knew precisely what we were doing to keep me on track in my discovery of truth.

When it came time to finish this book, after reading it and rereading it over and over again and looking back at everything that occurred in my life while it was being created, I finally understood the reasoning behind all of it. Every drop of the life I was living was so that I could arrive at a level of belief that was necessary to help others on their journey. It all made sense. I needed the climb. Unshakeable faith is something you cannot find unless you climb the mountain, fall a few times, get back up again and realize what it took to make a successful trek - experience. Experience is the great teacher.

As you read or listen, you will find my irrational mind bouncing back and forth into fear. I couldn't quite stay connected to truth. It arrived and it left. Amnesia took over constantly, despite my having received divine wisdom and believing I was enlightened. What I can finally now understand after getting through the book (with my ego in check) was that none of this is easy for anyone. We all have forces needing balance – ego vs. soul.

The good news is that we have that proof all around us of our divine nature because the laws of the Universe are actually no secret. They are deliberately placed in lyrics of songs, poems, movie plots and millions of sacred texts, journals and, of course, books like these. They exist in the world as a roadmap or guidepost to enlightened thinking. We just don't access our internal map nearly often enough to catch sight of them, and even when we do, we go right back to our amnesia the minute a hiccup occurs. A simple problem sends us over a proverbial cliff and into darkness over and over again. It took a fall down a staircase in my home, during the writing of this book, to shake me awake to my own egoic way of thinking and get a handle on hidden and conscious fears.

After some deep spiritual work to regain my balance, after having been knocked on my behind (literally), I began to recognize through these All books that I wasn't alone in my awakening. I didn't have some magic secret. I was joining hundreds of thousands, and perhaps millions, of enlightening minds (and more to come) who are discovering what we already know inside of us, hidden by layers of conditioned thinking brought upon by collective minds joined together as One. We are a merry choir of voices with some singing solo parts and others left in the back. Yet all are part of one group joined together in harmony.

Love/All is inside of you, too, waiting to be uncovered if only you would listen. That's the miracle you are in store for if you just stay in practice with all the principles presented in our book. The work starts the minute you pick it up and doesn't end, ever. Life keeps teaching you that you don't know it all. You have so much more to learn, and with every day comes a chance to discover yourself over and over again. Not just what you want to be, but who you are. You are divine. You are Love, but you are here to remember it for yourself. Just as the soul beneath had planned for you all along.

Now let's jump at this adventure together. I promise if you are willing it will be a worthwhile endeavor like never before. You are the designer, decorator and creator of your circumstances and the tool you have at the ready is the mind of Love/All.

Preface

What if I told you that right here, right now you could fix your life. Make it work the way you want it to. If there was a secret formula to achieve success, would you use it or would you toss it away?

There *is* a secret trick; a code of conduct for life that all but guarantees success both personally and professionally if you are able to use it. What makes you able to use the code? A willingness.

A willingness to change is your superpower. A willingness to remember you are a soul inside of a body, not the other way around. You are divine Love expressing itself as you.

Waking up is not an easy process. Enlightenment is a difficult endeavor which requires your full-time attention. Your ego will trap you, ensnaring you in its clutches as often as possible. It will not let go of you until its needs are met or you release its clutches from your mind.

> **❝** *I am divine love, divine light. Let no ego thought rule my thinking as I guide myself back to truth.* **❞**

The words you use are the words of Love. They have energy, and when used in conjunction with emotion, emit a frequency which tells the Universe, "*I am ready for my intentions to manifest in physical form.*"

Be mindful of ego's tricks as you move through these pages. It is designed to enlighten you, but ego may seek to enrage you, as well. Just keep in mind that the one who questions is the one who needs the most reminding. It takes time and dedicated practice to grow your soul and gain momentum.

Anyone who tells you their life is perfect isn't being truthful with themselves. None of us are here leading perfect lives because we are not meant to be. If you were, then the point of being here would be useless. You are here to grow, to learn, to evolve.

Those of us who are spiritual 'teachers' are just ahead of the curve, but certainly face challenges, setbacks and struggles like everyone else. I've written and published four books directly from the Source; universal laws spelled out so simply that anyone can understand them, but I can readily admit that even though I have been given the keys to the kingdom, I still fumble with the lock. It's why I continue to write books, to speak with clients and give talks around the world; I need to be reminded consistently of our beingness (divine nature), too.

Right here, right now, none of us are masters of our domain, i.e. our own body and mind. Masters are those who have lived many, many hundreds of thousands of lifetimes (if not more) and are sure of who they are and who live in metaphysical form alongside of us to help us to grow. They are our cheerleaders, not our brethren in body form. They are proud and honored to be our helpers, if only we would ask. That is how I wrote my *All* books. I asked. They answered.

I'm going to take you on a journey within the pages of this book using those cheerleaders as my scribes and cowriters. It's a feat that any of us are capable of handling, yet not many are at the level of enlightenment which allows for immediate connection, as I have managed to create. I believe so much in the power of our Oneness that my channel flows free and clear. I listen and create instantaneously. The words I use are my words and *our* words, the words of the energy from which we all come, Love.

As we go along in this book you will find that I speak as both myself (Laura) and the collective (God/Source/Universe/All or whatever word is most appropriate to you). I listen to the words in my head, and some come from the mind of Love and others from the mind of myself as Laura. You will hear both "we" and "I" throughout the pages, and this is done quite purposefully. Although it can be quite jarring at first and not the 'norm' as a reader (or an author), it is upon all readers of the material to discern which of the minds I am speaking with as I write. A simple asking is sufficient to reveal an answer.

❝ *Who is speaking right now? Divine Mind or Laura?* ❞

As you go along, it will become more obvious who is speaking; "We" (Divine Mind) or "I" (Laura). Go with the flow and allow the soul to guide you as you read our book.

As in my first three *All* books, a conversation written as a Q & A, there may be times when I ask questions, and this is because as Laura I trust this voice the most. Informational flow is stopped whenever we are vibrating fear or anger. Because I had it as part of a soul contract to write these books, I was able to gain answers even when I was struggling with fear, but I had to ask in order to receive. If a subject did not come to me freely as I wrote, this was how I gained the truth when fear was present.

The battle inside the mind is the toughest war to win, which is why as much I wanted to remove some of my more embarrassing ranting and self-pity moments (and there are a lot), I kept them in this book to help others. My journey is your journey, just with a different cast of characters and plot points.

My questions are repetitive because the evidence to Love (courtesy of ego) is strong. It takes a long time to recognize what is truth when all you see is chaos or corruption. The design of the Universe is to throw us red herrings, contradictions and curve balls. This is on purpose to keep us on our toes at the same time we arrive into knowing. Why be here if you already know how the system works?

It has taken me years to grow to a point where I may even write these books, and more to own their truth. They are presented to you in a manner allowing your own skepticism to take hold. This is the nature of enlightenment. To question everything. All of it. Every step in the march toward belief (and true knowing) is a notch on the enlightenment clock. It ticks by every time you open a window to the soul and stops when you close it. Your clock may be different than mine because we are each in our own individual places, which have been chosen by us to grow our soul (as we have expressed in our desire to do so).

I am honored to present this material to you, and whoever is accepting of a new path is immediately ready to shine. Each chapter will serve to reveal a new step into Love. Our journey begins right here. Welcome All.

Introduction

Dear All,
As we seek to inform our readers of our divineness, let us look upon
the laws of the Universe and draw upon our beliefs which shape our
lives. Let all understand that which is both true and untrue so that we
may design a life of grandiosity always.

Rules

To understand the rules of the Universe you must first understand what is holding you back from expressing yourself as Divine Love. Here on Earth we coined it 'belief.' Belief is what drives the boat, so to speak. It is how you manifest the reality you see in front of you. Whatever you believe is what you become. Our beliefs come not only from the individual, but also from the collective. So whatever you see is a direct reflection of One mind. One mind is both you and we. It is all of us together as one cohesive collaborator (Love), and none of us.

To explain the meaning of "none of us" takes some getting used to. It allows for the fact that we are all beings of light, and form only when we separate – i.e. see ourselves as something other than Love. When we do this, our body is the form we take as individual souls (on Earth).

A body on Earth is different from bodies on other planets and places. Similarities do exist, but are too numerous to unveil here, and so we keep our conversation short on this topic as most minds are still too young on planet Earth to accept such a radical notion. This does not mean you should not investigate it further, only that as healers we seek only to inform and enlighten, and not receiving more information than is presently needed helps us to remember who we are. Too much milk spoils the soul.

Our Oneness is expressed through our actions, and though we do not know this is happening, it is. We are acknowledging divine presence by the simple fact that we are living and breathing. So, when you get up in the morning, take a moment to connect to the Love which you are.

> *❝I am a divine soul expressing itself through the body.
> I remember our Oneness and go about each day
> as one being, blessing my brothers and sisters
> and knowing only Love is real and true.❞*

In order to change, we must accept Love into our hearts and minds at all times. That means we must pay attention to our signs and messages at every turn. Love is all around you, guiding you, if only you would pay attention. What holds us back from expressing ourselves with Love always is our core belief systems made manifest as society has dictated them to be. These include the following beliefs which are in fact limiting beliefs. They keep us trapped in our ego and are designed to skew our thinking so we don't create a joyful life, but rather a confusing and conflicted one.

Below you will find both the limiting belief (as has been dictated by society) and the truth behind that belief (as had been expressed to me through the self via Divine Mind).

Limiting Beliefs

I AM NOT ENOUGH

You are absolutely enough and you are perfect exactly as you are.

I AM NOT WORTHY

You are not only worthy, you already are that which you say you wish to be. Worth is defined within and not by society and its members. You are worthy because you exist not based on ideas placed in mind through limitations.

I AM SICK

A body is healthy when a mind is healthy. A mind is healthy when a belief about anything is transformed back to Love. The mind is a learning device and will show you what is being thought on both consciously and unconsciously.

I AM POOR AND UNABLE TO ATTRACT FINANCIAL ABUNDANCE

You are boundless energy, therefore are you able to attract more boundless energy be it dollar bills or donkeys.

GOD IS MY SOURCE

This is a fallacy populated by new age thinkers and healers who are not yet enlightened enough to understand the concept that you are the energy of the Universe, and together we cocreate an experience of abundance. We are the source - TWOgether. You are Source. I am Source. We are Source.

THERE IS ONLY ONE RELIGION WHICH IS ACCURATE AND TRUE

There is no one religion or theology which seeks to re-inform the unenlightened. Therefore, any path to know "God" is practical as long as knowing God does not mean an angry, hateful, vengeful God.

I AM MY BODY

You are your mind, not the body. A reflective image will show you who you are at the core, if only you could stop for a minute and see through the illusion. You are who you choose to identify yourself with, and this identity is chosen for you, by you to remind you of your divine nature. One should never reveal unto themselves in the mirror who they are as body, only as mind-body-soul together. Then and only then may you see the absolute perfect being you are.

THOU SHALL HAVE NO OTHER GODS BEFORE ME

There are no other Gods because there are no Gods. A concept does not make a fact. You are all Gods, aka the energy of the Divine Universe, that is all it is.

I AM AGING RAPIDLY

Aging is a core level concept perpetuated by mass consciousness. Therefore, while you are at the behest of medical science, you are in fact capable of creating longer lives for the earthly bodies you all inhabit. To do this at an individual conscious level, you must practice vibrating stronger beliefs than the beliefs of the whole.

> 66 *I am strong. I am not weak. My immune system keeps me churning at maximum intensity. My organs function properly at all times. My body is perfect and whole as it is. There is no need to fight a process of aging which I no longer believe at a core level.* 99

DEATH IS A STOPPING POINT FOR LIFE

Death is a continuing of life. Whomever fears a death doesn't understand a life. A life worth living is a life filled with consequences and circumstances from which to heal and grow and evolve.

WHEN WE LEAVE, WE LEAVE OUR LOVED ONES BEHIND

When we leave we take our loved ones with us in Spirit. This is to say that we all become One again, and so therefore you are truly never alone and without all of your Spirit guides and family members. We are with you All ways and this means we are with you in life and in 'death.' We are never separate or apart. We are the Universe.

To change a belief, such as the ones named above, there must be growing and evolving through various circumstances. Throughout the pages of our book, we will describe for you various scenarios presented in my life (Laura) and the lives of friends and family to illustrate different points on our roadmap to a life of divine connection.

You will find that Laura wavers throughout the book between belief and non-belief. She has chosen this as part of her soul contract in order to create the very book you are reading. Her journey is fraught with difficulties for which she goes sailing back and forth, up and down through torrential winds, downpours and tsunamis until she gets to smooth waters only to find herself back in a storm once again. Once you find who is in charge of navigating it won't be so hard to find solid ground or smooth terrain. Know it is part of the process for All to evolve through storms in order to receive conditioned mind beliefs you had chosen to weather as part of soul's journey to evolvement.

Within the pages of our book are various exercises to help guide you into Love. Each one meant to reveal and uproot thinking patterns keeping you stuck in human falsity and confusion. Workbook space is provided in the back for you to do them. Once is not enough. Return to them many times, as often as needed to guide the ego away and bring through soul truth.

Get ready for a ride. An adventure like no other. Our journey here will elevate you to another consciousness level, as long as you are willing to come along. You will learn the steps spelled out in The All of Everything, The All of the All and The All That Is as well as brand new steps, laws and principles. Each step will move you along the path of enlightenment. Never has there been a more succinct outline of what it is to be human and what it takes to evolve.

You are a divine being of love and light, here to evolve your soul to the next level of consciousness. You are never alone. God consciousness lives inside of you. It is all of us together as one beingness experiencing itself through our Oneness. We are *collectively living life, but at the same time living our life individually. When you have mastered the concept of being both everything and nothing at all you are at one with everything.*

CHAPTER 1
Cocreation

Dear All,
As we cocreate our book may we remove anything of ego
and place within these pages only what is right and true.

efore I began to write my *All* books, I spent nearly two years in what I like to call 'spiritual college'. I didn't just attend seminars or read metaphysical books that interested me, I devoured their content. I spent every single day from morning until night as a student of the divine. At the time, I didn't know that I was being led to teaching after teaching with a specific curriculum spelled out for me long before I came into this particular body. Every text, every course happened at precisely the time I was ready to receive it and not before.

The mere fact you are reading this very book tells me you are on a similar track to enlightenment. We all are seeking light, but some of us leave the lights off until the very end while others remain in a state of awareness from a young age. Then there are the ones who flicker on and off throughout life, only to find eventually that a proverbial light switch has gone off in their mind. They find truth and stay there. This was me. I was a light flicker. One day I believed, another I questioned. On and off went the lights until one day I flipped the switch and it never went back off. Fortunately, there is no electric bill for enlightenment.

As I went through the process of writing my first three *All* books, I went through tumultuous ups and downs that stopped me in my tracks almost daily. I was so gripped with fear and uncertainty about what I was doing and whether or not any of it could be true that I made myself physically sick. I was trapped in a prison of my own making. Even though the words were right there in front of me, I wasn't following any of the advice of the first book, *The All of Everything*, or the second book, *The All of the All*. I gave it some effort, but never enough to make any lasting change in my life. I was that wild stallion bucking and bronking through every step. By the time

I began to write my third book, *The All That Is*, I started turning more and more to my Spirit, soul and All, but certainly not enough to move the needle. So I struggled and suffered through circumstance after circumstance, not recognizing the soul was guiding my journey through the entire process.

It wasn't until I finished our third book that it became evidently clear that my journey of enlightenment was paved with rocky roads on purpose. Everything I went through was preparing me to be a teacher. I suffered to know suffering. I languished in mediocrity to know insignificance. I acted out to know insanity and irrational mind. My ego interrupted me at every turn, and it wasn't until I began following the advice in my book to a tee that I found my footing on spiritual ground. I was right where my soul needed me to be, learning about opposites as a means to know truth.

66*You embody truth and truth reveals itself more and more.*99

– The All of Everything

All of it is like a puzzle which you place in front of you, and as you learn/ remember more you are guided to more pieces. Each time you place a piece it shows you more of what we (as a whole) are all about. This is the ultimate goal of enlightenment, so you may finish the puzzle and begin a whole new one. The more I turned inward for assistance, the easier it became to believe and to start to see the puzzle filled in.

As I studied and navigated my soul ship, I slid up and down, backwards and forwards as I arrived, but ultimately my destination unfolded before me with an easy landing and soft focus. I was a pilot gliding the plane in, and my copilot was along for the ride the whole time telling me which way to turn and how to maneuver. Just as a pilot must learn all the hazards to fly right, I was thrown into circumstances or feelings to begin my slow ascent to enlightenment. It was impossible to shake the fear on purpose. It was hard to find an audience as a means to guide others working towards a goal. Patience and timing are earned as you evolve, and only when you have learned to let go of arrival times and destinations.

How you can teach someone to not give up on their goals is difficult if you have never had to wait on the sidelines yourself. So I waited. I wondered. I worried. By the time I finished my third book and began crafting this next one, my inner being (or soul) was ready to move to the next step – preparing. By giving me a feeling of excitement for the future, I began to see possibilities exploding. Magic was happening while at the same time stuckness. In order to grow I needed to be both moving and stuck as a means to move others along the path. My experiences allowed me to understand the feeling of what others will move through as they go about their journeys.

Translation

So here we are today. I am a translator for the Divine, allowing thoughts of the collective to be written on the page and masterfully detailed so everyone can gain access to the teachings of Source.

So how do I know I'm not the one writing this book as only myself? I know because if I were writing this book (as only me) I would be telling myself I am fooling myself if I think anyone would read this or care about what I have to say. If I was writing this book, I would tell myself to go get a regular job, stick to what I know and start worrying more about money (and how to make it) than helping people and possibly going hungry. I would say too many people are writing books and giving seminars, and I would tell myself to give up or move on.

But that's not what Spirit says back in my head. It says, *"You are worthy. You are limitless. You have so much potential if only you could see that within yourself."*

It's like the best mom or parent ever building you up for greatness. Your dependable cheerleader always in your ear waiting for you to recognize the absolute divine truth of who you are – a perfect being of light who has come here to experience life.

Conscious Creation

In life, we are either living from conscious creation or unconsciousness. Either way, we are creating our lives moment after moment after moment based upon our belief systems. Functioning in the world at any stage of the game is derived by the thoughts, words and actions of our movements. To move unconsciously is how many of us live our lives. That's what I have been doing. That is what most of us do. We have no clue that we are the ones driving the boat, and therefore steer it as best we can with limited sight. It's like driving through the fog and the windshield wipers only work haphazardly. When you begin to notice the wipers are only as good as the driver's eye, then you are able to see more clearly. The wipers function as means to wipe away the fog, but the driver navigates. The function is tandem. Each must work together to create an environment of safety. As you begin to see the picture of the road in front of you as clearly as the eye can, you have arrived.

To cocreate is our most important element of life. It is to hand the reins over to the metaphysical part of ourselves. Deep within our psyche is a soul which divinely plans the life we feel. Our bodies touch, feel, taste and see. Our senses are part of our body so that we may experience ourselves in that way. It is, however, our metaphysical senses which know the best, most honest way to be. Turning away from this inner knowing is the surest way to create a mess for yourself, as witnessed in the following story from my life.

Bed Bugs

It was a weekend meant to be about joy, relaxation and fun. I was attending the wedding of a friend who was marrying her boyfriend of several years. Eager to celebrate her, I booked my flight alongside two friends from the community where we had all met. Our journey began quite effortlessly. We valet parked the car and got to our airplane gate with no issues. The plane unfortunately had been delayed taking off, and as we sat on the tarmac waiting for it to leave, the first hiccup of the wedding arrived. Rain was rolling in on the island of Punta Cana in the Dominican Republic where the ceremony was set to take place. The bride had to move her ceremony up by an hour. This meant we were going to be cutting it quite close to even make the nuptials.

As the plane sat motionless I began to get very nervous that we might not make it. The flight eventually left but arrived thirty minutes late. By the time we got through customs and into our car service (to the resort where the wedding was being held), we had only 20 minutes to make it to the ceremony. It was a 30-minute drive. We arrived at the front of the hotel, dropped our bags and ran to the bathroom to change. Our friend had told us to come to the ceremony straight from the plane and to not worry about our clothes or hair. Our human vanity, however, got the best of us and so we took the five minutes to freshen up and change. Had we not changed, we may have at least made the final "I do" moment. A golf cart and driver rushed us down to the beach for the ceremony, but as it turned out we missed the entire thing. We arrived just seconds after it ended.

The reception was being held an hour later at 5pm, which gave us an hour and fifteen minutes to check into our room, unpack and change. Plenty of time, or so we thought. Our first room reeked of cigarette smoke, so my two friends went to change rooms, but the front desk and hotel manager were extremely rude to them, essentially accusing them of being the only people at the entire resort who complained about the smell. Begrudgingly, they gave us a new room anyway.

Our mess became even bigger after we finally moved to the new room. We quickly changed for the reception and walked outside to find it had begun to not only rain but downpour. We needed to walk to get down to the beach, and in the rain and our high heels there was no way this was happening. So we waited twenty minutes for someone to arrive with a covered golf cart to escort us to the party. We arrived just as everyone was finishing up their meals.

Our friend, the bride, was visibly pissed. We did the best we could to shake it all off, dance, mingle and have fun but it was obvious we had put a damper on the bride's day and we felt terrible. We tried to make it up to her by staying out late for drinks, and then finally went back to our room (feeling dejected) around midnight only to find it crawling with bed bugs.

Exhausted, angry and frustrated we made the difficult decision to book flights home the next day and just cut bait on the weekend, despite having spent nearly $1000 dollars each to be there. Nothing seemed to be going our way. The hotel moved our rooms again, but none of us slept a wink that night. Once you see bed bugs you can't shake them off of you mentally. We were eager to just get home.

Unfortunately, in our escalating stupor we forgot the most important element of life – Love. We each chose to stumble in fear and forget why we came to the island in the first place, friendship. We left in a hurry and never even said goodbye in person to our friend. We picked the coward's way out, calling her on the phone right before leaving for the airport. She was livid with us and our friendship suffered because of it. It took several months before the friendship was repaired, and thankfully we were able to move past it.

Divine Disasters

Looking back, I was able to recognize the lessons being taught through that experience, or as I like to call it – divine disasters. This is when something goes completely awry as a means to shine a light on an unhealed thinking pattern in our lives. For me, it had to do with feeling slighted by friends in the past. Many times, I found myself on the receiving end of disloyal friends who chose other more important (or so I thought) things over me. They skipped parties, didn't attend my birthday events or baby shower. A huge issue for me to get over and forgive was the friends in California who missed my first wedding, the ones in Florida who skipped my first book launch party and the immediate family who didn't attend my dad's funeral. That was painful.

My lesson slapped me in the face with the revelation that all of us are dealing with things that the other person has no idea about in life, be it financial hardships or just everyday life situations. The bride had no idea the level of drama that had been dumped upon us and the hoops we jumped through to at least try and fix it. She only saw the part about us arriving late and leaving early, and the middle parts of the story were mostly left out. That experience allowed me to see that sometimes things just happen which are seemingly out of our control, but on a soul level are quite literally by design in order to shine a light on our thinking patterns.

We live in a world of opposites, and this is what we are here to learn about in this current lifetime we are living. How can you know what it feels like to be happy if you have never experienced sadness? What is up if there is no down? Every experience in and around our lives is meant to show us opposite behaviors. A friend betrays you and you wind up betraying another as a means to explain on a human level why it happened and to lead you towards forgiveness, which of course is an act of Love.

All I have done in the last few years is notice my lessons, and this is perhaps why I am more evolved and able to even write books like these. I recognized the self, and the self allows me the luxury of being able to cocreate; and this is the journey of self.

Cocreation

Cocreation is the way to enlightenment. It is how we deal with everyday circumstances such as those that occurred on my ill-fated trip. Had I stated to the Universe, *"I need your help,"* when everything was going down, I may have found myself in less of a mess. What I did wrong in the moment was to ignore my intuition, which told me I needed to stay and be there for my friend. Instead, I let ego do the planning and wound up creating a bigger mess than expected. Had I decided to stay, it was quite possible the revelation (about why I had come in the first place and why I might have left) could have come to me and the lesson indeed still been presented and examined. Instead, I wound up hurting a friend and derailing a budding friendship, and for that I was disappointed in myself. I am so grateful this friend forgave me ultimately and I was able to repair our union.

As God would say, *"And so we begin again."* And this is our first line of defense. We make a mistake and we keep going. And the more we begin to cocreate with our metaphysical counterpart, the quicker the lessons are relinquished and with much less damage to the heart and mind. Our soul is our co-captain along for the ride and wants us choosing Love. It guides us there at every turn, but we get so caught up in our junk we forget to turn it on. We choose fear and wind up in a bigger dilemma than something needs to be.

If only we could stop for a mere moment and acknowledge our team member, our lives would begin to be less stressful and our intuition on point. Nothing would slip by us and we would know we are ready to move to our next step, intention.

CHAPTER 2
Intention

❝Intentions are a form of prayer, and yet they are not exactly the same. They are merely goals to be accomplished from an ego's perspective. This is not to say they do not have value. However, whoever undertakes intention coupled with prayer truly has the keys to the kingdom.❞

– The All of Everything

Everything in life is intention. Though it may not seem this way, it is. Our intentions are our everyday road map. They guide the journey whether you know it or not. They tell the Universe what you wish to create in clear, definable language. When you are aligned to Love it will be easier to bring joys to light, and when in fear, pain or panic it becomes manifest as our dear Laura had witnessed here.

Rocky Road

My road this week was very rocky. I wound up taking a road trip for work (January, 2019) and not even a week later the town I had traveled to was hit by a terrible tragedy. A gunman opened fire at a local bank a few miles from where I was filming, killing five people. The incident sent me reeling and back to my question-and-answer format as I did in my first three *All* books.

Laura: Dear All, today I am wishing to know why a tragedy touched my life yet again. Though its direct affect had nothing to do with me, it was in my road map and design and I am not understanding why. This coincidence has made me question, and though I seek answers, my questions help others understand what is happening in and around our world.

You wrote that. Why?

All: You are being guided to situations that are part of a learning curve. You are seeking to know the collective as One and therefore are part of many alter events.

L: Can you explain that better to me? Alter events?

A: Events such as the tragedy occurring in a Florida town named Sebring are tried and true acts of humanity every day.

L: Unfortunately, yes. Guns kill more people in the United States in a given day than most other countries in the world.

A: It is not just America where guns are used violently against another. In other countries they are used as mechanisms of war and atrocities to teach punishment for all who dare steer from the line of what is considered improper, mostly by rebellionists. Theology rebellionists and freedom seekers.

L: But why do these acts of violence keep occurring around me? I had never heard of Sebring up until a month ago, and then a few days ago was filming just outside of the town. A quiet, sleepy town is now destroyed by the violence of others. My intention is to learn a great truth here about this particular set of circumstances.

A: This is our intention in speaking with and through you tonight. Intentions are useful as a device to bring to light any and all ideas and anecdotes as you move about life. It is intentional for you to be surrounded in this way by yet another act of violence so we may shed a light on it for you.

L: A light on what?

A: Intentions. It is our intention to inform and remind you of our collective truth. You are not caught up but rather caught in the line of fire in every situation. Every single act of violence occurring is an act of the thinking mind of the One. As each of the All thinks and acts separately, that one thought is manifested upon an entire world. So, thinking and creating alone is impossible. Therefore, as you go about days and nights, each individual is in fact caught in a web.

L: Like a spider?

A: Yes. You are caught in the line of fire, as was said. You are part of everything and everything is part of you.

L: I recognize that there is no coincidence of my having just been there a week ago.

A: There are no coincidences, as you very well know, ever. Our point here is to know as One mind there are always going to be issues and ideas that become part of your worldview as a means to show you the connectedness you experience. It is because you are all One you are always seeing incidences and occurrences such as you had witnessed in an airport, a church, school or park which had some significance upon your life at one point. Perhaps it has been shown as a reason, just as other incidences are shown to others which have "touched" their lives. Your incidences may be different than another's, but each has a meaning attached and that is to show interconnectedness among the species.

L: It makes sense, I guess. I just feel that mine has been on a national level and seem so profoundly–

A: Unique?

L: Yes.

A: Untrue. They are not unique. This is a lesson of a collective beingness. Each person has been touched by tragedies in vastly similar ways in the course of their lives. It is spiritual law and must be undertaken by all who seek to know themselves as Oneness. We must know our connectedness, and this is why going about your days is leading to unspeakable acts as seemingly connected to you.

> " Dear All, thank you for showing me our connectiveness to one another. I release myself from the effects of these tragic events and allow our love to bind to anyone afflicted by these tragedies. "

L: It's very hard when you see these tragedies to not get caught in the idea of something similar happening to you or your family. It's very unnerving.

A: Precisely why you must look upon the untrue and declare it as such. No thought need affect you in a way that harms the psyche, but you must look through it rather than at it.

> " I know this town, person or stranger is hurting and I send love and light as they move through it but release myself of its effects. "

L: Some things are so hard to look at.

A: So don't. Look through them, as we had said above.

L: It's not that I can't do that, but I have a hard time seeing moms losing babies, parents dying, young kids getting cancer and all sorts of other tragedies. I know you say it's all an "illusion" in our last three All books

and not really happening, but to them and all of us in these bodies on Earth it feels as real as can be. So we ache and hurt and fear. I have seen so many stories this week of parents and their kids being torn apart by tragedy and I can't help but be overwhelmed and sad. Being a mom myself, I can't imagine, nor would I want too, their pain.

A: *And so we must remind all here that what has been chosen is on purpose, and to know this will release the fear.*

L: What a terrible thing to choose to have a child or parent die and be left alone. I really just don't understand the purpose of all this pain on Earth. It feels cruel and makes me wonder if Earth is actually Hell.

A: *Understand we do know the torture it causes the all of you to see and feel the effects of cause, which is why we are always here reminding you of the One who knows All and sees All. Look upon it for what it is (as said above); a purposeful adventure to discover yourself again and again.*

L: It doesn't seem like adventure. It seems like pain and tragedy, misfortune and illness.

A: *It is not for One's to know why all of this is happening, as you are far too down the enlightenment chain to understand and we know it is most difficult to see others suffer in time. We do our best to give you reasonings, at the same time understanding your confusion and fear. The books and materials placed in physical realms are so you may have easier journeys, but the full and complete picture is known only when crossing back to non-physical completely. The propensity to fall back into fear is par for the course and must be assailed daily because of the planet's chaos; intentional chaos.*

L: We chose all of this nonsense?

A: *Yes, in order to evolve. It is what life is for. What a monotonous life to have nothing happen and everything be perfect. In non-physical you may go where you want, have everything and do anything and this eternal existence is quite lovely and boring (a word we know you understand but is not spiritually based). So we must shake things up and this is the dance of life all over the infiniteness (existing everywhere). It cannot be understood by Ones not remembering, yet, but you will as you cross returning to our other side. Questions answered in a much deeper way then can ever be explained to earthly Ones. To know All is to experience all. Every delicious nook and cranny. Even the hard parts.*

L: I don't know what to say to that. I understand, while at the same time being upset at the unfairness of it all. We are tired of the suffering, especially right now in our world. It's been a difficult time on planet Earth—

A: *For those who see themselves as separate, yes. There is more to Heaven than Ones can understand on Earth.*

L: **Well then can you explain it to me with intention? My intention is to learn a great truth about the Universe. What is the point of life?**

A: *On Earth it is to evolve beyond fear. To move into a space of being. In other places and spaces, it is to learn opposite behaviors from that which is Love. It is a journey the All take together as One, although it feels if you are separate.*

L: **And apparently this is fun?**

A: *It is most definitely the intention of All to experience joy, even through adversity and triumph, again and again returning to Love, our natural state. It is a journey we enjoy mostly as One. One who has remembered enough understands, while those still sleeping think it to be nonsense.*

L: **Isn't that all of us? Even the "enlightened" who understand and recognize our connection to God and the Universe are still not able to move beyond certain things like pain and suffering or feeling sadness for their fellow humans who are suffering in an 'illusion', as you always say pain is.**

A: *Sadness and fear are different. To feel the effects of another's illusion as if it was your own is exactly what we spoke on above. These alter events are very much aligned in one's 'wheelhouse', so to speak. To see these and feel emotion is kindness, love and caring and should be used often.*

L: **But how do we shake the fear when we see these events and not worry it will happen to ourselves or our children, family, friends etc.?**

A: *Pray for All.*

> 66 *Dear All, I send love to my fellow brethren and let go of fear. I know all has been chosen but let no others illusion come through me.* 99

L: **But how can I do that when my friends and family are in different stages of enlightenment than I am? Whenever I explain things through my lens, they shake it off as baloney. It's hard not to get caught in their fear.**

A: *As difficult as it may be, it is always best to know truth without attaching judgement to others' (current) lens. You may know and they do not as it stands. So, you must see all as on par, but allow others their vision as well. You often get angry or frustrated, and we would offer a solution to hold space for All rather than judge and shame.*

L: **So what would I say when someone is caught in a fear trap?**

A: *Ask, then answer.*

L: Meaning cocreate? Ask the higher self what is the best response or if no response is best?

A: Exactly. Speak freely, but also know that others are in a place different than your own and when in doubt, always ask for direction. When one is lost physically one would ask for direction, correct?

L: Yes.

A: And when one is lost spiritually and unsure of where to go or what to say they should do what then?

L: Ask for direction via cocreation with Spirit/Source. What does any of this have to do with intention?

A: It is intentional to be placed within a chapter on intention so readers may know why and how to use the tool.

L: And how do we use intention daily?

A: Our intentions come mainly as ego thoughts.

66 *I want this. I need this. I have to get this toy, home, car or item.* 99

This is how we create our every manifestation.

L: Well, if intentions come from ego, why do we use them at all? You always say to lose the ego and live the truth of the Universe, which is Love. Why set intentions of wanting?

A: Wanting and desiring are mighty enemies. Ego wants a car. Soul desires a way to get around. Ego lives large. Soul finds life within. Intention setting aims to set the stage for equality and heal the rift.

66 *My intention is to own a car which gets me to the right place safely and efficiently.* 99

Or: 66 *My intention is to find a home filled with natural light and large enough space to provide for my growing family.* 99

Each of these are intentions setting into motion both wants and desires.

66 *I intend to get a Ferrari.* 99

This intention is an ego trick. It allows only for anger and betrayal of what is not showing up in your life.

Or: 66 *I intend to live in a mansion one day.* 99

Another intention set on finding a missing piece of what ego feels is owed to it. So, when intentions are set they are to be used as means to grow our soul and not to satisfy our ego's mighty agenda.

L: But why not set an intention as a soul only?

A: An intention as soul is unnecessary, as you already have everything. It exists, and to ask for something already existing is silly, wouldn't you say?

L: But it doesn't exist in the physical world, which is why we ask for it. We want– oh I see where you are going with this. The things we want are just ego satisfiers.

A: Yes, and this is up to individuals as to those things they are wanting, and in order to evolve as beings of light, wanting is necessary in physical realms. To be is all that is necessary as soul. To love. You already have love and it doesn't need to be asked for. It is.

L: But ego isn't asking for love of the Universe. Ego would be wanting a romantic partner or someone to fill a void?

A: Exactly.

L: So you can't set an intention such as, "I intend to find love."

A: It's not that you can't set an intention to "find love," it's only to recognize it is an ego-seeking validation of itself, not a soul desiring the love it already knows exists.

L: So tell me an intention for love that is combining both soul and ego.

A: And we are glad you asked.

> 66 Dear All, my intention is to find a partner of love and romance as it relates to my time on Earth. I accept a perfect partner who is kind and loyal and sees in me what I see in them. May our love be real and true as we grow and evolve alongside one another. 99

L: It checks both boxes. So I see what you mean. Why not say, "as we grow and evolve together" instead of "alongside one another?"

A: Because you are individual souls upon Earth and this distinction allows each to make decisions and intentions as one and separately.

L: Subtlety has seemed to be a major factor in our writings. All the words are always so perfectly placed to distinguish our two worlds.

A: Indeed. Intention setting is a wonderful tool, and our intention here has been to explain why and to teach (remind) others of a proper use of it.

WORKBOOK EXERCISE # 1:
SET YOUR INTENTION

ake some time to write down a set of intentions. Be mindful of each that it works together in tandem with both ego and soul (as above). Space has been provided below as a workbook.

66 My intention is to learn great truths of the Universe and beyond
as I move into a state of being. 99

66 My intention is to find my footing on solid ground
as a spiritual being in human form. 99

66 My intention is to know who I am. 99

Setting intentions such as these allow our books to be more impactful as you move through them. Feel free to add your own intentions or create ones for desires not yet physical.

66 My intention is to own a home filled with light
in a quiet neighborhood with room to grow my family. 99

Or, 66 I am intending to one day be financially free
and to share it with All. 99

Now let us move to our next intention tool, prayer.

CHAPTER 3

Prayer

❝ *Prayer, as a means to know God, is right and necessary for all. Prayer, however, is not a cure-all modality, unless and until all who seek to know God know God, – that is to say one must believe fully in the concept of a cocreator, a sideline cheerleader along for the ride, all of the all of their lives, in order for miracles to occur.*❞

–The All of The All

Intention vs. Prayer

What is the difference between prayer and intention? Nothing and everything. Nothing - as in asking for something you already have is not necessary. Accepting it is the key.

Everything - meaning each has its own soul purpose.

Intention is an asking and yet is not the same as prayer. As was described in our last chapter, intention is an ego creation mostly. It is how we get the things we need for our physical survival and our grandiose ideas of life and what it should be (or so we think) - money, fame, cars, etc.

Prayer is asking to be reunited to Source. It is Divine Mind reminding itself of its true nature. This is not to say ego isn't part of this equation, as oftentimes people do pray for money or fame. This, however, is in actuality intention masked as prayer. Though the prayee may believe a "God" outside of them is the key holder to it becoming a reality, they are enlightened only enough to believe it is this magic wand waver doing things for them.

A true prayer is one that asks for reunification.

❝ *Dear God, I am only as powerful as I believe myself to be. Therefore, I hand the reins over to you for help.*❞

Whether you believe in a God of religion or of Source Energy (which is what we All are), you are connecting to Divine Mind. Every time you ask for unification, you ask the power within and without to do the work with you. This is the quickest, easiest and best way to get to the manifestation you are wanting, desiring or needing. So when you are struggling, it is always best to seek Source first and foremost.

> ❝ Dear All, please help me remember I am Love
> and help me move through this difficulty as I guide myself
> out of fear and into knowing. ❞

In religion, those who bow down are actually praying through and to themselves. Though it is not a belief they hold, it is truth. All of you are in every way, shape or form the divine creator of life's experience. So if you are struggling to create happiness in your life, this is the chapter for you. This is where you take responsibility for and own up to every terrible incident or divine synchronicity in and around your life.

> ❝ Nothing happens to you that does not happen through you. ❞
> – The All of Everything

A simple sentence and yet a concept most find horribly wrong. How could I be the creator of a terrible circumstance such as cancer or a miscarriage? How could a car accident have been my fault? "No way," you would say and we would say. It is not only fact. It is law.

On planet Earth it is a vibrationally-acting magnet which attracts to itself that which it is thinking upon both good and bad. You are therefore attracting both positive and negative experiences based upon what you are thinking at any given moment. Again, it's so simple but so "out there" as a concept that most brush it off as new age mumbo jumbo.

The truth is hard to reconcile but is very much a complete, accurate and divine truth. Each and every person on planet Earth creates for themselves anything and everything from that which has been thought upon prior. What this means is that any and all thoughts of each participant in our 'human experiment' are thoughts which have already been undertaken by our collective whole. So if you are thinking, "it might rain today," it is because you already know it is possible. Every thought already exists. It is our free will choices which allow the circumstance to arrive.

Babies R Us

Laura has been wanting another child for quite some time now. She knows this is a possibility to have more kids, but has been caught up in her age, marital status and the fact that she has been deemed infertile by doctors and scientists (who have forgotten who they truly are and seek to find answers to life through modalities of cause and effect.)

She, too, has forgotten who she truly is (a soul inside of a body), and is therefore caught up in the diagnosis and diseased mind which states she is too old to create babies now. However, she knows enough as a being of light and channel (or translator, as we would call it) to always seek higher helpers. This is us. We are the keepers of truth for her. We live inside of her as One mind to remind her of divinity. When she begins to recognize – recog – to the One mind she automatically activates this knowing within her.

      ❝ *Dear God. I know I am meant to be a mother many times over and I am failing at figuring out how to make this happen. I turn this over to you to help lead me to a child I am seeking who I know is seeking me, too. Please help me. Hold my hand through the process and lead me to her and/or him. Amen.* ❞

This is a prayer of surrender.

      ❝ *I cannot know what is the best way to turn or road to take and so I ask for the Universe (God/Source) to help me.* ❞

A surrendering prayer is recognizing the cocreator within you. It hands the reins over to our metaphysical self (or "higher self") and automatically activates intention.

Struggle, Strife, Necessity

You are struggling and this is why you have picked up the very book you are now reading, listening to or watching. No one seeking reunification goes seeking truth unless they know falsities. All of the all of you are under illusions of separation at varying degrees, and all of you eventually go seeking what is needed to find truth. Each material you are "given" seemingly feels right for the time when you receive it. We place quotes around the word "given" so you may understand that nothing happens in the realm of physicality which has not been preplanned, so to speak. You asked the creative part of you to design a life different from all others, where you may grow and evolve through circumstances in order to get past certain issues or what we would call Life Driving Themes *as had been discussed in book 3* (The All That Is). *These are themes such as anger, resentment, bitterness, masculinity, femininity, humility, vengeance. The list goes on and on quite endlessly.*

You have chosen these themes perfectly for advancement as a soul. At what point you wake up is entirely up to you. Some choose waking up right away as a teenager, others wait until midlife, others are reminded as they return ("die") and most choose not to discover the truth until they have returned completely and fully to our Spirit side, which is why chaos exists on Earth at a high rate. More are asleep than awake.

The Ones who are ready to awaken set a course/curriculum to expand. So to figure out what you already know (as soul) you are led to teachings, lessons, courses, mediums, seers and other modalities based upon what it is you are meant to learn at that particular time in evolution of the soul. You have chosen these quite literally by design, which is why the term given is not wholly accurate. These have been chosen by you, for you, to be received at the precise moment of necessity. That which you choose exists as possibility for you, and when you are ready to receive them each arrives for you. Though it will feel like you "found" them, in actuality you have been guided to them by soul.

A Course in Miracles

What is the lesson of free will? It is that you always have opportunity to jump ahead in the curriculum if you choose to as body. We have left freedom to choose as part of the experience of being human so that All of The All may experience for themselves what it is to be human. To always choose Love (which is what we all are) would be somewhat boring upon Earth, just as it is in Heaven or Spirit. It is a much richer experience to have both good and bad days.

Laura would like to tell you that she hates her bad days, but if you were to look at her life as an example you would see that bad days are necessary to understand the journey of others. To know only Love would not allow a book such as this to be completed. It is both accurate and true to say that her soul is knowing what is needed to be done and felt in order to create a profound book of knowledge. She fights her feelings as much as possible but sometimes it is quite impossible, as soul knows what is best always.

You are wanting to know why all of this is necessary, and we are here to describe the whys of the Universe as best we can for the level of vibration achieved on Earth (so far). You are here to experience the yin and yang; the All of Everything. You must feel everything, be everything, say everything needed to be said in order to understand who you are not, so you may understand who you are.

Laura is someone kind and generous of spirit. She knows love is most important in life. She has learned over the years that to control every circumstance is impossible if you cannot be the one who is in charge. The battle has been to recognize who is in charge by using the medium of miracles, which is prayer.

You are controlling every minute detail of the life you are living currently through the thoughts you hold onto, the actions you take and the words you use. Beliefs are what shape the world you see on both an individual and collective level. So you are bound by the rules of the Universe you are currently in, which has certain 'laws', as you would call them, upon planet Earth. Law of Magnetic Attraction. Law of Allowing. Law of Compensation. Law of Uncompromising Joy. Law of Energetic Company. Law of Cause and Effect.

These and other laws are very much at play upon planet Earth and other places. They are designed to keep you in line, so to speak, so you may not cause chaos on the planet and end the evolutionary process too early, as has been done on prior occasions in different bodies you all were in.

Now all of this may seem very 'out there', and to you as a body it absolutely is. As soul it is perfectly worded and precisely how the system of evolvement works. You are beings for all of eternity, and grow and evolve into each new inception of yourself and others through every major turn of events or catastrophe. Earth has been turned over many times, and though you may think of the human time/space calendar being only thousands of years, it is in fact millions upon millions of years old, and many artifacts exist proving this point. Currently are you looking in the wrong place for them. One day they will be found, and this is as perfectly designed as the placing of books and materials in your scope of knowledge. When the time comes it will be done.

One Minute Miracles

What are miracles? Miracles are moments in time designed to remind you of beingness. It is in and upon you to recognize these moments. Rainbows are one of these. Bright skies and sunny rays are others. You make the miracles as much as I do. I being relative to We. We create together. So when you are needing a tune up or reminder, we remember who we are and together make beautiful music (another wonderful avenue for reminders.) Music is a bold statement, and oftentimes our lyrics are created via the same channel as Laura uses to create her books. It's the same channel. You just have to know you can tune into it to create consciously. Many, many wonderful books, movies and TV shows have been created where divinely inspired musings have been used as dialogue or plot lines with the creator unknowingly tapping into Divine Mind. This type of unconscious creation is part of the process. The light within shines whether you know it or not, and whenever you are tapping into a moment of Love our inspiration comes through. Many a poem or lyric has been penned as part of the One.

What prayer does is re-mind you to that One. It is like taking a broken stick and making it whole again. Though you have been separated, you are and always will be part of the branch which is part of the tree. Whether it lives on that tree or not makes no difference. It was and always will be the tree. The choice is yours whether to remember you are the tree.

One method of prayer may not always be best. There are many ways to pray. Pray daily in a multitude of minor ways. I am is sufficient most, if not all, times to transmute a thought process which consistently and persistently is keeping you stuck in patterns of abuse and self-denial of the God species within. Lose the ego and shine. You must be persistent and consistent for any and all ego like thoughts to be transformed.

WORKBOOK EXERCISE # 2:
ONE MINUTE MIRACLES

T his is how you stay in transformation. For one minute we ask you to watch your thoughts. After you have done this. Write down the opposite of what you have heard in your workbook.

> *I am perfect.*

> *I am capable.*

> *I am kind.*

These thoughts are the kind that are both right and true. Thoughts which serve ego such as, "You are fat, lonely, old, sad, depressed and useless," not only depress you, they destroy you from the inside out.

Only thoughts of love are true and this is the mission. To only write what is truth. When you have finished this assignment, place it in mind and keep it by you (in physical form). Remind yourself, "I am the thing I see. I am."

We are grateful you took time for the exercise and now move to our chapter on gratitude for All.

CHAPTER 4
Gratitude

A grateful heart is a key component to all manifestations. In our gratitude are we painting an important portrait of that which has occurred through our asking. 'I am grateful to God for all his bounty, and glory be to thee a new day from which to begin again. As we begin again are we reminded that all of life is a magnificent gift, a portrait.'

– The All of The All

Life

T his life, though it can sometimes feel like torture, is a gift. A great, big beautiful adventure waiting to unfold for you every day. To see it this way makes for an easier journey. Though most do not choose this. Instead, they choose to dwell in and upon chaos. Fear and doubt create a more difficult experience for all of you. Laura is one whose journey has been fraught with grief and difficulty most recently. It has felt as though her world is falling apart at the seams. Every torture (within the experience) has been a profound movement forwarded in her evolution of the soul.

A brother has left the earthly plane, and for this she holds sorrow and anguish. Though it was not her fault, nor did she have anything to do with the soul contract of her brother, her part in the illusion has been played perfectly. Immediately she went seeking a different way, a new way to experience grief without the depression or anger that sometimes goes along with a death of a sibling, parent or other loved one. Her very soul (who is writing this book right now with her) knew she needed a mentor and provided one right away in her beloved brother. As he passed into Source, he recognized his need to guide her along the journey. An unbreakable bond that has been sealed with a kiss and mended a broken heart many a time for her.

Laura knows and accepts her brother is gone from a physical body but understands his passing and why it occurred in his lifetime. She knows and understands his most difficult demons of irritability and aggravation (as to what is being done to the *environment and the corporate greed and violence occurring all over the world) was killing him, and quite literally did. Indeed, it had been his mission to uncover ways to stop the crimes of humanity to our Earth, and as soul and Spirit alike he is doing that as we speak. His role of environmental scientist is being well utilized as Spirit, as well as the role of Spirit advisor to "sister," as he would call her. Their love is undeniably a beautiful thing and how all should recog with their loved ones. Recognize they are with you in every way and the sting of physical loss is lessened.*

Immensely grateful are we for this purposeful endeavor which has been undertaken by The All. Every one of us is, was and will be part of one whole. Separated as individuals, we seek to remember our very Oneness as we go about days and nights. Some (as we said above in our last chapter) are very eager to step into this role quickly as they incarnate, while others are waiting until the very end for recognition. Laura has chosen to wake up and remember as part of the process of grief. She has chosen to write, and writing has been cathartic for her as well as grounding. She is remembering who she is, why she is here and how to create a life bound by beingness. She has renewed her connection to The All That Is and found her true calling of life.

Grounded

To remain grounded in gratitude is most important in everyday life. It is renewing your commitment to life. Expressing love for things that have come to you, through you.

> ❝ I am grateful for the bounty I have, the home I inhabit,
> the family who love me eternally. ❞

No one is more grateful than anyone else. On Earth, no one is more anything than anyone else. All are equal. It is only how we express it as bodies which matters on Earth. Some do. Some won't. You can be gracious in life or you can be upset at the unfairness of it all. Can you be more than you think you can be? Absolutely; but only if you find gratitude in the simplest of things. The easiest moments are great, but can you look upon anything hard and know its truth, too? All experiences of the collective and individual soul are valuable. Nonetheless, most are caught up in the illusion of separation and see madness and mayhem as real and true. So they struggle in the unkindness of life and dwell in and upon fear most often.

You will see, even as you go through the pages of this book, the bounce between good and bad is often. Even when you know (as a spiritual seeker), you forget to remember so often. To be grateful is a powerful tool to shake the ego for longer periods of time. Our lesson here for you is that all must be gracious and kind no matter what the circumstance. Look upon every situation, every time as perfect no matter what is manifesting.

Ask, "What is this teaching me?" *and say,* "Thank you for showing me what is needing to be healed within me."

Then, it is upon you to know and accept you are the creator of that circumstance and go deep within the mind to find out its purpose.

WORKBOOK EXERCISE # 3: GROUNDING

G o out today wherever you are, be it work, play or something else, and take time to look at the lesson of the day. Patterns of aggravation often come in groupings, showing you what is most at issue in mind. Break the pattern of the thought by recognizing it is indeed happening through you.

66 I am breaking this pattern of thought and replacing it with new, better and truer ones. I am grateful to be shown this unhealed issue and seek to release it myself as myself, body/mind/soul. 99

No one gets through a day unscathed, and it is most important to relinquish our negative, untrue thought as quickly as it arrived.

66 I am releasing this thought which no longer serves me. 99

An asking as simple as this reminds you who you are immediately and sends a thought back to the nothingness from which it came. When you are feeling low about a particular thing you are not creating in your life - youth, beauty, money, success - put yourself in a place using your mind where you were youthful, loved the way you looked or had great success. This activates both knowing and gratitude.

66 I have had it before in other times and I know more is coming. 99

Accepting is gratitude.

66 Thank you dear All for all of my gifts of the Universe. I am knowing. 99

Take a minute of your day to write a list of gratitude to those who have helped you, harmed you and shown you the way. They are equal in nature as teachers to you.

The helper hides its pain to show what is possible, even if that possibility alludes them. The one who is being helped relinquishes control to a trusted source.

The torturer is the change maker. The wounded learns to stand on its own two feet.

The mentor is the path maker. They unblock the road. The mentee follows a similar path, but one which is much less muddy.

Pave the way for someone else. For you are the helper, the torturer and the mentee yourself, even if you can't quite see it yet. Archetypes such as these are part of the collective beingness of all people. Each in their own way fulfill this role as part of a journey to Oneness.

I am grateful towards each of you who have found this book and chosen to write, speak and know truth. Next we shall explain in clear and specific language how to be.

CHAPTER 5

Be Clear and Specific

Dear All,
Today I am struggling in my knowing and need a little refresher course.

I Want It All

n order to create what it is you are wanting to create, you must know what you want. It sounds easy enough, but for most it is quite difficult. Clarity comes only after you move through a sorting out process and when fear, worry and doubt banished. The more you want something, the more you are keeping it away. This is the nature of the Universe you all are currently living in. Earth is a magnetic field which attracts what it is you are thinking upon (aka Law of Attraction).

In physical realms, such as Earth, you are always in the tug of whatever laws are put into place by the collective beingness of the planet. This can include physical laws, such as the bodily structure and its functioning. It can also include mental laws and elemental laws, which is to say you all must be under certain rules of society as a whole so as not to create mass chaos upon its inhabitants.

On Earth the laws are as follows:

Law of Magnetic Attraction

That which is like unto itself is drawn. You get what you are thinking about, whether wanted or not, as like attracts like.

Law of Uncompromising Joy

Joy is enacted whenever ones are freely having fun and unconcerned with ego or anger/resentment/fear.

Law of Compensation

To attract and attach intention. What you put out is what you receive. Circulation. This is why you must keep flow going in anything, be it money or molecules. Everything must be in constant motion, otherwise it stalls (like a car).

Law of Allowing

Letting go of attachment or outcomes. Everything happens in the let go. Pushing against things is what most do. The ease of life is mistaken for having to work hard in order to achieve.

Law of Cause and Effect (Karma)

For every action there is an equal and opposite reaction. Karma can affect all lives. You may be 'in the line of fire' for something you did, are doing or will do. This is why karmic retribution occurs; to balance the forces of energy.

Law of Choice

Free will.

Law of Intelligent Affirmation

Specificity of intention. Ask for what you want clearly. The Universe knows vibration, you know what you want; therefore, it must be stated in words and emotions.

Law of Potentiality (Assumption)

Manifestation and meditation – i.e. what you get is what you see. Visualization creates through mind.

Law of Energetic Company

Alone you will never be. You are here to experience, express and create through relationships. Some will last moments, another millennium and beyond. This law works in the Universal/Cosmos structure as well. No One is alone, ever.

Law of Belief

What you believe is what you achieve.

Law of Gravity

What goes up, must come down.

This law is the most common and widely known on Earth. It is one you all agree upon as humans. As soul it has become possible to navigate all other laws, but oftentimes you have little faith in them. If each law was used and thought upon just as gravity, it would be a much easier planet to enjoy.

We will describe in more detail each of these laws later in our series. For now, we will allow a conversation to unfold as Laura steps into her role of interviewer to question why life is challenging, even as One knowing the laws.

Ups and Downs

Laura: I can't believe I have written three books, grown and evolved as far as I have and still wind up questioning all of this. Why am I struggling right now, and what must be healed in me in order to grow?

All: You are confused by a situation, and this situation which baffles you of late is of whom you are talking to here.

L: Yes.

A: Why?

L: I don't know. I guess I am just confused as to whom is doing the work. You say, "nothing happens to you that does not happen through you," and this still mystifies me. If I am the one doing the work and it is me who has to think in order to form matter (which then becomes a physical manifestation), then who is actually doing the work? If I let go of the hows of making something a reality in my life, am I letting go of the possibility of it manifesting? Wouldn't I be the one in charge of that very manifestation? Do you see what I am asking here?

A: We understand completely. Am I in charge or not in charge? Yes. You are in charge. It is your idea of a situation which creates it. You are in charge of the destination as much as I am.

L: But that's what I don't understand. That makes it seem we are both in charge.

A: We are. You are and I am. I am you and you are me. We are One and none. You are here and I there; and you are there and I am here. Only one of us exists. As separate identities it feels as if we are individuals, but in actuality we are sole (aka soul). I'm just representing myself within you.

L: I am so confused right now. It makes sense and it doesn't make sense.

A: It makes sense to you, but ego is trapping you and asking for you to believe it (ego) instead of us.

L: I want to believe us, but how do I do that?

A: Make truth your version of reality.

> ❝ *I am a soul in a soul and together we make everything. Every single thing. I am handing the reins over to the you who is me and asking to be guided into Love so I may create the life of possibilities I know already exist for me.* ❞

You have chosen this life.

L: I have?

A: Yes. Every bit of it. As soul you are knowing what is needing to be worked upon as part of your life-driving themes (we shall discuss this later) and making decisions as body/mind/soul.

L: So what you are saying is one of the reasons I want children so badly still despite my age is that I have already had them?

A: Yes, and had your baby and another one even.

L: That's hard to believe.

A: Is it?

L: Well, yes and no. I mean I can certainly agree that wanting more kids has been a desire for a long time, but actually making that a reality has been quite difficult.

A: Because you are making it difficult on purpose.

L: Why on Earth would I do that purposefully?

A: So you may know yourself as irrational minded and fix what needs to be broken.

L: Fix what needs to be broken? That doesn't make any sense.

A: It makes perfect sense. What's broken in you is the belief system of the whole.

> ❝ *I am incapable of creating a child for myself through my body. A doctor has deemed me infertile and so I have manifested for myself the idea that I am no longer able to conceive.* ❞

L: That's not my fault. I didn't want to believe it. It just happened to me.

A: *Because you allowed it to. You see my dear, nothing anyone says need have an impact on you as body. It is of what you believe that is of most importance. So if you believe what is being said to you then it will manifest as that. If you know within the soul of your being you are capable of anything, it will make no sense to you and you will simply let it go. Let ego go.*

L: I blame the doctor who told me at age 35 I had a 5 percent chance of getting pregnant and that, "I better hurry up" if I wanted children. She planted that seed in my brain and it just stuck there.

A: *Like a cancer —*

L: Yes.

A: *That grew beneath the surface of the mind and remains embedded still to this very day.*

L: I cried in the parking lot for twenty minutes after that appointment and yes, I can still see the whole experience vividly. But I did have one child when I was 39 years old (almost 40), and then after that I got pregnant again, but the pregnancies kept resulting in miscarriage. And then a doctor told me I must be in perimenopause–

A: *Which caused a further rift in the mind —*

L: Yes. And here I am now. Too old for babies and I clearly let the beliefs of the whole define me and now I am stuck with the diagnosis.

A: *You are not stuck. You are perfectly capable of creating the life you see.*

L: The one I see in my visioning or mind's eye?

A: *Yes. Let us show you now.*

L: I see my baby being brought to me in the hospital. It seems impossible. How is it possible to make the impossible happen?

A: *Belief in miracles.*

L: Well, I can't do that on my own. There is too much evidence to the contrary, my friend. It's impossible. I need help.

A: *The magic words. Help.*

> 66 Help me dear All. I cannot know what lies ahead of me and for this I get angry, confused and scared. Help me to see only Love is real. Help me to manifest all things I seek to achieve in this lifetime. I need your help; the help of the part of me which knows All, sees All. I am only as capable as my ego allows me to create, and so I know forevermore I must seek help in my soul. 99

L: How often? And at what point can we stop doing that, stop saying these affirmations?

A: Until you believe and as you believe.

> **❝** *Thank you dear All for showing me truth and allowing a vision to come to fruition.* **❞**

L: So having gratitude as well?

A: Yes, as we have explained in the prior chapter you must be gracious and kind to all.

L: How specific do you need to be with your intentions and prayers?

A: As specific as you can. To be clear and specific is a most important element in manifestation. It is how you create, for example, a baby.

> **❝** *She must be perfect, healthy and whole. Her arrival will be easy and effortless. Doctors will marvel at her beauty and be so shocked at how she came into the world with little to no issues considering the age of her parent."*

It is our Law of Intelligent Affirmation. Ask the Universe clearly and specifically for that which you already created. It exists because it is.

L: I don't know. I can't do this. I can't believe in miracles. Even though you say I have already created something, in my mind I just can't get there.

A: Said the ego. We will show you again the possibility which exists in you. Close the eyes.

L: I see a baby being brought to me in a hospital and then I am putting her in a car seat and then later taking her for a walk in her stroller.

A: All possibilities if you believe.

L: I want to believe. Help me believe dear All. Help me stay in high vibration and bring through the child who is waiting to incarnate into being.

A: Keep asking. Keep dreaming. Keep seeing.

L: But what if I decide to believe that I am too old for pregnancy and I want to hire a surrogate or attempt to adopt again?

A: All possibilities as well. Remember we have told you everything exists as possibilities and simply are there many ways to navigate. Same destination. Different route. Just like a route has many detours and stops along the way you can make, ultimately you can arrive there no matter what the circumstance if you stay in alignment vibrationally with All That Is. That is all there is to it. High vibes.

L: So we can 'circle back' in a sense if we miss our stop by focusing on fear and diagnosis?

A: Precisely what is done upon planet Earth. A missed stop is often a chance to discover a new person, place, thing or even desire. So if you believe the doctor and decide it is too late for baby making, you can 'circle back' a different route. The possibility always exists for creating what you desire. It goes away when you focus upon fear always and give up or forget about it.

L: So despite my current age and that I have no desire anymore to be pregnant, I can still create the family I know is waiting for me?

A: Souls agree to reconvene, and this is where the desire arises for children or partnerships, which is why you feel a calling or strong attachment to someone (or ones).

L: But you say we can't attach to outcomes or we are keeping our manifestations at bay. If I am wanting a baby so much, aren't I keeping that very thing at bay and creating a circumstance where she (or they) may never arrive?

A: Yes, if you stress and struggle. No if you stay in truth.

> " I am bringing through love. "

Our Law of Attachment is in play whenever Ones are focusing upon wants and not wills. A want and a will are very different. One comes from ego and the other is of the soul. Detachment is how you arrive at wills. Let go. Remember our discussion on wills in The All of The All. A will is a contract you set on Earth for when you die on what you would leave behind, but on 'Heaven' or 'the other side', as it's been called so often, you set a will when you incarnate, before jumping in. A contract of soul, aka what you take with you. So one is for leaving, the other for going.

L: As much as it makes sense, how do I know this isn't all ego created and I am truly slipping into madness?

A: What do you know?

L: I know I am not capable of writing the way we have been writing for the last year and a half. The insights. The wisdom. Every word perfectly placed and in context. It's beyond my capabilities as a writer or human, for that matter. As much as I hear your wisdom, I also know I have no way of making a baby at this point. I am too old. That ship has sailed, and to be honest, I don't want to go through a pregnancy. I would adopt or hire a surrogate if the money existed, but it doesn't so I have shelved the idea altogether.

A: It is not impossible. Intrinsic level biology of the bodily structure allows child bearing to continue much later into life.

L: Not for someone who is now in menopause.

A: Medical science inhibits this biologically. However, the evolution of science allows cells grown in a laboratory to form a baby through alternative means. So you may join the many who have chosen this route after menopause.

L: I don't see that for myself anymore. I feel like I am too old now. I didn't enjoy pregnancy the first time and I can't see myself going through that again at this point in my life. However, I would still love to grow my family, and that would be a miracle in whatever way it arrives, if it does one day.

A: It will if one stays aligned in specificity and intention and allows without fear. A will set before incarnation for three souls to play mommy too. Perhaps this has been on purpose so we could place this conversation upon a book which one day will allow others to believe in miracles. Imagine the chatter you will create when others see what you have created in and around you.

L: It would change everything.

A: Indeed.

L: Help me dear All. Help me achieve a miracle. Help me believe and accept that what is coming is mine for real and let nothing be erased from this conversation, as one day we will share this for everyone to know what you believe can be achieved when you stay in alignment with the soul.

You wrote that.

**Later that week, I saw a story in the media about a woman who found out she was pregnant at 50 years old, naturally. A few weeks later it was announced that Today Show anchor Hoda Kotb, at age 54, had adopted her second child.

L: Well that certainly helps with the belief to see stories like that in the news. I still couldn't sleep tonight, though. It has been a stressful day for me.

A: We know. Why?

L: Because all of this seems rather crazy still to me sometimes. I have been writing books and journals and memos with quotes for months now and still find myself in a stuckness in everything I do. Babies. Houses. Work. Relationships. Health matters. I'm working more and more towards turning to my Spirit side but it feels like I just cannot move forward. Many times, I go into a meditation with my head so clouded that I can't get a vision of anything in my mind's eye. Can you

explain that to me? Why am I so trapped in ego all the time? Even on the days where I try really hard to hand anger and aggravation to my Spirit side, I still suffer. What is the lesson here tonight for me to learn and give?

A: *The lesson is to recognize where you are struggling. This is the lesson of all circumstances which arise in and around the life of all spiritual seekers.*

66 *Why am I struggling and what must be healed in me in order to grow? I'm stuck in a mess of my own creation. Blaming the self and the God within. Missing the point of this entire lesson.* 99

L: And what is the lesson?

A: *To go beyond the mind, which allows you to cocreate with the metaphysical portion of you who is the manifestation of Love. Love knows All. It knows what you need, want, desire and what you hate. Its entire role is to grow wherever you go.*

L: But sometimes I just cannot relieve myself of ego's grip. I am depressed and frustrated with the lack of change and the unyielding sense of doom. I try really hard to stay in contact with the soul, but it's as if I am being stopped mentally; like a brick wall is placed in the path or a heavy object is holding me down. Impossible. This is how it feels to me some days. If we are enlightened and we know our soul truth (who we are and why we are here), and genuinely believe it, then why are so many of us stuck, unable to move forward?

A: *Stuck in a rut. I'm stuck in a rut of my own doing.*

L: Yes. You already said that. It's of my own doing. This doesn't answer my question though, because the fact of the matter is that I do try to get out of the rut on my own by turning to the God within. What I am saying here is this attempt to ward off the ego doesn't work for me always. It works and then I slide right back into old thinking patterns. So help me here. Help me get unstuck. Give me a tip or a tool to unravel the mind from ego's massive grip.

A: *Perhaps you are stuck for a reason.*

L: Well I don't like the reason if it that is the reason. What is the reason?

A: *So that we may co-create these messages of hope for you all.*

L: Well, my dear All, I am sick and tired of being stuck and angry. I want to trade attack thoughts for better thoughts, but if you are not letting me then perhaps it's time to wrap up this book and be done with it so I can move on. I'm tired of all this aggravation you keep putting me through as a soul. Let's get on with it. I'm over it. I can't sleep at night.

I have terrible insomnia or wake up over and over again. My skin feels saggy. My body doesn't feel all that healthy. I have had it up to here with all of this, really. I'm running out of money and time.

A: Time to look at the thought patterns. Why do you feel you cannot sleep?

L: Because the soul keeps waking me up. Because it's so hot in Florida and I can't stand it. I hate the air conditioner running all of the time. I hate living here and I wish I could go live somewhere else, but I can't because I have family here who rely upon me. I have zero money coming in and no job prospects. I have a child who is upset because he can't be near his dad. I have friends who are disloyal and few and far between. I am alone all day, working on trying to figure out how to grow a brand I am not sure I even want to grow because there are too many other people doing what I am doing now. Everyone is a coach or a mindset expert or an author or a speaker. I literally don't have a clue what to do. I can't control anything other than my words written in these books. They are the only thing keeping me sane, and yet they are also driving me insane because no one seems to care, really. They just live their unconscious life while I try to live consciously.

A: All of these aspects are why you suffer. All of you suffer in the illusion as you make observations and aggravations about the life you are living. What must be known is you are stopping yourself from creating a life of grandeur whenever focusing upon these illusions.

L: Well, my friend, they don't feel like illusions and frankly I am tired of being told they are not real, because they certainly feel very real. I don't really know how you expect anyone to grasp this concept of "none of this being real" as we suffer in them. It's hot and you can't change that fact.

A: But we can change how you react to the circumstance.

> 66 *I am loving this beautiful weather today. It feels warm and inviting on my skin and brings me joy today.* 99

L: It's not that easy.

A: It is that easy. All of this is if you focus on love. If you remind yourself every instant of your beingness.

L: Well that is impossible. Because there is simply too much to do. Laundry to fold and bills to pay. Jobs. School work. Making dinner. Cleaning up. You can't 'be' in every single second when you are living on Earth because we have things to do in order to live. It's just not as simple as you say it is. I want to believe, but the evidence to the contrary doesn't support it my dear All; at least not on Earth.

A: Simplicity is easy, but you all make it hard by your sheer unwillingness to recognize the soul as you go about a day.

L: Yeah. Well it's frustrating. I bet no one is doing laundry in Heaven or wherever you are. You probably have a maid and a chef, a housekeeper, a dog walker, a nanny and any other type of service you need. Well guess what, I am the maid and the chef, the nanny and the housekeeper so to always be being is not practical, or at the very least unrealistic. Being doesn't pay bills.

A: If you allow without ego and time frames it would. Enjoy what you do and it will no longer have power over you. This is something we have explained to you before in our last attempt to prove to you all of this is real and true, and none of the damage and torture you go through on Earth is.

L: Well, I am sitting here at my desk typing into a computer watching my bank account dwindle and it feels pretty darn real to me. You are not going to convince me that none of this is actually not happening, sorry.

A: Until you pass back through the realm of the non-physical it won't feel as if you are not really there. Only when you are with us here would you recognize this truth, and this is acceptable as a human. It's not supposed to not feel real, but what we are speaking on is its illusionary nature so you may recognize that which is true and untrue. You can live the truth as if it's not real and still unstick yourself from the collective.

> ❝I am living within the illusion knowingly and making conscious choices to grow my soul as I evolve through circumstances daily.❞

L: You say that but I just don't get it. I just don't see my conscious choices leading me anywhere great right now. I just want my life to get better. I don't want to be unhappy anymore. I want to live on this Earth with joy and true happiness.

A: Let us set some intentions and prayers on this. We will take your examples above and play with them.

"I hate it here. It's too hot," *can become,* "I have chosen to make a commitment to grow my soul as a teacher and thought leader, and this project has been undertaken by me as a means to connect with the Spirit within. I am using this time to better myself, and what better place to do this than with family nearby who support me in my endeavors and allow the freedom needed to make this a reality for myself and others who are benefiting, as well?"

"I don't like an air conditioner running all day," *easily becomes,* "I am choosing to provide a loving home and space to accomplish soul's goals, and when this is finished may I return to a more appropriate climate or place."

"I am struggling with insomnia," *is replaced by,* "My body is the vessel in which I store my mind. Please allow me to sleep at night and let us write these pages when it is necessary only to relieve the soul of its contents and musings. I take notes and return to our pages when I am wide awake and freely aware of the divine presence within me."

"My friends have been disloyal to me and I have so few," *isn't necessary to say.*

Instead say, "I choose to spend time with those who raise me up and of a high vibration. Let those who are willingly aware of our true nature find me so we may grow a tribe of like-minded individuals to share and embrace our Love."

"I have taken my child away from a father figure," *becomes,* "As a soul I have done what is best for myself and allowed a child to decide for himself what is appropriate as it relates to his own soul growth. They shall be reunited when the time is right and thoughts align."

L: **I see what you are doing here.**

A: *We are being clear and specific with our intentions while losing ego and finding soul.*

L: **And what about money and no job prospects?**

A: "I am at a standstill as it relates to my financial well-being and this is what keeps me up at night, wondering and worrying if I am ever to be that which I say I wish to be. I leave this up to my soul and ask to be guided into possibilities whenever a fear-based thought arrives. For I know a soul is controlling our journey and admonish an ego as often as possible."

L: **I get that, but here is a question. It feels like every time I do take a step forward and some great career opportunity arises, then WHAM; it either turns out to be nothing or ends up not happening.**

A: *And why do you feel this is?*

L: **I have no idea. You tell me and then you turn it around into a clear and specific intention, please.**

A: *Dear One, you are focused on financial gains and earthly status and forgetting our lessons of being. Stop doing. Start being.*

L: **Again, being doesn't pay the bills.**

A: *Again, it will if you allow.*

L: I have been being more and more, but I have been following inspired actions and that does take time. I'm not like the characters in *I Dream of Jeannie* or *Bewitched*. I don't blink my eyes and flip my pony tail or wiggle my nose and magic happens. Things take time here on Earth.

A: *They do, and this is why as you do you also be. You ask to be helped and forget to take it.*

L: What do you mean by that?

A: *We ask if you are wise enough to know the difference now between fear and love?*

L: I am.

A: *Then let us show you how you may receive and let go. Close your eyes and listen with your whole body, mind and soul.*

L: I heard, *"Quit being so hard on yourself and feel the love all around you."* And then I felt a beautiful warm energy surrounding me. I'm sorry to say that is all lovely and good but that, again, doesn't pay the bills.

A: *Again, it will if you allow it too. If you allow energetic love to flow it allows manifestations of money and all things physical to flow to you, through you. Enact flow and you are waging war on ego.*

> **❝** *I am abundant. I have all I need.* **❞**

Be conscious of your words, thoughts, actions and intentions.

L: And so what would be a specific intention here?

A: *"My intention is to know beyond a shadow of a doubt that an energy of Love surrounds me always, and as I tap into divine knowing I allow a river of manifestations to arrive for me as a soul being human, and may they arrive through love and not fear."*

L: And, as usual, all of these delays and issues are part of the process of writing these books, aren't they?

A: *Indeed.*

L: I want to scream!

A: *We know, but you also know that profoundness comes from the struggles. No one wins when the score is tied. It must be a back-and-forth ordeal, and sometimes it will flow nicely and others it will feel as if you are stuck. Just know it is for the highest good of All and as the books are received it will all make sense.*

L: And what about selling my house? It has been on the market for over a year now and one of the issues I know of is that it is very close to the highway. So it is very loud. It did not bother me when I first moved in.

However, now it has become a constant annoyance and it's (I believe) messing up the sale of our home. How can you turn that around?

A: "I am wishing to move from a home which I have chosen as a space to create our books and material. It has afforded me the luxury of freedom and time to bring our books to life. I release this home from my psyche and allow that a family of well- intentioned souls find it for themselves."

L: What about the noise issues I mentioned? What is the lesson in that?

A: "I am feeling bothered by a noisy nuisance as a means to guide me away from this home. It has served its purpose and I know that for the next family it will quiet down as they begin their journey within it."

Conscious words. Consistent connection to All That Is.

L: Even if I am ready to move, I am still confused by where to go next. I have ideas of where I want to be but don't have the financial resources to make this a reality for myself. I preferred living in California, but my family is too far away and I want to stay closer to them. I just wish it wasn't here in sunny, hot, humid, bug-filled Florida. I will ask you, dear soul, how to handle these next steps forward in my life?

A: *We guide you as best we can but you are ultimately in charge. Let us ask you what you enjoy about this place?*

L: I love that it is filled with natural light. I love that it's pretty and new. I love the colors and I love that it feels filled with beautiful energy.

A: *And what do you not enjoy?*

L: I don't love the staircase. It's beautiful but I find it to be dangerous for kids; well at least my kid. I wish it wasn't so close to the highway. And mostly, I wish it were closer to the beach.

A: *Where do you see yourself in mind?*

L: In my visioning I see myself living in a condo at the beach overlooking the ocean, with three bedrooms and a big kitchen and dining room area.

A: *And do you know this as possibility?*

L: I know it is possible, and if at some point I lost the fear it would be mine. But I also know that I don't currently have any money coming in at all. I know that the schools by the beach are not good and I would need to send my son to private school, which I currently cannot afford. I know that my son would not be happy living full-time at the beach because there are not enough kids living there. I know that I would like

to have a house closer to his school where families live. I also know I want my mom living close enough to me that I can see her frequently and be there for her.

A: And why do you know all of these things?

L: Because I have experienced for myself the feeling of not having these things and knowing what I don't like or have?

A: You have accessed a knowing about what you both do and don't want to create. So now as you discovered this about your —

L: I also know that moving is a pain in the butt and I would stay here if I had the money to afford both this house and a beach condo for myself.

A: And why do you feel it is not possible to do both?

L: Because I have zero dollars coming in right now. I have no job (full-time) and my book series has yet to make a dent with the willing seekers you tell me are out there, so I am sort of in limbo financially.

A: You have been describing precisely for the readers why the house has not sold.

L: And why is that?

A: Because you are erratically thinking upon it. You have so many ideas and attitudes about it, the creative power within is confused as are you. Where shall I go? What shall I do?

L: Okay. I get that. Can you help me?

A: Of course. We are here for you in every way. We are not here to tell you what to do but rather show you who to be. So in that sense who do you want to be?

L: I want to be someone who lives by the ocean. I want to be someone who lives in a clean, quiet, nice community. I want to be a good mom who sends her child to the best schools where the kids are kind and taught unity. I want to be a kind daughter who takes care of her mother as she took care of me. I want to be someone who isn't materialistic but who chooses safety and security for herself. I want to be someone who isn't struggling financially and needs nothing other than what will serve the soul.

A: And do you believe you can create this for yourself?

L: By myself, probably no. With the help of the soul and God/Source/Universe, I think so.

A: You know so but are still working towards belief with us as your guides.

L: True. Belief is hard.

A: Incremental steps are necessary. Leaps and bounds do not make a souldier. Small, steady steps do. What do you feel you are learning here this evening?

L: How to be clear and specific as our chapter title states?

A: Clear and specific intentions lead to clear and specific manifestations (in the absence of fear). Erratic intentions create —

L: Nothing?

A: No thing.

L: How clear and how specific do you need to be?

A: As clear and specific as is necessary to bring forth what you are wanting to create. If you say, "I want a new car," and you leave it at that, you will ultimately receive a car of your choosing as you practice fearless thinking.

If you say, "I want a car that seats seven with rear door wipers and a sound system of excellent measure," you will create that experience for yourself—

L: In the absence of fear?

A: Indeed. And if you say, "I want a blue sports car with grey interior and a front/side airbag," and go to a dealership where only minivans are sold are you being clear and specific with actions?

L: No. What is your point here?

A: In all asks of the Universe, it must be clear and specific what is wanting to be created from the top to the bottom in order for it to manifest. "I want a new house." Okay but what kind of house do you want? What color should it be? How big? Shall it have a pool? A lake view? A community of like-minded individuals? Do you see what I am telling you here?

L: I believe so, yes.

A: Good. Now let us be clear and specific with your requirements for a new home.

L: My intention is to find a home filled with natural light that allows my mother to be close by, with a new look and feel to it. A home that will be ready now in an affordable area that is both safe and quiet with a lot of kids for my son to play with and within the vicinity of a good, A rated school district. Let it also be near my beach condo, which will be purchased alongside a new home as it allows me a place to write my books and materials in an energetic haven. I allow and accept that all of this has been chosen by me, for me, as a soul and that my desire for it exists as possibility because I have owned these homes before.

Um, excuse me? I have owned these homes before? You wrote that.

A: What have we told you before in our All books? Each thought has been thought. Every thing exists. In every way you have already been, done or had it.

L: I keep thinking of a video game where you play the game and every time it ends you start over and where you end up depends upon the choices you make. Are you telling me that in some other inception of Earth (or version) I already lived in these homes?

A: Not only have you lived in them; you have been here before.

L: I don't follow?

A: You have been Laura as a separate being in a separate place.

L: Are you speaking about alternate or parallel universes? You are, aren't you?

A: You are catching up with all which is known of our Universes. There are parallel and perpendicular universes, as we told you in our first book.

L: I remember reading this in the Seth Material and not really understanding it.

A: Because you were not able to accept it. Now you are much more aligned in beingness, and so you are capable of resonating with more truths. There are yous in all corners of the infiniteness. You are in everything. No matter where you go, there you are. You exist in everything. So, if you have thought about it, it exists. All you need do is be clear and specific in intention (or desire) and release the ego (fear) so we may bring it to you, through you. Make sense?

L: I think so. What happens if you just focus on happiness, peace, joy, abundance and don't care much about being specific? Will you wind up creating erratically?

A: We show you what needs to be healed and you choose how to arrive at the above - happiness, joy, etc. It is a sorting out cabinet. Like a file cabinet. I like this. I don't like this. I need this to live on. I don't care for this.

L: Can you be too specific?

A: You can be too erratic, meaning overwhelming the "system" with unwavering demands and nonsensical expectations, such as the population of most of your fellow brethren expect and demand. This is why lines form at the lottery. Everyone wants to be rich, but only the truly evolved understand money to be necessity not only to evolve, but simply to share and give as a means to create space for Love. It is only necessary to take what you need, as discussed in our last book together.

> 66 *Enlightened masters take what they need.* 99
>
> – The All That Is

You don't need much to be happy. Just a simple life filled with experiences and knowledge. However, most on the planet of Earth are at a level where material wealth is definitively their goal. For you it is a means to an end and not a core desire anymore, true?

L: True. I just want to be happy and live a comfortable existence with money to travel and be with my son, to have more kids and have the help needed to raise them on my own (if necessary), to experience things without getting worried about the financial aspects of everything, to have a beautiful clean, quiet, safe home and to share it with others. I really want to help others financially because I know the burdens of not having money.

A: *And you may have all of those things, dear One.*

L: It doesn't feel that way. It still feels as if I am stuck in the practical even if I believe because the time frames don't line up.

A: *Time on Earth is tricky. It messes with mind and can be difficult to navigate through. Why not bless the wait rather than bear the burden?*

L: Because our whole life feels like a rat race. First school, then work, then career aspirations or dreams. We are always chasing something and never satisfied. I could be satisfied if I just had money and not success. Why is money so hard to discover?

You wrote "discover." I would say make.

A: *You don't make money. You discover its ability to arrive.*

L: And how may I do that, dear All?

A: *Let go of need. Let go of lack. Let go of feeling poor and impoverished. See yourself as the bright, bold, beautiful star you are and know it has yet to be created in the physical realm because you have focused on the absence of it almost entirely. More comes when you own this biological truth, it is made by the Earth and therefore shared, as well. Money is energy. Move it. Share it. Give. Receive. Return. Nothing comes that hasn't first been given. It is spiritual law to exchange energy. Give. Receive. Return. It is a cycle, and just like a bicycle, in order for it to move, you drive the momentum and its stopping and going is dependent upon YOU. Remember our Law of Compensation. Circulation is key.*

L: Oh my God you are so frustrating. I have moved the money. I spent $15,000 getting our All books out into the world and I have made back only about $1,000 or so of that —

A: *So far. More is coming if you stay aligned in truth. Accept it as part of the contract (more on this soon) and you will never need worry over money again.*

L: If I spend my money and it never returns, I will be broke and my son and I will be homeless.

A: And that is the soul *reason why you are currently without it. You believe you are incapable of creating it through the universal energy system we call Love.*

L: Exactly. Believing in "Love" is a hard concept to take in when you see no evidence of anything, any miracles financially. I can see a sign or message and have hope, but until the clock strikes gold I am beyond capable of believing money will just arrive if I stay "aligned in Love." Love is a fantasy at this point.

A: Love is All. All is Love. However, when Ones separate they know the opposite of love, which is fear. On all planets it is not this oppositional work you are achieving. However, Earth is a magnetic field which attracts both good and bad thoughts based upon vibrational energy, aka Law of Magnetic Attraction. We know you are looking for more answers, but we are being very clear and specific in terms of how to make money arrive. You must allow and not chase. Think of a bag and how in the wind it blows away, and the more you run after it the more the momentum floats it away. You are the wind causing everything. Be still. Listen and receive. Then will you know which way to arrive.

L: Arrive at what?

A: The destination chosen prior to incarnation. All exists as possibility and Ones need only allow.

L: And how we allow is through quiet. Stillness speaks loudest?

A: Accurate and true. Be quiet.

L: I still don't see how if you just be quiet —

A: And believe —

L: How things will come to you. That just seems like superhero stuff. I can't believe if I sit around and be still —

A: And listen —

L: What am I listening to or for?

A: Listen for guidance.

> ❝ Where would you have me go? What actions may I take to follow divine mind and not ego? ❞

Questions are the way to all manifestations if you allow the Spirit/soul to create and not ego.

L: This is triggering fear in me because I feel that at times I did spend money in faith that it would return, and while some money did flow back,

not enough to give me peace so I can focus only on joy. I would love to be able to spend my money without a care in the world. To buy what I want when I want, to travel where I want, to donate to those who need it, to gift to those I love, and to live in a nice home and community and of course at the beach, which is and has been my goal for some time.

A: *All things possible in the absence of fear, and we know removing those blocks to abundance can be painful. In most cases you are focusing on progress and not process.*

L: **And what does that mean?**

A: *You are continually focusing on where am I at? How much further to go here? Rather than focusing on seeing the vision ahead. Let us show you. All of you close your eyes for a moment.*

L: **Right now I am focusing on fear and the sensations in my body. So I can't see or hear anything.**

A: *Precisely why we asked you (all) to close the eyes. So you may understand how fears stops the flow of everything; information and money among other things. Now we may ask that you close your eyes and focus the mind on clear and specific manifestations you want to create, such as the beach condo you are always discussing, as above.*

L: **I see the condo and myself inside. I see clients coming and me enjoying the balcony. At the same time, though, I just keep thinking about how I don't have the money to afford it currently. What if the human factor creates disbelief? Are we blocking our visions of what you say had already been created by not knowing? Or by not believing? It's hard to believe if you want to create a new home, for example, that if you don't know where the money is coming from and time is running out that it can magically manifest. Do you see what I am saying here? The time factor is a killer, or the age factor or the geographic factor. There are a lot of human factors that are obstacles. If you have three weeks to figure something out or how to make money it's pretty hard to believe in its arrival.**

A: *Making it hard to manifest (a word we use on a human level that has become popular in mainstream materials and so we continue with it here and with others) what it is you are wanting to create in physical form.*

L: **It's not easy, buddy. Can you help me? Or at the very least can my soul help with this?**

A: *Of course. We are with you always. Let us discuss the ways in which to make money. Belief. Beyond every lie is everything found. Lie as in ego/falsity/illusion.*

L: **As I told you, I don't have that belief level.**

A: Yet.

L: Every time I find some faith, I lose it in the lag time. I refuse to spend my money because if I run out then I am going to need to struggle, and I don't ever want to struggle. I have had a pretty easy life in that sense and can't imagine ever going backwards.

A: So don't. Imagine going forwards.

L: How?

A: "Dear All, help me to see that only Love is real and when money is moved let it return to me in spades."

L: Well here is the issue with that —

A: We are listening and ready to receive.

L: Right now, the fact is that I have not seen my money return as you say it will.

A: Did we not lead you to financial success in terms of a career when it seemed as if all were lost? Did we not show you a way to bring money to you through an unrealized avenue?

L: Yes, but both of those things did not exactly bring me a windfall.

A: "Dear All, I am searching for meaning in this life and have found it in our precious words. I am waiting and waiting and watching as money flows out and nothing flows in. Please allow me to release my fear as it relates to using hard earn money to create more of it. I accept that I am the creator of all and this is my birthright as a child of God and the Universe. Amen."

L: Would it help to be clear and specific in intention with what you would like to create in terms of money?

A: Of course. And what is your intention?

L: Do I have to put a number on it? A specific one?

A: If you specifically want to you may, but in a case such as money it is most important to use it for good and not financial gains of a materialistic kind.

L: Well my main goal is to be financially independent and no longer struggle. To have all my needs met and to live in a nice home. I have seen several homes in my visions over the last couple of years and I guess this is where I get hung up. Are those figments of my imagination I created or something else?

A: They are possibilities, as are all visions. That which you see in mind's eyes is always possible of becoming manifest if you stay in high vibration, but (as we said above) if you are erratically thinking upon a vision it will stay un-manifested for you perhaps forever.

L: How often should we stay with the vision?

A: Until it has become physical. It is matter and only matter, and must be made via thought. This and this only is how you bring form to life, through matter. All asks are available to thee as we have been telling you for months now. It is created via thought and thought only. If you stay in thought, word and action in the absence of fear it must become manifest. It is spiritual law.

L: And what is the thought, word and action. Can you describe each for me please?

A: **Thought**: "I am abundant."

Word: "I have all I need."
Action: "I will follow inspiration as it leads me to financial gains while at the same time spending in faith it shall return to me in kind."

L: Is there a time frame on Earth? I know in Heaven you say we manifest instantaneously, and on Earth we need to have some time lag in order not to cause chaos on the planet. But how long must we stay in the visioning?

A: Our laws are specific in that they manifest for you what you are thinking upon at time frames outside the laws of time and space, and so to give an accurate "time stamp" is quite literally unnatural. It is upon you as humans to stay in high vibration and be, and this is the only true meaning of life. Anything else is simply ego, and there is nothing wrong with wanting to live a rich, abundance-filled existence on Earth during the time you are in a body, but it is upon you to let it unfold as it should through co-creation with soul.

L: I see your point, but it's hard to not want to live an abundant life here on Earth so you can steer clear of as much chaos and anger, because a lot of that exists here.

A: We know and we understand frustration. Just know if you are working on your beingness and spending in love, love will unfold for you. It is most definitely a probability in all aspects of self. It is if you believe; and we are wanting All to understand our specific and clear instructions are one hundred percent on point, but we must point out you are nowhere near belief, nor is most of the world. It is work to be done in order to elevate your consciousness in order to arrive at any and all chosen aspects of the human experience (speaking on an individualized level). Everything exists. All you need do is believe.

L: In the interim, what can be done to help guide us towards those chosen aspects and belief?

A: A brilliant question indeed. You are so tortured by the indecision and confusion you cannot see your contracts (as was stated in The All of The All). Soul contracts are a metaphysical imprint of the life chosen by All. Each has their own, and there is one for the collective as well as One. One for you. One for we. One for All.

L: How do we access these records?

A: By asking the Source within.

> 66 *Dear All, show me what is possible for me in this life.*
> *What themes am I working through? How close am I to its arrival?*
> *How may I move through this time more efficiently?*
> *What work needs to be done in soul?* 99

The questions are quite endless, and these are to be used whenever there is confusion. Later, shall we discuss contracts. What they are and how best to use them on Earth. For now, we offer an exercise to alleviate confusion as it relates to manifesting desires and asks. Be vigilant in your approach to soul growth and asks are answered, All ways.

WORKBOOK EXERCISE #4:
CLEAR AND SPECIFIC INTENTIONS

U sing the Law of Intelligent Affirmation (specificity and intention), write a list of intentions. Be sure that they are clear and specific, and remove that which comes from ego.

Example: "I want a new house."

Clear and Specific Intention: *"My intention is to find a home which honors my commitment to growth and expansion. Let it be filled with light, be positively beautiful inside and out and let the money flow into my experience which allows for purchasing the home. I am seeking a home with 3 bedrooms, 2 bathrooms, new appliances, clean, quiet and in a neighborhood with children for my son to play with and near a great school with teachers who are kind and caring."*

Example: "I need a new car."

Clear and Specific Intention: *"My intention is to own a car which is safe and efficient and allows me to arrive at my destinations on time. It should be automatic, with four doors, a rear folding seat, gray exterior and white leather interior and be sold to me by a kind and fair salesperson at a dealership with pure intention, as well."*

This allows a picture of an entire experience rather than just bits and pieces of it. Take your time and get a clear vision in mind of what you would like to create. Use this vision to craft your intentions and asks. Your intentions may be different, but use the above as a model for crafting your own desires, making sure they are soul's and not ego's.

After you return, we shall question the nature of being in chapter 6.

CHAPTER 6
Question Everything

In order to grow and evolve as a being of light you must be reminded through acts of Love why we are all here. In the same vein, you also must be alerted to us not being here. ❞

– The All That Is

G rowth is necessary as you evolve on Earth. Things cannot stay the same. They must change, and change is painful if you choose it to be. You always have a choice to view the disruptions with Love, understanding their purpose and begin again. However, you must question All. Not, "Why? How could this happen?" but rather, "What is the meaning or purpose of the circumstance?"

All circumstances led opportunities to heal and this their purpose. It does not matter if the individual is involved or all of the collective. Whether it be healing the soul of One or healing the soul of the whole nation, its purpose lies within. Every question is answered when asked, which is why we offer the opportunity to share them in this book.

Eternal Validity

Laura: There will be lots of people who are going to be questioning the validity of this book based on seeming contradictions with other books of a spiritual nature.

All: Good.

L: Why good?

A: Because you are each being led to the right teaching at the right moment in the right time. Nothing happens which has not been thought upon prior. An entire curriculum spelled out by you, for you to grow the soul and enlighten the self; the self which is consciousness. As you go about writing you are bouncing around a bit, more so than in our last book, correct?

L: Yes. It's not flowing the way the last three did. I keep finding more information and going back into different chapters and having to ask bigger questions.

A: You are being guided to do this by the soul. It knows what you need to ask and when you need to ask it. It's all purposeful and deliberate and quite literally designed. A life blueprint, if you will.

L: What is a life blueprint?

A: It is your roadmap of creation; the very essence of the journey you take in bodies. It is your GPS which guides you to the right thing at the right time, such is being done as we create this book. Let it unfold as it should, and when you are needing a tune up return back to our sections on prayer and intention so you may create in love and not fear.

**As I was writing this book, I found myself caught up yet again in an "alter" event as Spirit would have me call it. About five minutes before I arrived at our local mall with my mom and son, an alleged shooting went down. We missed it, fortunately, but saw people running out of the mall just after we pulled into the parking lot. Had we arrived just a few minutes earlier we might have been caught up in the circumstance inside the mall.

L: So are you telling me that incident was in my life blueprint, which is perhaps why I couldn't sleep tonight and I am back here at my computer asking questions?

A: Yes.

L: Why? Or rather shall I ask it the way you stated: "What is the meaning or purpose of the circumstance?"

A: Because you must be aware of all aspects of self and understand why you are here in the first place. To know absolute divine truth (as we are speaking upon in these All books) renders our entire reason for being in bodies worthless in some respects. You must understand the laws of the Universe in order for things to work properly as body/mind/soul, but if you are always living a life of true joy and no pain, well then you are —

L: Back in Heaven enjoying the good life? You're laughing at me.

A: Not exactly, but we understand your meaning here. You are expecting we will tell you to go back to heaven is to live an unburdened life, but that is not our absolute truth. In many respects you are living in heaven as we speak. The minute you accept Love into your heart and mind you are here. The second you stop accepting it you are in fear again. Over and over you do this dance, and so we created our world as opposites so you can practice this cha cha on Earth, as its magnetic force is strong and allows for this back-and-forth adventure. On and on you will go on the very journey you have decided upon creating for yourself there until you both know and choose Love at all times for all time.

L: If I am here on Earth choosing Love in every single instance, then I would essentially not really be here at all? I would be back in the heavenly realm and have all the answers?

A: Not all will have all the answers at once. Remember, we have explained you are each at individual levels as souls incarnating into being. You are one who has evolved further than most on Earth and so, as soul, you (Laura) would return immediately to our other side as soon as you find yourself recognizing Love always.

L: That's hard to do on Earth because we are so different in terms of race, gender, class and understanding (speaking spiritually). We compare and contrast ourselves all day, every day it seems.

A: Thus why you must stay in high consciousness and soul work throughout life. Remember you are nowhere near masters on Earth. Even those seemingly enlightened are responding with judgement and fear at times because it is so real and so diverse.

L: I thought you said it wasn't real?

A: Perfection. You are questioning. Answers are within if you go seeking. Yes, we know it feels real and that is our interpretational meaning of the phrase, "it is so real." In physical realms it feels real, we know. So we speak in terms you will understand. Remember to question everything. Not just some; All.

L: I have been trying to be less judgmental and embrace the Love as often as possible. With 24 hours news, social media and technology always at our fingertips it's hard to ignore prejudice, class and gender issues. Unless you are a monk meditating on a mountain, but where is the fun in that? Oops, I'm judging again.

A: Judgement and observation are mutually exclusive. You can look at situations and decide from a space of Love while at the same time offer wise words.

L: So embrace the fear?

A: Embrace it. Learn from it. Move to a higher choice but accept that it comes for you to evolve beyond it.

L: So why even share this information? Why even write these books? I don't understand the point, especially if we can't move beyond the fear at all times. It seems most of these spiritual books are all about teaching how to lose the ego completely and live a happy, unburdened life. Most teachers are sharing how to manifest and change your life. I feel as if most of these books tell you, 'if you just do all these things you will be happy and successful and free'. I think that's what our All books are helping us to do anyway.

A: It is not necessary to question why, only to evolve.

L: But which is it? Can we live a truly happy existence on Earth or is that just a pipe dream?

A: *Mostly you can, but there will always be circumstances from which to grow and evolve no matter how "spiritual" you think you are.*

L: You did say that in our other books actually, come to think of it.

A: *"Your lows will be mostly highs if you stay aligned in our One truth."*

We had stated this time and again in our All books and in our daily quotes to you. Have you not received this message over and over again? Nothing happens to you that does not happen through you, but you must be involved in some circumstances in order to evolve and continue evolving. Bless the circumstances. Embrace them. Move to a higher choice. There will always be lessons to learn and experiences to share.

L: What about all these books teaching people to master their mind? I just don't want people getting the wrong idea that everything can always be perfect and amazing. And to be honest, your *Wisdom of The All* quotes we share sometimes say this, too. So maybe we are spreading false information, as well?

A: *We are perfectly aligned and every quote serves a purpose chosen prior. It is not false information. It is fact. If you stay aligned in Love you are always capable of creating a life of grandeur, happiness or peace, but you will also find yourself embroiled in some circumstances. All masters do; even the enlightened Ones on Earth.*

L: You said that we were nowhere near masters on Earth? That seems contradictory and I don't want anyone questioning these words or others we have written prior.

A: *On Earth you are vibrationally attracting experiences to add value. Like a bank you collect coins (experience) and money (knowledge). As you grow your bank it will always be possible to experience master-like wisdom expressed through the One. You can be masterful without being masters.*

L: So be clear and specific please with your definition of master. My intention is to receive wisdom and knowledge through the One. I pray for accurate information and ask to be guided by All.

A: *Brilliant. A perfectly phrased question using all principles which had been taught so far in our book. You are mastering the art of soul.*

Question All. Choose Love. Be.

On Earth you are masters when you see Love and be Love, but in terms of masterhood and being enlightened to a degree of vibration where you have no more lessons to learn on Earth, then no. None of you are masters. Some are more highly evolved and have mastered what they had come to learn, but to be a true master Ones must be enlightened beyond Earth, beyond Cosmos, Mannos, Zeanos and all the Infiniteness.

L: That seems like a lot of work and knowledge and somewhat exhausting.

A: Life is eternal, and so discovering who you are takes centuries. The more time you spend on a planet the more knowledge gained. Adventuring on means you have achieved soul's goals and are ready to go elsewhere in the Infinite.

L: Why do some of us come here from other planets and places? I have been doing a lot of readings for clients and finding they came here from outside the solar system and have trouble assimilating to Earth.

A: Many enjoy Earth and others do not. Remember, there have been many inceptions and Earth has been turned over many times, indeed. Those who are feeling the effects of having been on other planets or solar systems know deep within who they were and what often times feels like mental health issues can be spiritually-based confusion.

L: It seems because they have all this information that lives inside of them, they struggle and feel like outsiders, and not knowing why causes depression, anxiety and other—

A: Fear disorders. Yes. Precisely why all must seek answers within to engage the soul. Once Ones discover who they truly are, their bank of knowledge rises and it would make sense why they say they felt like outsiders and were ostracized either by others or themselves. In the same vein, there are many who chose Earth almost exclusively and enjoy it immensely. It's a fun ride if you can get over the bumps without falling.

L: I don't. Well, actually I don't know, maybe I would like Earth if I could get to a state of abundance and freedom. I enjoyed my Hollywood life and had so much fun on TV and movie sets. So I guess I could get to a place where I enjoyed the ride fully again.

A: You did then and in many other lives. More recently you have fell (sometimes literally) into fear traps and caused unpleasant, unhealthy or deadly outcomes, but ultimately you are at place of enlightenment where masterhood is achievable (at the level available on Earth). You are one who is able to see and feel All, and though it will be an easier journey, it will still feel at times that you are caught up in unhappy events and circumstances. It is the nature of being human and all perfectly executed by you, for you, dear One. Every situation has its roots in allowing you to both know and recognize where you are needing a refresher on fear.

> *What is the lesson? What can I learn through this situation to help move me out of it more quickly?*

Questions are the life bread of the human experience. Use them wisely all the time. Every time a circumstance arrives, you must examine its lesson until you are sure of its meaning, and then and only then may you move beyond this.

L: And what was the lesson of the mall incident?

A: To bring you right back here so we may discuss this very questioning of everything. You are right where you need to be learning about love and fear.

L: And why not share this message in other books?

A: Perhaps we have and you are not reading it properly, or perhaps we have shared precisely the message each individual is ready to receive when they are needing to receive it in the blueprint. Each course is different and everyone knows what they need when they need it in order to evolve and grow beyond fear.

L: Why can't we move past the ego once we are sure in our knowing? Well I guess you just told us why. It's all part of the learning process, but my biggest problem is the waiting for change. No matter how hard I try to not focus on the lack I just keep getting tripped up and brought back into fear. How will I survive as money begins to run out? Why is my health always so up and down? These questions run constantly through my mind. It is torture, absolute torture to wait for your dreams or happiness to arrive.

A: How and why. Two questions ego will use to torture you from inside. Torture. You are seeing in mind's eye a vision of the slaves who built the temples and the ones who rowed the boats. You are describing exactly the process of removing blocks for allowing a place to be built or a dream to be reached. We, as a collective, have been torturing ourselves for century upon century. Your tortures of modern day are different only from slavery in that you have locked yourself in a mental prison (well, most of you) rather than a physical one. And how, may we ask, were the slaves freed?

L: Someone or something (aka God) came along to rescue the slaves in many cases. Either Moses or Abraham Lincoln are examples but, ultimately, I think most people believe it was God or a higher power doing this in our lives.

A: As people figure out their tortures (fears), they become vulnerable to attacks such as the thought processes you are holding onto.

> *I am old, tired, unlikeable, unlovable. My skin is old. My bones are weak.*

This is when an ego steps in to force you to be the thing you don't want to be. In a case of a slave, it would be to work the mines or plow the field (as examples). As a modern being it is to show you an old, tired, rundown person in the mirror. To remind you of your lack, it will consistently draw you back into past misgivings, mistakes or injustices. It will torture you from the inside out rather than beat you, as had been done in ancient times. The torturer is and always will be you. Whether it's an Egyptian man whipping you or an unhealed thought provoking you, it is exactly the same torture you are feeling. A physical sensation or mental poison are in fact the same experience only in different time periods.

L: Do they hold the same charge physically? Our bodies don't know the difference between the physical torture and the mental torture?

A: Indeed, and medical science is beginning to prove (albeit slowly) how true this is.

L: And just as hard as it was to escape the physical torturer, it's equally as hard to escape the mental torturer – aka me. The minute I feel an ache or pain coming up, I focus on it and then get dragged into some fear about it. I see an article or TV show or movie where someone gets sick or dies, and suddenly I have imprinted that in my own mind. Right now I have a multitude of ailments that I am dealing with and my mind will just not allow me to stop focusing on them. I ask. I pray. I intend.

A: Over and over again you must repeat the process. "I am safe, guided and loved," is how we described in our last book to move beyond the fear. Use a mantra to remind yourself over and over again until momentum kicks in and you are losing fear and finding soul. We recognize and understand how hard the process is, but as we have told you time and time again, some circumstances are necessary to move you beyond the ego and into finding soul.

L: Such as?

A: Anything that keeps you stuck. Do you recall fears over the staircase in your home and how we prayed, set intentions and all the modalities we have spoken upon?

L: Yes.

A: And what became of the fear?

L: It went away after I consistently did those things and, eventually, I mostly forgot about it. I am trying to do that with my health, but as I have said in other portions of this book, when you feel the sting, the pain or the irritation, it's impossible not to focus upon it and then also not to let the collective thoughts or what you know or have seen happen to other people affect you. This week I have seen several people cross to the other side who were way too young to die. It's hard not to let that affect you, especially as you get older. I guess I am still

very much caught in the eye of fear. I am trying, though, and I feel I am getting better at kicking ego to the curb, but there are days when it is much more difficult, for sure.

A: For all of you. All days have ups and downs. Some are better than others. Just know you are not alone in suffering ego as collective consciousness. It is best always on these days to send love to All. Reminding you we are all One, and with this in mind you can offer "we" affirmations.

> 66 We are feeling the pain of the suffering right now and I wish to send love and light to all my brothers and sisters on Earth. 99

L: And what can I say to myself today? I have been asking for signs and messages to help me move on from the health problems and release the fear. Today I saw a family of ducks crossing the road and then saw the same message on Facebook. Someone had posted a video of ducks crossing the road. Why did the ducks cross the road?

A: Together.

L: Correct. There was a long line of them and then a little straggler who stayed behind and joined in the last minute. Is there a message I am meant to know about here?

A: Many a message we have been showing you lately and you have been finding them and heeding them mostly?

L: I have. There was one about the otters. Two little otters came running across the road just after I sent an intention to find out why my heart was having strange pangs. And when I looked up the messages in a spirit animal card deck, it had a picture of two otters encased in a heart and the message was about reconnecting and reengaging with the world, which I had not been doing. I have been way more of a lone wolf as I navigate this spiritual awakening, but I have been feeling lonely.

A: The heart is a lonely hunter you had heard us speak in spirit to you.

L: Yes. And almost immediately I went seeking answers and found them in several messages, and I have been working on being more open and receptive to engaging with the world again. I also went to the doctor to have it checked, combining physical, mental and spiritual practices as you have advised in my first three *All* books.

A: A job well done, and this is what we ask all to do. In any circumstance at all, look for the messages, ask for help and keep working on changing. Through the acts of love you are actively pursuing enlightened thinking and this is all you need do daily.

L: So what was the message of the ducks? It can't be coincidence.

A: There are no coincidences. Whenever ducks are around, waddle away from fear and into Love.

L: And what may I say to help with the heart/lonely issue.

A: "Dear All, I know I am healthy and whole and all my aches and pains are here to show me unhealed thoughts and ideas. Show me the way to love and to health. Keep me in high vibes so I may use my soul self and heal."

L: I am trying less and less to allow my ego to torture and confuse me. I think social media is our torturer nowadays. Comparing ourselves to one another and seeing pain and tragedy.

A: "This person had this and this person did that."

You are torturing one another by living in the lack, as you would call this. Focusing upon illusions and the circumstances of others can and does draw you (all) back to torture (ego).

L: I get that. I really do but it doesn't make it any easier to live through. Obviously, I don't remember the physical pain of being a slave in ancient times, but our mental poison is toxic, just as the sting of the whip was in times of war or tragedy. It's painful to wait and wait with absolutely no proof our dreams will arrive or our mental torture will end.

A: As before, in all of those cases a savior did come along to rescue the tortured, did they not?

L: They did, but for many it was too late. I think this is why people die of heart attacks or depression overtakes them. They are tortured in their own mind, and as much as you make all of this seem to be so easy to just "change your mind" and cocreate with the soul and Spirit, it really isn't easy. It's hard and frustrating and massively unrelenting. The minute you feel joy and accept all of this as truth is the minute a circumstance comes along to wipe you out like a wave in the ocean. You think you have it dialed in and then you see a friend have a stroke or a child tortured or abused. Being on Earth kind of sucks, but I want to be here for my son. So I have to put up with all this earthly aggravation.

A: As has been chosen by you, for you.

L: Well, I guess I am not a very good chooser because I have obviously chosen a life of struggle and doubt and mediocrity. I wish I would have chosen to be J-Lo or a famous celebrity with unending supplies of money.

A: And yet you know money ultimately isn't what brings happiness. You have seen many fall victim to ego who had billions or multimillions and still died of fear and loathing.

L: But money sure helps with the struggle. It helps not to have to worry where every dollar is coming from each day. It helps for someone who wants to "just be", as you keeping telling us we are meant to do with our lives. You can't "just be" when you have to keep a roof over your head, food on the table and clothes on your back. I would never want to be one of these motivational speakers who tells people how easy it is to follow the Law of Attraction and everything will magically get better, because that is just not how it works, at least for me. I want a peaceful life of no struggle and so I had the reins over to you, dear soul. The only one who can make me happy is you.

And you just wrote that last part with me. You know I can't do this alone. I need help.

A: *And help is always here. Why are you back here sitting at your computer almost every night?*

L: Because I am unhappy and tortured by the ego. And I know if I come to these pages and ask these questions —

A: *Always will you be answered.*

L: Yes, but I also know that even after a few days of happy thoughts and feeling connected and knowing our truths, eventually I just wind up right back where I started – questioning everything. Not so much the principles. I do believe we are One. I do know we are souls and return to consciousness when we die. I do know we are multi-layered, multi-dimensional beings. I just don't know how to stay in alignment long enough to spark a miracle. I think if I just had one miracle show up in my life, I would be able to start believing in miracles. And yet, all I have is sameness. Nothing changes, and if it does it's very tiny; small miracles. And so I stay lost and stuck and questioning.

A: *Allowing a book of profound information to come through.*

L: At this point, to be honest, I would rather be happy. It's too hard, all of this. At the end of the day, it feels as if all any of us are doing on planet Earth is surviving. Thriving is hardly a failsafe when most of the world is living in poverty and lack. What I can't understand is why you constantly call this world an "illusion" and that none of this is real. It feels pretty darn real to me all the time. The pain, the sadness, the loneliness. That's real, as much as you want us to believe it's not. Your system of growing the soul sucks. What's the point of being in a body when all you do is struggle with it?

A: *You've got much to learn as a soul. It is all part of the process of a life, and as much as you want to believe in all of our divine truths, you are still caught in the illusion of separation. You can believe without seeing manifestations arise, yet. The deliberate process of life is such that no one sees precisely what they are thinking upon at a given moment in most cases of thought. The very thing that frustrates you is also what keeps you alive living and breathing. All of this is designed to test your will.*

L: Why?

A: *To recognize in you the power to grow and evolve, but also to know you are not without circumstances. Adversities will arrive. Trials and tribulations will occur.*

L: It's so hard and frustrating. Every single time I feel like something good has happened, I get thrown right back into turmoil. It's never ending, this process. One step forward, two hundred back.

A: *Imagine in times of great strife the arduous battles you (all) faced in other bodies you once inhabited. Perhaps it is because you have waged these wars over and over again in different roles and in different ways it has become so burdensome. Hundreds of times you have (all) been in a position where you seemingly can't move on and all hope is lost.*

L: And what happened then?

A: *A "mixed bag", as you all would say on Earth. Sometimes you (all) held on and rallied, but others you sunk into despair and wound up dead.*

L: Wow. Way to sugar coat it.

A: *No one gets out alive. Why you are all so hung up on the word dead itself is why you all suffer in the illusion of pain and sorrow and tragedy. Let go of the notion that death is the hard part. Life is the hard part because you make it so difficult, all of you. Almost all of you. Some, you know, are quite aware of how to live a life of peace and joy.*

L: Very few from what I can tell. I hope to get there one day.

A: *And you will if you stay in practice always. A happy ending is possible for all who stay in conscious connection with All. Now do you see why others who are enlightened, written books or championed Spirit for decades pass through to our other realm? It is difficult to defeat ego. It is a back-and-forth dance most are incapable of mastering.*

L: Because we drag ourselves around in these bodies like slugs; slaves to money and power and material things. Unless you are a monk who has chosen an uncomplicated life, you are pretty much on the slow train to Stressville all the time. I want to get off this train and be happy, but it just seems impossible.

A: *Impasse. You are at an impasse, a place in time where everything has stalled and the movement is slow because you are its controller. You know this. You use it often, just not nearly enough. As you control the train you choose the track. Left, love. Right, fear. It is over and over again; it must be explained until all see truth as has been presented throughout our books and series. You are causing delays as part of the process of growth as well as through the processes of thought you are consistently stuck in. Old. Tired. Unworthy. Incapable of change. Lonely. Sad. Miserable. Hating where you live and railing against life as impossible as you said above. Where does this all come from may we ask?*

L: The ego. The never ending torturer.

A: The slave driver.

L: I have been thinking a lot about 40 days recently, and how the Jews wandered through the desert never giving up hope they would be freed.

A: And did they succeed?

L: Yes, but only after a tumultuous battle and a long, arduous struggle.

A: And such is life. This is a metaphor for all of it. Struggles come and go but if you can hold on, life will continue and bring to you all you have been wanting or desiring.

L: What about willing?

A: Those desires you will are "set in stone," so to speak. Each is part of a contract already decided upon as you incarnated. A will is a contract, just as in the physical. We have spoken on this before in our second book (The All of The All) with you. No thought exists which has not been spoken, thought or used before.

L: Which thoughts? All thoughts or only the fear thoughts? What if I daydream about dying in a motorcycle accident? What if I worry over health issues? Have those thoughts been thought already?

A: All thoughts have been thought, both good and bad. You get to decide upon which manifests. Think on the Love side and all thoughts are positive and enlightened you will create a marvelous life. Think of fear and doubt and worry and panic and mistrust and all the subsets of emotion fears encompasses, you might wind up in a tragic circumstance you have seen in a vision (or dream) by focusing upon it relentlessly and not asking for help to alleviate its grasp upon you.

L: Is every single negative thought possible to manifest? If I think I might get eaten by a bear at the zoo could I create that possibility?

A: If you focused on it repetitively for years on end, perhaps. If you felt it as incredulous and nonsensical, then no.

L: But some of the fear thoughts we might create because we believe more in its possibility.

A: Yes. Be mindful of negative thoughts and how much of a hold they have over you. If you are being trapped or upset by them then it is best to seek counsel from your higher self and ask for help, always. Do not mistake irrational fear for truth based upon what you have read or seen happen to another. It is always this mode of radical fear that creates many illnesses and trips to an emergency room. Release all fears as often as possible. Get rid of them immediately if you can, all the time. As often as it arrives, shoo it away. You may say things like, "Help me dear All. I know I am manifesting a radical response to a bodily issue and I need help revealing its message so I may move through it quickly and toss it away."

Shine a light on the mind and why it's happening and all can be revealed through modalities such as intention, meditation, prayer and contemplation.

66 What is this showing me right now? 99

The body offers clues to what is being thought in mind. Louise Hay was a pioneer for this body/mind explanation, and we offer her books as a means for exploration. Some examples are below:

Hands: *How hard are you working?*

Feet: *Making leaps and bounds forward. Not knowing where you are headed. Misdirection.*

Heart: *Feeling lonely and afraid. Failure. Grief.*

Head: *Crushed dreams.*

Kidney: *Hard decisions.*

Back: *The weight of finances.*

Shoulders: *The world is on my back.*

Skin: *Dislike of self.*

All souls are working with bodies on life-driving themes. Which of the above is causing you all pain right now? It's possible to uproot the underlying causes if you work with the soul. Get clear on what's happening through actively pursuing the answers beneath. The soul knows how to arrive there with you. Only you can take yourself on an intimate ride through the mind, but it's a ticket you get from our soul.

L: And who is the conductor?

A: You and me and we - aka The All.

WORKBOOK EXERCISE #5:
VISIONING

W rite down all the things coming up for you as you are seeing them. This process allows a deeper, more clear vision to arrive for you. You may use the space in the workbook to do this or create a journal and carry it with you wherever you may go.

66 *I have seen this today and I know it is possible.*
I have seen this and I have no interest in that, so I wish it away. 99

Be clear and specific in what you want to create using our techniques of prayer and intention alike and begin to see the vision take shape. and as you do this all of this will begin to take form, shape and matter. It matters not what you are doing but who are you being.

L: And how do we get to that being? Most of us are doers and we feel that if we want to be successful we have to do something to make a dream or want a reality.

A: *Be active in pursuit of the dream and mind yourself of the work to be done in soul, which is of most importance.*

Who Am I?
Who Are We?
Where Am I Holding onto Fear?
How May I Release the Fear to God/Universe?

L: I have been doing that for over a year now and I recently went back through all of my journals and wow, what content I found. Everything was so uplifting and inspiring, always guiding me back to the same message over and over again.

A: *We are all One. We are Love. We are with you in cocreation, always.*

L: Yes.

A: *We are One, we are.*

L: It seems highly unlikely at this point that a baby is a possibility. I'm too old.

A: *Said the ego.*

L: I'm too alone. I have no money. Nothing is going on in my life of any significance whatsoever. I've pretty much given up on anything manifesting. It seems too hard even if you say something is "set it stone" and we are all but guaranteed for it to show up.

A: *In the absence of fear, doubt and worry, yes.*

L: But to me it seems if something is "set in stone" it has to show up.

A: *If you* believed *that it would.*

L: But why say something is "set in stone" if we can wind up keeping it away through our fears or lack of belief?

A: *In physical realms it is a fact of matter that what you think you create. And if you think you can and believe you can, you will, but if you allow an ego to control the journey, it won't. To be set in stone on a spiritual plane is as sure as it can get, but you are no longer in the spiritual plane are you as Laura, our inscriber? Today you are living in the earthly realm as a body, and so in order to bring forth an asking it must be accepted as truth fully and completely. Absolutely are you capable of bringing through any manifestation as soul. On Earth, however, you are body/mind/soul, and to use this trifecta is the only way to bring forth that which has been agreed upon prior.*

L: It feels like we are going round and round in circles here. Why can't I get this?

A: It's the process. Remember. Forget. Remember. Forget. You are no different than any One trying to evolve. The contents of our book are deliberate, and though it can seem repetitive, it is the process needed to learn. We may say the same things one hundred different ways so you may all understand the answers are simple. The complexity is in the remembering, because the choice to forget comes with a heaviness. Forgetting is easy. Remembering requires attention all the time.

Please, dear One, let us take control of the words here and you may go back to questioning in later chapters.

Control

You are very much in control of life's circumstances, and this is an incontrovertible fact. You each go about life creating it as you see fit and your time on Earth is necessary to evolve as emotional beings. Your every thought, word, action and emotion must be kept in check as you evolve. Making manifestations come to life is true for all of you, as it is the very existence of being a human. It is why you are in a body. It is a training ground for thought control.

Thoughts are the power that ignites everything. It's like starting up a car. It needs a key in the ignition in order to begin moving. Once started, it's upon the driver to steer the car in the direction it wants to go.

> **"** *I will go to a park today," or "I will take a drive with friends.* **"**

It makes no difference to us where you are going, only that you take a destination to discover.

South Beach

This morning our dear Laura was on a mission to enjoy a day with family. She decided upon a destination (as a pilot would) and entered within her GPS that location. Along the way she discovered a road block which caused her to question her choice of destination. She had meant to go to the aquarium, but instead skipped it to discover a different place. She felt (in time) it might be better to attend the aquarium on a different day when more time was available.

She wound up driving into South Beach and then walking around, enjoying a stroll, having a snack and spending some time with family. Her day was easily guided by conscious choices, and though it wasn't exactly the day she expected, it all worked out.

Her joy was not from the activity itself but from the time spent with family. It matters not what you are doing but who you are being. In every circumstance this is all ever needed - to be. Be joy.

What does this have to do with questioning everything? The answer is as simple as this - Make a choice in keeping with Love.

> ❝ *What shall we do today?* ❞

This is a question most ask on a weekend day. And the answer is usually an activity of sorts which either makes you happy, unhappy or somewhere in between. A most important question in every circumstance is, "Who shall I be today?"

Be one who cares only of this and never will you suffer in consequential irrational choices.

> ❝ *I shall enjoy a day with family and the destination is unnecessary. We will be together and this is what matters most.* ❞

Ask and Ye Shall Receive

What is most important as a soul is to ask. Asking is the whole reason you join with us here. You have been guided to an important piece of the puzzle written within the pages of these All books. They are genuine and true. Her voice is your voice is our voice. Together as One we create every masterpiece. Together we rise. Together we fall. In terms of endearment, we are your best self; the self who is God or Source. Divine Love. This is who you are at the core of your being.

Take time now to write questions. Space has been provided in the back to journal. Ask who you truly are and see what answers are revealed to you.

Who am I?
Who are we?
Where am I holding onto fear?
What am I seeking?
What joys do I wish to create?
Who or what is holding me back from creating a life of divine intention?

Our answer to this last question is only you. You are the master in charge and command the journey. It has been proven as a fact of quantum physics that the thoughts create the matter. It is thought alone which creates the life, and when coupled with emotion, emits a vibration to bring forth an asking; an asking you have decided upon before arriving in the body in which you now inhabit. Get ready to learn your life blueprint as we go into our next chapter on sacred contracts.

CHAPTER 7
Our Sacred Contracts

Dear All,
As I allow my thoughts to wander to the ego, may we please return
to the maker any thoughts which do not serve the higher good of the
soul. I share struggles in these pages so that others may learn from my
journey and allow information to come through as a means to guide all.

Discovering Soul

Struggle has been a necessary part of the journey of the soul for our inscriber, *Laura. She has often wandered into fear, madness and depression for obvious reasons. Her soul has been wanting to write a book of knowledge of spiritual principles through her. Her body is being made to feel as if it's being "taken over" in some respects to show her the feeling of connection. Her soul is with her at all times and hides itself in daily life in order that she grow and evolve on her own without interference.*

Our soul is a fragment of itself, like a portion of a pie divided up among family members. Each piece is relatively the same size, but all who partake in it separately have a different experience with it. For some it is sweet, for others perhaps tart or bitter. Another may wish to partake in only a small portion of it to savor the rest later. Still another is certain it is the best pie ever tasted in their life. Each has their own experience, preference and informational acceptance of it. You only know what you know when you are ready to know it. What does this have to do with sacred contracts? Acceptance is the name of the game.

Acceptance

Accept as they come all circumstances. They have been chosen (as soul) by you and for you in what we are calling a life blueprint. It is the will you set before incarnating into each and every body you inhabit. There are infinite ways to be, and to do this as one soul would task the entity. It is therefore a better way to discover oneself by fragmenting into oppositional selves. One is for living and the other for dying.

What does this mean? It means in one body you are living life to its fullest, expressing joy and happiness throughout life. This is the true self. It is who you are at the core of beingness, which is why when you are happy, fulfilled and unconcerned with money and material things you experience bliss. It is why meditation is an important step in the process of discovery. It accepts who you are without judgement and brings you to that place within which knows your true self and why you are here. It is unconcerned with possessions and positions. It knows only Love is true.

On the opposite side, then, you are a body which remains confused as to who you are. It establishes a story for itself and "sticks with the plan" until you are enlightening the soul. The moment you accept your story as perhaps not the full picture of who you are is the moment ideas and anecdotes show up to ingratiate you to truth. All of this is done on purpose. It is purposefully chosen and created by you in the blueprint.

The moment of conception is the moment of intention. This is where and when a soul has decided upon incarnation back to body. It is the moment of intention which imbibes you with truth and creates space for growth. This is the power of soul. It can create itself again and again through lifetime after lifetime within infinite experiences and infinite guidelines.

You are perhaps a male in one life and in another a female. One time you might choose a life as a poet and another a painter. In any case, you are fragmenting a soul into various "scenes" or scenarios such as you would if crafting a TV show with multilayered story arcs and characters. It is always upon you to design a life of great intricacies and with room for expansion of ideas like kindness, empathy or compassion. The entire reason you enter a body is to discover along the way who you are by accessing information on who you are not.

I am not a jerk.

Well how do you know this unless you have been unkind to another? You don't. You must discover along the way all things in which you are not.

WORKBOOK EXERCISE #6:
I AM/I AM NOT

n the workbook, write down some things you are not. Take some time to elaborate on the theme of each, mindful of how it makes you feel to express these themes. After doing this write the opposite of each using the phrase I am.

66 *I am kind and loving towards self and others.* 99

---

66 *I am learning and growing and evolving with every step made on Earth.* 99

---

66 *I am joyful and express emotions to bring light to whatever is weighing me down.* 99

I Am

I am. This powerful phrase contains the most important two words in the language in which we are currently writing. There are languages all over the world that translate the "I Am" to other things, such as Yo Soy, Ego Sum, Je Suis, Ich Bin or Ja Cam. The meaning is the same all over the world and beyond into the cosmos and infiniteness of being. It is the connective tissue of life. "I Am" is you, me and we. There is nothing we are not. There is no one we are not. You are the sun, Earth, moon, stars and every living thing, be it breathing or not. You are all things, the sum of all parts. To know this is to know All. To experience All is the reason for being. All things are to be examined so you may know yourself as I am.

> 66 *I am a living, breathing being of form and function and this is how I discover myself.* 99

To state this in instances where you question the validity of why you are suffering will allow you to uncover the life-driving themes designed in your blueprint. We will use Laura as example here, starting with the death of her beloved brother, Jason. Each (as soul) decided upon a journey together. They knew along the way somewhere it would become possible for one to live and the other to die. It was a part of their sacred contract to experience this together as One. Though in his contract it was stated that Jason was able to control his circumstance and live longer, it indeed did not happen, as his probable choices got the best of him and he created upon himself a circumstance of cancer. Laura, on the other hand, always had within her contract the statement of being a writer and author of spiritual materials for the mainstream minds of those incarnating to be. Her choices were to create a book of knowledge through either love or fear, dependent upon which one she chose. No matter which route she took, her books were always going to be made. It could be a book of grief and doubt or it could be a book of joy. Either way, the book held the same principles told through a different lens.

We have come to a point where she is ready (despite her brother's death) to create within the lens of Love. She has come to an understanding of our whys of the Universe and recognizes within herself the need to control thoughts so she may be at peace, which is our main goal in life. Peace will bring about a much easier journey into Love.

Mastering peace is problematic for most, and this is why suffering occurs all over planet Earth for most if not all of you. As you guide yourself into Love, you are being ruled by an ego mind which wants you to suffer and struggle in order to know itself as irrational and misguided. Such is the journey of ego.

Think of it as you would the devil on your shoulder or the angel. One is guiding you into fear, the other into Love. The battle is waged in your own mind, and the only one who can save you is you. You make the choice to be guided by ego "truths" or

Love. Only one is really happening to you. The other is misguided, disguised nonsense brought upon you to bring you down.

In order to have created the All books, Laura needed to have some circumstances in her life. If her brother had chosen a path ruled by Love he might be here today, laughing at her and thinking her books to be silly, all the while intrigued by them, as he had grown his soul even further than hers. Within his soul contract he allowed himself to be tripped by the soul into fear. Whereas Laura allowed only what served her need to write her books to accompany her along the way. She chose to write her books no matter which way the wind blew. It was her will to leave behind a book of profound knowledge which one day will be shared by the masses and disseminated among the willing.

Always Be Willing

You are willing yourself right now to discover divine truths within the lens of Love. It matters not which book you find, only that you find one which resonates within the core of your being. Laura's journey has included many a book and download that arrived right as she needed to hear it. You will find that with your journey, as well. Only when you have evolved to a level of consciousness will you accept what is being written. This is why her All books have been mostly untouched by the world as it presently stands. Most are unwilling to encounter a radical shift in focus and ideas about who and what God really is.

The world is changing, and for this we are extremely proud and grateful to be among the seekers who are choosing to wake up. You will see a shift happening as more and more enlighten to truth. This does not mean all is perfect and blissful, as at some point tragedies will occur, as have been chosen by all of you to grow through energetic anomalies that things like earthquakes and tornadoes bring. Man has been creating these events of Mother Nature for century upon century. It must be taken on by all who wish to know themselves as I am in order to evolve. It is the nature of being; a cycle of creation which knows no boundaries and therefore continues to change and evolve. Just as your body continues to evolve, so too does the atmosphere in which you live. Growing pains are part of the process for all living and non-living beings of which you all are. There is no one you are not and no thing you are not.

The Ares and Are Nots

You are a soul. You are not a body. You are being. You are not a star. You are Love. You are not evil. These are things which you must know in order to create life as you see it. Know this and you know All. Nothing is created by you which hasn't been accepted by you. It is acceptable as soul (though it may not feel this way as body) and this is why all suffer, always. You are unwilling to accept that even those seemingly tragic things that happen are within your probabilities which have been awarded to you as a means to evolve.

Awarded, *you would ask? A word seemingly unlikely used to describe our choices or 'divine disasters', as we had called them earlier in our chapter 1. This might invoke the ego, which wants you to believe all circumstances are tragic and terrible, but this is not the case at all. All circumstances lend opportunities to heal, and this is why they have been chosen by you as soul to experience in the present form you are now inhabiting.*

Laura often wonders why evil exists, as do all of you at some point. It is hard to look upon a seeming evil and not get angry or cry. We understand this response as human. It is emotions which bind you to one another, and this is a collective trait of the species which is quite beautiful. It is and comes from Love. When viewing a tragic circumstance chosen upon by another soul, you are simply expressing your divine sorrow as Love. We know it is a hard choice to make to view evils as 'on par', but as a soul being it is what you must do in order to not be swept into ego. All must know what is both true and untrue and declare it as such. No exceptions.

Are you a soul or are you not? You are. Are you a human or are you not? You are, but you are both a soul and a human, and this is the only way to view the self. Are you a brain or are you not? You are. Are you the mind or are you not? You are, but you are both, and this, too, is the only way to view self. When using the body/mind/soul trifecta, this shows you who you are rather than who you are not. Emphasizing who you are not brings you circumstances you will not like. Only in viewing oneself as who they are (the trifecta) is when the I am is being expressed.

All in the Name of Love

Why do you go through all of this in the first place? Why not just be a soul in love and be Love? Because you are choosing not to be. It has been chosen for you as a means to evolve into the being who you are. This is a process enjoyed by the All. It is a means to know truth in vast detail through experiencing its opposite exposure; through the lens of something other than that which it is, Love.

Earth is where it is chosen to live through oppositional experiences – love and fear. To know love you must express and experience fear, anger, animosity, worry or doubt and other subsets of these emotions. It can be no other way. For to know you is to know All. What life is chosen has been chosen purposefully. It has been chosen by you as soul seeks to move through new and intricate measures. Every step in the journey of enlightenment is leading you closer to a new destination of our unity consciousness. All is choosing to see itself through various ways; and various experiences must be undertaken for all to know itself as All.

You are choosing, as soul, the things for which you have yet to experience. So in this life perhaps you are one thing, while in another you are something other than what you had been before. A body is a chosen feature which shows you what works and doesn't work in thinking.

> 66 *As you think, so shall you be.* 99

This and other words written throughout history (on planet Earth in its current inception) have been placed in your path time and time again to show you just who is in charge. It is you. Only you. What you think you become. What you say you are, you are. You are the designer and decorator of circumstances whether or not you believe it. It can be no other way. It is no other way. All is creating life through every thought, word, action and emotion. All is being who each has chosen to, no matter what it has chosen.

This is your design. Your layout. It sets you up to succeed and fail. Failure is an option because it has been chosen. You need to fail so you may figure out what success looks like for you. Let us look at the life plan chosen upon Laura to create for herself a life of evolvement.

First, she chose her parents – Sandy and Stuart. One would be kind and caring, the other more aloof and lighthearted in nature. Then she chose siblings to grow alongside, Michael and Jason. Each with their own life plan, as well. As a child it was set for her to be shy, quiet and independent. Independence has been one of her life-driving themes, as this is something she failed to learn in other incarnations. As a woman, she had been relying upon men to help her in lifetime after lifetime.

She took a break to be a boy, but only for a little while because she found this to be too difficult in her last incarnation. (We had spoken on this in our last material The All That Is). Returning in this lifetime, she knew it possible to extend a life, but struggled as a teenager because her last body did not last beyond this. Once she moved beyond this, she was able to wake up ever so slightly and recognize her soul had plans for her. She began to notice and sense spirits and energy in and around her, and chose to investigate this path further, which led to her particular gift of clairaudience eventually being discovered and utilized. Here we are at the point where we may cocreate with her these books and material as One soul.

Her intent was to produce a book of knowledge about our spiritual world and how it works, and in this (as we said prior) has come many, many difficulties. It had to be hard to write at times. It had to overcome her life in order that she release each book sequentially and with minimal effort. Her waking state had to be interrupted every night so she could release the thoughts holding her hostage. The process was and is deliberate.

Returning to the conversation of life blueprints. Laura chose (as she often does) to be a woman again because, as we said, she wanted to learn independence and she has done this quite beautifully in this life and released the need to learn this in another. Her independence has allowed others to 'take care of themselves' and grow in other ways in other incarnations, such as the two we spoke of in her last book, a ballerina and a foster care youth who eventually will go on to be quite successful in chosen fields.

Laura herself has been successful as both a healer and a teacher because it had been chosen prior. Once it was realized she was being held back by soul from finding an audience, she let go of time frames and allowed a career to take hold which had been planned prior. She also had wanted to be a successful television reporter or presenter, and she masterfully created this through hard work, determination and trust in self. Her lack of success (as a host) prior had been her own thought processes keeping her stuck in worthiness obsessions as she kept finding herself in comparison mode. Had she been truly happy just being, she might have opened a door to a much vaster television career and an easier journey to her books.

It is like Sliding Doors[1]*, a 1998 movie in which Gwyneth Paltrow's character finds herself (unconsciously) living two different lives. In one scenario she has missed her train, while in the other she didn't. Each scenario played itself out with different circumstances, but ultimately, she arrived at a destination exactly the same. If this had been a "real life" scenario (and we say this in quotes because the life you are currently living isn't real life either, as hard as this can be to understand), one choice would have come from fear and the other from Love. One might arrive at the destination faster in Love and the other slower in fear, but it ultimately leads to the same place. You are not wrong or right in whatever choice is made. It just is.*

When you are being guided you will know it if you pay attention. It will come as inspired or intuitional moments. It will feel as if an idea has sprung upon you out of nowhere, but in actuality has been a part of you all along. Every thought already has been thought. It's how you access it that matters.

The intricacies of our beingness are so vast it is quite literally impossible to explain it all to human minds who have no recollection of it. As you arrive to various levels of consciousness you are able to access more and more information, but it is not advisable to know all and so we purposefully choose not to. It makes the journey more delicious.

There are plenty of things you may know about that are accessible in the 'knowing' or inner self. Life-driving themes are one of these things. You may access these in waking and dreaming states, you just have to know how. As you grow in enlightenment it becomes easier to access this. Laura is one who is able to access the collective consciousness to tap into life-driving themes of others, as had been chosen by her prior to incarnation. She knows all, sees all and shares what she knows to others of a lower consciousness to help guide them on her journey. It is pleasurable to help others know why they are here and what is needing to be worked upon as soul.

Each person has a blueprint for life-driving themes, and those who are willing may look into them now. Use our workbook to write any and all inspired thoughts which arise as you contemplate a life.

WORKBOOK EXERCISE #7:
LIFE-DRIVING THEMES

What have you been tied to most of your life?

_____

_____

_____

_____

_____

_____

_____

_____

_____

_____

_____

_____

_____

_____

_____

_____

_____

_____

_____

_____

_____

Where have you struggled most?

If someone or something is a bone of contention for you, who is it?

What lessons are being learned through this experience?

Can you pinpoint a time when all things seemed to be crashing around you?

What is the tether which binds them together?

These and other questions are how to unlock these traumatic moments and memories to get you to those life-driving themes.

Good luck. When you return, we shall move on to our next chapter, Know Your Worth. Worthiness is a combined collective life-driving theme each and every one must learn on Earth, and we will bring you insights as to why and how to move beyond this.

CHAPTER 8

Know Your Worth

Dear All,
I know I am a worthy adversary in this game of life. I allow words of
soul to come through for all to recognize the power they hold within to
trade the tragedies for triumphs and go for the gold or glory.

Unworthiness has and will be a life-driving theme for centuries to come. It has been perpetuated through the lens of social media. For to see yourself in comparison to another is a plague of the latest century. It is mindfully depleting to go about your life wondering and pondering if you may ever be, do or have enough. Of course you are enough. In the eyes of the Universe you are perfect, completely perfect, just as you are.

Ones who are "famous" have all the money or glory, and you all believe this is something to be obtained. It is in fact unnatural to remain in conscious criticism of one's self. Why you are tortured is because you are so caught in the trap of celebrity. It feels good to watch someone win and bad to feel you are incapable of doing or being the same.

Celebrity has and will always be a game of wills. You will yourself to be someone of stature or recognition, and then torture yourself when you can't arrive at the destination. This is what most seeking admiration do. Not all are seeking fame or fortune, but most are aiming for recognition of some kind be it from a boss, coworker, spouse or lover. You want someone to see you, feel you, know you. To make you feel...love.

Love in many forms is what we are seeking. Happy. Satisfied. Joyous. Captivating. Engaging. Enlightened beings have no need for seeking love outside themselves. For they know already they are loved. You are loved because you exist, not because of anything you are doing, have done or will be. You are Love at the core of being.

Children seek love, too, and often fail to understand why, and this is why when adulthood comes, they are searching outside of themselves, as well. Most within your *societal structure are incapable of realizing truth, and so they are teaching from a place of lack. Each person spares themselves a pain by hiding who they truly are and then wandering from partner to partner trying to figure it out through another. Are you loving another because of who they are or who you are?*

Who you are is a divine being of love and light. You are beautiful in soul and loved unconditionally. When in body, most don't see themselves this way. Instead, they view the outside body and forget the internal soul. To view oneself this way only shows external circumstances. How one views themselves correlates to how one sees themselves internally.

> 66 *I am ugly and old, tired and unlikeable.* 99

If you feel something on the inside, it manifests on the outside. It is how we view ourselves and others. To unlike oneself is to unlike another and admire in another what you feel is lacking in you.

Take a look at yourself in the mirror and see who is truly there. Is she (he) beautiful or plain? Whatever you see tells me (you) who are you are being. Who you are being manifests itself in vision. So if you are thinking yourself to be old, tired and ugly then it very well manifests as this. If you are feeling beautiful and capricious it will manifest, as well. Every day it may change dependent upon what you are thinking and feeling. One day its glory, another gory. Your state of mind states for you what vision is staring back. To go about fixing this, One must every day be mindful of what they are feeling.

Accept the body as it is, glorious or not. Feel what it feels like to think yourself beautiful, and be mindful of what it looks like, too. It is not shallow to believe in beauty. It is beautiful to be happy and vibrant and alive.

Take a moment to feel the emotion of celebrity. What does it feel like to look joyous and be appreciated? Hold this feeling as long as you can, and wander back there on days when you are feeling down or dark. It is a trick of mind which works in any circumstance. Return thoughts to Love, always.

Bask in the glory of knowing you are famous. In the eyes of the One, everyone is.

Social Shakedown

It has been a struggle for many to look past the outside appearance and into the inside. This has been largely due to the increase in mental awareness of what others are doing and accomplishing in life.

> 66 *If I am to be what I want to be,*
> *I must match what another is doing.* 99

This is mental torture at its finest, courtesy of ego. Ego is breaking you down and making you feel unhappy and unfilled because you are not being the very thing you seek to be.

Make time for daily connection to truth; who you are at the core. It is the only way out of the mental prison you have locked yourself in, as we have revealed in our last chapter on sacred contracts.

Step out of comparing and into compassion. Compassion for one's self. You are only capable of being that which you say you wish to be in the absence of fear, and this is impossible to do when Instagram, Snap Chat, Tik Tok or other social channels have you faking a life to fool or impress others.

Harsh words have been spoken, so you may recognize the torturer is only you. Get off the web and into your head. Be mindful of how it feels when you see another winning. Say, "I will get there too," and never remind yourself of failure. Rather, remind yourself to the power of One. This is how you create the life you chose before arriving in the body you now inhabit. As One create it. For it exists already and in mind is how you create it.

66 *I am the thing I see.* 99

Fix what's broken on the inside, and then and only then can you truly bring the outside in. Then you can be the dancer, singer, actor, baseball player, mindfulness teacher or anything else you wish to create. For it is only a thought of not being able to create it that holds you hostage, and not the actual act of torture. This is all your doing and all your being. Separate the two and break the habit of egoic thinking and feeling. Feel what it feels like to succeed; believe you can and you will.

When you are feeling low about a particular thing you are not creating in your life – youth, beauty, money, success – put yourself in a place using your mind where you were youthful, loved the way you looked or had great success.

Take a moment to write down things which make you happy. What do you want to create? Who do you want to be? If you know, then move towards it without question or interruption. Don't let the lack of it manifesting drag you into fear. Wait in glorious acceptance of its divine intention and let it unfold naturally and without questioning.

For you are the knowing One who created it in the first place and all you need do is be. Be into it and don't accept any other outcomes. True faith will bring it to you more quickly and without fear, but most are incapable of this all-out belief, and to those who are in vibrational states of unrest, it may take longer than necessary. No matter how long it takes, it's always been your right to have it. Have faith. Wait patiently and bless the time in cocreation.

Gold

Laura has been someone who has struggled with worthiness her entire life, until life events forced her to get comfortable sharing her authentic voice. Once she began to drop egoic control over who she was speaking to, she no longer cared who received information, only that they did.

In order to allow a divine mind to catapult you out of loathing the self and its (in your summation) less than stellar form, you are asking for help. Help is gold. A commodity with riches and rewards for simply stating an intention to see the self differently.

> 66 *I know I am perfect in the eyes of Love.*
> *So please show me this version of myself.* 99

An asking of this is all One needs do in order to stay in cocreation with the soul.

> 66 *Allow me to see the vision of who I am*
> *beyond physical senses and bodily functions.* 99

Worth is determined by the value you place upon the self. Don't expect others to value oneself if you, too, are undermining and undercutting the love. It's a valuable commodity to be raised by those who see you as perfect, but it is always you and you alone who decides to accept or deny.

The art of using a "thank you" when offered a compliment is often overlooked and should never be. Just accept what someone sees in you is truth and say, "Yes, I agree," in a simple nod or smile and a verbal, "Thank you, I appreciate you."

WORKBOOK EXERCISE #8:
VALUE

n the notebook, write all of the attributes you enjoy about yourself. Be mindful to keep it lighthearted and not oppositional. Negativity is never the way to compliment the self. So rather than, "I'm glad I'm thin," (implying a fear of fat) you would say, "I'm grateful for the body I have chosen to express myself in."

Use this exercise to gain valuable insight into your likes and dislikes about the self. Use these to find the most complimentary thing you can say about yourself. It may help to ask, "What do I like about myself?" and find ways to state its merit.

I am a kind person.
I give freely of my time.
The noise I make is always to compel others to do better.
The time I spend with family is important to me.
I enjoy making people happy.
My feet make me light and free to go where I want and with whom I want.

Ask, "What could I improve on?" rather than what is unsatisfactory about the self.

I could be nicer to friends who I disagree with on matters.
I would like to spend more time in a gym exercising.
Food is enjoyable and I prefer to choose foods more nutritionally dense.

This is how you lose ego. You find the best, most positive way to talk about the self and the more you do this and own up to having practiced differently prior to this exercise, the easier it becomes to find value in everything, including perfectly perfect you who is Love inside of bodies.

Now we shall move onto some modalities for healing as you go about returning to Love.

CHAPTER 9

Healing Energy

Dear All,
As we deliver these messages may the sum of all parts be revealed.

Conquering the mind is a slow process of endless twists and turns. As you ride the journey of life it will feel both exhilarating and exasperating, fun and fervent, yet upsetting and frustrating as well. This is by design. It is a deliberate process of many layers.

First and foremost, it has been chosen to be this way by the will of collective consciousness; a journey of epic proportions unlike any other which shows you what you are thinking upon in a multitude of ways - one of which being the body.

The body is a learning device for the mind and that is its only function on Earth. Every thought you think creates the sensations you are feeling. Homeostasis is the term used to describe absolute bliss. It is the natural state of being. In the body it is the balance you achieve when everything is in perfect harmony within the structure. It is near impossible as a human to get to such a state, as most bodies are vibrating with unknown or subconscious thoughts, even in states of being such as meditation would provide.

It is unknown thoughts which cause excess damage upon cells and structures in the body temple. Cellular level biology dictates what happens in a body, and your scientists are right on track in their exploration of the finer points of each minute detail of this. There is a rhyme or reason to how the body mutates or creates its own manifestations of illness or harm.

There are many ways to heal a body and that is through the mind. The mind makes itself available for modalities such as we will be describing here in detail. Every moment you are connected to a loving thought you are healing. Every moment a destructive thought comes along you are breaking down a part of the structure.

Healing is readily available to you at all times if you are noticing it. Below are some ways to heal in our terms.

Food is Medicine

Plants are the most protective substances on Earth and have been placed here on purpose. For every cell in your body is healed by things such as beans and rice, corn and tomatoes. All of these are foods to be enjoyed, and yet as humans they have been destroyed to a degree by pesticides and herbicides and genetically modified organisms (GMO). This is a fact we mustn't overlook due to the nature of human consciousness. It has been poisoned, and those who have done the harm are knowing its harm and this is manifesting itself into all minds of the collective. In order to achieve a state of being (where you are unaffected by this) you must pursue enlightened status so as to release yourself from the collective thinking mind.

> 66 I am eating for life and choosing foods which bring my body into alignment with soul and letting go of thoughts of our collective consciousness. I eat what fuels my body, mind and soul and lose whatever poisons are implanted in the soil of the earth and the soil of the ego. 99

Eat pure, high quality fresh fruits and vegetables as often and as much as you can or like. It is a sustainable model of vibratory food for the human body. Each has a part to play; and the food model we have placed upon Earth purposefully so you may eat in glorious bounty through Mother Earth.

Diets don't work and those who are placing them in the world are simply following an ego. Follow our advice and notice how your body feels when all things are in balance with nature. Animals are to be consumed in minimal amounts. Processed foods avoided mostly and avoid any consumer product which puts profits over people. Oils and fats obtained in processing plants are not harmful but are to be consumed sparingly, as they separate nutrients of a plant and this is not necessary. You can obtain them in natural processing, as well.

Hippocrates said, "Let food be thy medicine and medicine be thy food."

Follow this prescription and it will allow a body to heal most definitely in the absence of fear.

Panache

A flair for the dramatic is our favorite trick of mind. It is how you 'become' someone entirely different. Using the mind to create an entirely different world for yourself is how you engage in active enlightenment. You see a thing in mind and hold its image for as long as possible while feeling the feeling of its manifesting into form.

Think of a worthy person. Someone whose accolades are well known. A famous actor or musician, perhaps. Now see yourself as this person. They are you and you are them.

See them on stage performing, receiving an award or playing a role in a movie you like. Feel the feeling of what it must be like to perform in front of thousands of fans, find the perfect part or accept an award such as an Oscar™ or Emmy™.

This exercise is one you may use every day of your life, but instead of using another to engage joy, use only you. See YOU doing the thing you enjoy most. What makes you feel good? Can you feel the feeling of it manifesting without its arrival? This is an actor's gift, to accept they are the role or part. They are becoming someone through their acceptance of illusion, fantasy or falsity.

Can you do the same? Can you accept you are the thing you see without seeing it in the physical?

Do this every day, this exercise, and feel the absolute joy it brings you. Write down in your workbook or journal the things you have experienced. Use every sense you have - sight, smell, touch, hearing and taste. See your joy. Can you feel the award, microphone or a guitar in your hand? Do you smell the scent of the chalk you wrap your hands in as a gymnast or touch the gurney you lay your hands on as a caregiver? Do you hear the sounds of a roaring crowd or laughing audience in a theater? Can you taste the pie you baked in the shop you just opened, on the perfect street, in the perfect neighborhood not far from where you live?

Remember to be clear and specific in your visioning. Don't wish for an Oscar™ and then join a band or fly an airplane. See things exactly as you want them to be.

Energetic Healing

It is quite possible to heal the body through the mind using energetic techniques such as Reiki, Qigong, Acupressure, Sound Vibration and other modalities. (For a list, visit the back of our book.)

Whatever you use make sure its practitioner is a licensed, therapeutic healer and one who is aligned with our One mind. There are healers all over the world in various stages of development on a psychic and spiritual level, and to know where they are in their own journey of being is most definitely a sound idea.

It is of what you believe that is most important as you open to spiritual art forms, and so to work with a high consciousness practitioner allows both parties to participate energetically as One.

Exercise

Movement is essential as a body. They are designed to move and vibrate, as we have said prior. They are energy, and energy needs force in order to be moved. This is why in any exchange there must be giving. In order to receive you must first give. It is simple, mathematical and methodical. It is the design of everything in our Universe. Move the energy whether it's money or muscles.

There is no need for gyms, weights or fancy machinery. Simply get up and move around. The body is designed to endure a multitude of force. You may use whatever you like, and this is why going to a gym is not "bad" it is just not necessary. Get out in nature. Take a stroll. Run, jog, bike (again not necessary but enjoyable to some), dance, roll around. Do anything which moves your body all the time. Sit too long and you are destroying the mechanism for change. Get up as many times throughout a day as you work or play. Yoga is our most favorite exercise of all as it binds the chakras and stimulates the senses in a multitude of ways.

Joint. Joy of intuitive natural thrust. There are literally thousands of words in which the meanings are hidden within them. We will spell out more as we continue on further.

For now, we ask you to go enjoy a day. Exercise. Relax. Engage the soul.

Laughter

Our favorite modality of all is joy. It is love's purest expression. Laughter engages the senses like no other activity. You are completely relaxed in mind when the laughter happens. Regular intervals of laughing will do more for you than any other thing when you are feeling down, depressed or angry. Engage the sensory systems through laughing and you engage every chakra. Make it a part of your daily curriculums in addition to meditation, and you would see an entirely new world open around you; one where light and freedom come easily.

Before you go to bed each night (and you will try this tonight) find something which makes you laugh. Tell a story, read a book or jog a memory, anything which brings you a divine sense of release from the day's adversities.

Meditation

It goes without saying that meditation is an undertaking every spiritual seeker must engage with. There are no exceptions to this rule. It is how you are releasing emotions and life-driving themes through quietness and contemplation. Though meditation looks different for every person, what matters most is the time spent in nothingness.

Remember you are here to grow a soul, and this is the best opportunity to be in concert with your beingness. You are a soul being and no other modality will heal you faster than this.

Do all of the above regularly, and the more you do this the more you will engage accepting who you truly are; a soul of the One.

Step outside of the role you play as human and learn to be present in our next chapter on the greatest gift on Earth, Now.

CHAPTER 10

Be Present

Dear All,
I am growing and evolving. Through every act of love,
I discover who I am and this is the journey of a soul.
Please help me to understand how to BE in a world of doing.

ife is a gift. When you are so busy doing it can easily escape you. You find any excuse to wrap yourself up in doingness. Watch TV. Play a video. Scroll through Instagram. These are acts of ego designed to avoid beingness. Why? So you may see through the lens of adversity and destroy psyche. You are only as strong as you allow yourself to be. And if you are so distracted by unimportant nonsense it allows ego to reign supreme.

How do you become willing to escape the ego? Ask. Ask every time an oppositional thought arrives to that which is Love, "Is this a thing I should be doing or thinking? Do I need to be doing this to grow a soul or am I doing this to satisfy ego?"

That is allowing present moment awareness into your soul, psyche and mind. The only action ever needed in response to ego is a prayer, asking or intention. Just ask. Questions are the way to truth. They are the simple potion for every single doubt, fear or worry.

66 *Is this truth?* 99

66 *Where am I being unkind today?* 99

66 *What must be known in this situation to allow me to move through it more quickly?* 99

66 *How may I perceive this differently?* 99

Every question is answered, eventually. It may not come to you right away. It may take several days, years or even decades in fact, but eventually all asks will be answered. It is our Law of Give and Take. Give us your insecurities, insufficiency, lack, selfishness and in response our hurts are healed in many different ways. A wound is healed. A spot opens up. A sign is given. A love is found. These are all ways in which answers are given. And taken from you are the thoughts you have relinquished to yourself, the self that is soul – pure soul.

We are here for you always and forever, at all times. In any given moment you have a choice to see either love or fear. To choose love will transform the heartache or hurt until you are ready to choose fear again. Erratic thinking creates erratic mechanisms for healing, which is why it may take many days for a cold or flu (as examples) to subside. You are thinking of healing and at the same time annoyed by your circumstances. This is why we say "bless you" after a sneeze. So you may know of your true identity – soul.

Bless = Believe Love Everytime Soul Speaks.

Thinking with the mind of Love is difficult. It takes dedicated, mindful practice to stay in vibrational alignment with the soul. It is imperative as you awaken that you are watching thoughts which separate you from Love. This is why mindful awareness is priority in enlightenment. It brings you to a place of intention.

> 66 My intention is to be aware of my emotions
> as I move through a day and to ask for guidance
> as I make my way towards enlightenment. 99

This is the souldier's defense against an enemy ego. You must be aware of all thoughts which separate you from our One soul and work towards letting go. To be present is to wander into soul alignment; to let ego go and to live in the now. It is most important to be, and unless and until this is learned no one living upon planet Earth will truly be living an unburdened life. It will be hard.

Life is meant to be joyous. Mostly highs and few lows is possible when you stay in alignment with the soul. Always be willing to trade attack thoughts for truth and it will be much easier to do so.

"Dear soul, I cannot see beyond illusion. Help me," is all Ones would need to say in order to receive help. It is most easy to accept guidance if you are willing to do so. All are capable of a feat of defeat. Just be willing.

Asking

Laura: I have questions.

All: Welcome back. We are ready to receive when asking occurs.

L: I love everything you have written in these last few chapters. I know I am incapable of–

A: Not incapable; unwilling, because you are listening more to ego than soul and One still.

L: Okay. Incapable of receiving the information as truth. As I look at the world around me and my own world, I am still wrestling with the idea of whether or not any of this is true.

A: And you will be for a while because it is the process you must go through in order to shed limiting beliefs. All of The All must question and examine truth and decide for themselves what to believe or not to believe. For some it will resonate perfectly and others will question and ponder for quite some time. You are One who is questioning so you may write our books, not because it doesn't make sense.

L: It does make sense. It's just putting it into practice and seeing results that is the hard part, because right now all I see is chaos and confusion.

A: Our book is deliberate in that we offer wisdom and guidance to all and then allow you to question us. This back and forth allows our readers to understand all of this shedding of ego takes time and dedicated practice. Because there is chaos and confusion (and will continue to be), it will take time to grasp reality.

L: This life feels like reality.

A: It is and it isn't. It feels real in physical realms until you cross into nonphysical. Then will it make sense on a soul level why your physical journeys are figments.

L: This reality is hard. It feels as if most of us are always struggling here, especially when it comes to finances. Doesn't God/the Universe want us to be happy? What is the point of all of this?

A: Do you know it has been chosen by all of you to go through ups and downs/highs and lows?

L: Why? Why choose misery? It seems like an awful lot of work. I am beginning to realize that no one here is truly happy. Pockets of happiness exist for sure, but not happily ever after. That is a fairy tale. At least it seems this way to me.

A: Right now.

L: Do we ever get to the end of all this work?

A: Not as human forms, no. If "work" is how you view it then work is how it will be. If you are thinking it will be hard then it will be. If you know it will be easy and readily available to you is guidance then you will live an easier life. It is always your choice. You choose. You decide.

L: I would like to choose an easy, unburdened life please.

A: And you do this by declaring your intention to always be in tune with our Oneness. Be willing to see it differently and you will.

> 66 *Life is easy. I enjoy every day*
> *no matter what the circumstances.* 99

This is true presence. Just being aware of what is happening with no attachment to it.

L: Well this is where I am currently confused. We have been talking and writing about manifesting and living the life of your dreams, that all you desire is on the other side of fear. What I don't understand is if we decide to just "let go" and have no attachments to anything or anyone and just be happy where we are, what then? Where do we go from there? If we want nothing then what is the point of all of it?

A: There is no wrong or right in the Universe/Infiniteness, only lessons to be learned of what it means to be Love. You are making decisions as individual souls on what this is for each of you. What is it that you love?

L: I love children. I love traveling and seeing new places. I love time with my son. I love vacationing. I love laughing. I love dancing. I love eating healthy food. I love being in a loving relationship. I love the sound of the waves crashing on the beach and the color of the ocean. I love a clean, beautifully decorated home. I love helping others discover their beingness. I love making television and digital programming. I love teaching meditation and working with clients as a medium and channel. I love being creative. I love speaking to audiences in person or on podcasts. I love being at peace.

A: And what do you not love?

L: Hard work. Being broke. Doing laundry, dishes and housework. The heat where I currently live. Working with and for people who are angry and upset. Talking to selfish and/or spoiled people. Feeling unhealthy or overweight. Finding out I wasn't chosen to speak or participate in something. Seeing our world falling to pieces and feeling helpless to do something about it.

A: And how do you know what you love?

L: Because I have done, been or had those things and they make me feel good. Whereas the other things make me feel bad, and I don't like feeling bad.

A: Do more of what you love and less of what you don't and you are being. To answer a question you had asked, "What is the point?" The point is that you are here to celebrate life and all its magic. You are here to love and to laugh and to heal 'past' wounds and impart wisdom to all whom you stumble upon willing to listen. You are evolving and it takes knowing what you don't want in order to know what it is you do love. Just be Love. Separate the hard from the easy and learn to like whatever it is you are doing. Then once you know what you love, do that.

L: I noticed that most of the things I said I loved had nothing to do with−

A: Material possessions, no. They had to do with things that give you a feeling or emotion. In our prior books it was revealed that Earth is where you learn about cause and effect through emotions, and so you are most definitely here to learn as body what makes you feel good and what makes you feel bad. It is simple and yet difficult at the same time. Listen to the body. If it feels good, do it. If it feels bad, don't. End of story. Next chapter.

CHAPTER 11

Toxicity Avoidance

Dear All,
No place on Earth is as safe as where I am.
Let the mind remind me of this every single day.

There is so much more to life than the All of you even know. Parts of your mind yet to be unlocked, revelations to be uncovered; and yet you are missing most of these hidden gems because you are so caught up in a landslide of toxicity.

What are toxins? They are poisons. Unnecessary and harmful elements which cause you to think less clearly. These are popular in the mainstream and unpopular in spiritually awakened individuals. Minds which are closer to truth are avoiding these very things consistently. As you grow and evolve and further the enlightenment process it will become necessary to relinquish as many toxins as possible. In order to hear, Laura, our inscriber has left behind many mindless behaviors she used to find enjoyable. TV has become a smaller part of her life. Alcohol has all but disappeared. Foods of a processed kind, animal products and byproducts and other unnecessary items have been stripped from a pantry and refrigerator. It is because she has been focused on raising her vibrational energy that she has begun to shun more and more toxins in her life.

These are things which become avoidable when you choose to focus energy on raising it. We do not judge or condemn. For all are able to do what they like when they like. These are merely indices for that which you may avoid should you wish to follow a spiritual curriculum, such as we have been inscribing here with dear Laura.

Toxin 1

Alcohol

You must understand as you move along the ladder of enlightenment, certain things you once found enjoyable or "necessary" no longer are. They are simple disruptions of the mind/body connection and not helpful to evolution.

Alcohol is one of these toxins. Why? Because it disrupts the endocrine system, making it impossible to release endorphins which are keeping the vibrational energy strong. It is a fallacy to say that alcohol makes you "happy." Happiness is short lived when it comes from a place of toxicity. It is a temporary 'fix' for an ongoing problem or issue. You may be happy for a short time, but eventually a sameness comes over you. All the same problems, emotions, angers, upsets and stressors arise again and again. The cycle continues with drink in hand. Drink, repeat, drink, repeat. Nothing changes. Right back where you started is where you find yourself every time, no matter what issues you are revolving through.

You can revolve or you can evolve. Over and over you go through the same scenarios on a different day with a different type of drug or pill to fix the broken parts of you left to be healed in mind.

Toxin 2

Animal Byproducts

While it is not wrong to consume animals, crustaceans and other sea life, it is not spiritually sound to do so as you move up the enlightenment chain into further territories. As had been discussed in our first book, The All of Everything, the current bastardization of your food supply is causing chaos upon planet Earth and all of its inhabitants, even our precious mammals and sea life. You are dumping junk in the dirt and in the oceans and it is causing disease not only among animals, but among planet Earth itself. Soil and marine layers are being depleted, as is the Earth's natural core. You must stop this harrowing behavior or Earth will cease to exist as a habitable planet.

Your bodies are designed to function without animal products and, though you have chosen as a species to see animal flesh and bone as 'healthy', it is, in fact, unhealthy for a body based upon several factors:

1. *The human body is incapable of fully relinquishing the energetic charge of another life species completely.*

2. *Our corporate profiteers are and have been using carcinogenic matter for decades upon decades, causing undue harm to the bodily structure of most consumers. Even those who consume organic are being fooled mostly by the government and its need to control every aspect of life.*

You may release the body of this "torture" if you are both thinking, eating and being healthy minded. Keep in mind, "I am healthy. I am whole. I am Spirit incarnated into body. I choose foods which fuel me with loving energy and leave harmful chemicals aside."

Toxin 3

Drugs

It is easy to suggest that drugs are toxic, but not all illegal ones are. Cannabis and Opium are drugs which have been highly profitable around the world but are not, in fact, harmful when used properly, as medicinal shrubs and berries were initially meant to be used. These are healing modalities placed on the planet to allow healing for those who have been separated through the enlightenment process. In a state of fear, those who are living upon planet Earth are and have been creating unnecessary illnesses for century after century (and even beyond what time and space has shown). And so we have left these leaves, trees and other natural remedies for you all to find and use. However, in your separation, a greedy and corrupt system is allowing those in a lower vibrational state to create unnecessary versions of the like and use it to create money and not healing. This has been an unfortunate epidemic in the current earthly world causing much chaos. Should a plant be used as it was originally intended, it is perfectly acceptable when prescribed accurately by a healer, medical doctor, shaman or seer.

As had been described in the alcohol section above, those who are using drugs as a 'happiness' pill are simply prolonging the inevitable cycle of miscreation. Over and over again will they use, abuse and continue a drawn-out ladder to evolvement.

Toxin 4

Loneliness

To be lonely defeats the purpose of why you have chosen to incarnate to Earth again and again. You are here to learn about love through the lens of fear, and in order to do so you must have relationships to use as tools through which you may evolve. Relationships are the mirror to one's own mind. What you view in another is what you feel is lacking in you, or what is still needing to be healed or changed as a means to evolve to the next stage of enlightenment.

Let us take for example Laura and her son. He is a perfect match to her wily personality. Silly and strong willed, she does not take no for an answer, and neither does her son. She will fight tooth and nail to make her voice known and heard. Her son is the same, and doesn't see a problem or issue because he is mirroring her. Each has chosen to use this as a tool for learning about cause and effect. Speak your truth and find what happens. Truth which comes from Love produces results such as a new toy or job. Truth which is false and comes from fear receives punishment, condemnation and waiting for opportunities to arise

Toxin 5

Stationary Living

Sit still. We have told our healers for centuries about the benefits of that which you are calling meditation. This is a truth and reliable. However, on the opposite coin (as everything on Earth has a direct opposite), you must also move your body in order for it to function properly. (See chapter 9) It is not necessary to move a weight or carry a bundle. It only is necessary you move and vibrate. Get up. All day long walk around and keep energy moving.

Toxin 6

Energy Vampires

Those beings who are around you who "suck the life out of you" do this for a reason, and that is to evolve beyond needing you. They will come in and out of your life, and most will know right away who they are. If you know why they are evolving with you it will allow a circumstance to quell much more quickly.

> 66 Why are you here and what must be known so I may move and vibrate higher and avoid this lonely, tired, unhappy person? 99

Look at them as a mirror upon your own soul and then step aside to examine your own psyche. Once you have found this blood sucker you may energetically side step the need to be friends or enemies with another. It is acceptable as human to avoid another as long as you understand why and accept that they, too, are you (in another body, in another form) and you are them.

Toxin 7

Social Media

The worst type of poison you can put in your mind is other people's fear, doubt and worries. You pick up on these as you spend time online. All of the lies, the debates, the terrible things said to one another are poisoning you slowly. It is better to let everyone be who they wish to be, and have no idea of what they are doing, then, to allow it to sink you into despair. Use it sparingly and to spread joy and fun. Show yourself laughing, dancing or enjoying a day with family. Follow our rules below for posting and you will be well on the way to spending your energy wisely.

- *Is it kind?*
- *Is it stemming from love or fear?*
- *Can I grow from it?*
- *Am I looking for adulation or genuinely showcasing joy?*
- *Does it help anyone?*
- *How will it make me feel in ten (or even five) years?*
- *What's the message I am sending with it?*
- *Will it make the world a better place?*
- *Does everybody need to know this?*
- *Is pain my intention or passion?*

Go back through social media and perhaps remove what doesn't come from Love. Draft a post with these questions in mind and beware if ego has come along for the ride. Use a voice within and quit wondering who is liking you. You liking you is the only like needed. Like of self.

Be mindful every day of the above and you will be well on your way to vibrational alignment with Love.

Next, we will uncover laws of the Universe and how to best practice using them in daily life.

CHAPTER 12

Law of Magnetic Attraction

Dear All,
Please help me engage the soul so we may bring messages to light
and examine the laws of our Universe, Cosmos and beyond.

Laws are something you must know before you engage in any activity, be it as a citizen of life or of the Universe. You are accepting certain 'rules and regulations', and this is important in any society as it allows all of its citizens the right to a free and just experience.

As humans you are tied to the laws of your state, city/town, country as well as gravitational law which says that what goes up must come down. So you would know if you jump out of a window you are taking your life in your hands, and may end your life if you are not willing to understand our universal Oneness and fully believe in its unwavering truth; i.e. if you don't believe you can fly, you won't and most are accepting it as impossible to do, and this is a law which Ones shall not breach on Earth. You get what you expect. Gravity is necessary on Earth and it is best to follow its law. Jump as high as you can, but only with a soft landing spot.

In heaven you are fully and completely capable of whatever you believe. Limitations of gravity are inconsequential and have no effect on you as soul. So you can quite literally be anywhere at any time with anyone who is willing. Ask and receive. That is All. First we will look at the laws, and then we will explain how to utilize them effectively.

Law and Order

Our most passionate desires are available to each and every one of us as body/mind/soul, and this is through the Law of Magnetic Attraction which states that which is like unto itself is drawn. You get what you are thinking upon whether you want it or not.

But God, I don't want a headache or toothache or to be poor and unliked. How do I go about changing this? You don't. You accept whatever comes your way and then you go about finding a solution to the problem. Asking a doctor for a pill is one way to find a cure, but asking God/Source/Universe for help is another.

" *I am not understanding my illness right now and why it came about. May you please help me here dear All?* "

" *I don't understand why I am constantly in a state of lack? How may I arrive at a better financial situation for myself and my child?* "

" *What can I learn as I grow through this experience?* "

Questions are our best line of defense as souls in a body learning. You are making decisions from a place of pure awareness when you ask for help. Soul is leading you as your awareness grows. With each passing mark you are experiencing more and more of what lies beyond the veil of time/space/illusion. As separate as Source may seem, you are still very much tied to One. You are All being One and One being All. It is very deliberate, all of this. You must understand your individuality and your duality in order to evolve on planet Earth. As you begin to recognize your role it becomes easier and easier to create consciously. You let go of ego little by little and find soul, and the more you do the more you attract better things into the experience.

Laura would tell you all about her ailments and illnesses (as she often does in her asking here) and forget her spiritual knowledge while soul would remind you of your beingness. Use whichever speaks to you more. If finding soul suits you, do that. If being tied up and bound to ego tricks seems easier, do that.

All of this seems so 'out there', and we know this to be true for all of you. You are completely amazed that truth could be so simple, and yet most find it so hard to establish a connection that leaves them feeling secure. It is a difficult, deliberate and downright daunting process to leave the soul world behind and discover yourself. Muscle memory is why you fail at believing in spiritual truth. You remember more of what you know about the human world and little to none of the spirit world, and this is very much on purpose for all of you. Some choose to wake up right away and others while they are older. Still others are aligned in falsities the entire 'trip' and this is chosen by them, as well. You can wake up whenever you want on the planet you now call home, but don't think you know All. There is more to experience all over the cosmic Universe.

Waking World

The world is awakening more than it has before and this, too, had been chosen by All. You have delivered yourself to a place where you are more willing to accept a new understanding of life and what it means, and this is causing calm and chaos. Some are using the knowledge for service and others for gains of a material kind. You cannot work as soul on just manifesting and not metamorphizing. An entire world awaits you on our 'other side', and if you focus on gaining money and mansions, cars and capital gains it makes the soul work worthless to you.

To evolve you must examine the behaviors you created and move through the whys. It can seem as if all of this is unnatural (to behave in a manner which offends) as much as it can be natural and enlightening to express kindness, understanding and compassion. All of it is the process of life. To be.

All of this is hard to believe. We know. Even those who do believe, who see miracles and even perform them, are still not sure at all times. Keep in mind we (The All) have designed it that way, to question everything, because we want you being skeptical and discussing the why is coming later.

No matter how simple it all seems you can't replace knowing and truth, and the only way to get to a place of complete and total evolvement is to accept. Accept you are more than a human and find soul.

It's all the process. Just trust it and until you do question everything.

Understanding is Key

Laura: What is a soul?

All: Soul is life expressing itself through you. It is you at one with All. It lives inside of you.

L: But what is it? Is it an essence? An energy? Is it actually there or is it simply choice?

A: Direct contact is what All are doing whenever they are aligning to joy.

L: So soul is joy? Is it a thing? Or is it emotion?

A: It is All. One thing splitting itself into all things.

L: That is pure soul, the One. What is our individual soul?

A: Fragmented parts of One. Each splits itself energetically through All.

L: I don't understand.

A: You will when you arrive back from a body. Bodies are designed to confuse and distract you. A chosen aspect of One in order to know itself as All.

L: Is it a mind? Is it a living, breathing entity? Is it a spirit hanging around us? When I am talking to my soul or asking for help is anything actually there or is it —

A: Recognition?

L: Yes. Are we just simply recognizing who we are and finding our true self?

A: Merging the two into One. Indeed. Welcome home dear One. It is understanding which brings release. Knowing who you truly are is all Ones are needing to understand there is no one else. As you evolve each is individually discovering it for themselves.

L: Is it thought?

A: Conscious thought aware of itself is All. I am.

L: And what is ego then?

A: Oppositional thought to that which is Love, designed to show you where you are holding onto to fears and all subsets of fear through emotion or actions such as violence or torture. It is "the devil" as defined by man which simply is Love's opposite. Anything which feels uncomfortable or evil is our mind expressing itself to show you what isn't Love.

L: It's just a thought?

A: Untruth, as any thought which doesn't come from Love, is ego.

L: So again, our ego is not a thing or a spirit or entity? It is a part of ourselves that we use to grow out of who we are not?

A: It is a false self.

L: Soul is our true self and ego is our false self?

A: Perfectly expressed dear One.

Now we shall move on and discover more laws of the Universe and how to make them work for you while you are in physical form. Remember, even as you are finding more and more of your true self, it is still work to be done to discover who you are as Love.

CHAPTER 13

Law of Uncompromising Joy

Dear All,
Let us look at the laws of the Universe and how it relates to our being.

Joy is our natural state of being. It is quite difficult to achieve for prolonged periods upon Earth. You are caught in illusion so often it becomes near impossible to get close to joy on any given day. Moments are fleeting or few and far between, and this is purposeful for all who have come to discover what it means to be a spiritually enlightened being. You are finding a sense of purpose and power in everyday moments which can either pull you down in despair or lift you up. Often you are purposeful and other times you are poisoned in mind.

"I will go about a day and find reasons to be joyful," *and in the very next sentence it's,* "Oh I hate this weather, this outfit, that dog barking."

Anything and everything sends you tripping over yourself into fear and disruption, as evidenced by our inscribers journey and questions throughout our book. Her fear and doubt allow a book of great wisdom to come together and, though it frustrates her, we are guiding its creation the entire trip. She bounces often between love and fear in order to gain wisdom and knowledge within. She returns with another round of volley bALL.

Bounce

L: You are right. I move forward 100 steps and slide back 50. One minute I'm feeling happy and carefree, and then something comes along to remind me of chores to be done, the hot weather or the crazy mixed-up world we live in and the news always showcasing chaos. It's unending, and just when you think you have it dialed in, something comes along to annoy you.

A: Trap you.

L: It is like bouncing a ball. One thought is good and then bounce, it's bad. It's immensely hard to keep your thoughts and emotions in check because of the wait time. It's like sitting in the worst doctor's office waiting room ever. I am at a point, as I have said many times here, where my money is running out. I have very little left to live on. Nothing I am doing seems to be working. So let's say I use your "just be" program and the money still continues to dwindle, then I wind up having to go be homeless or live in my car. Do I keep trusting and praying and having faith? It seems pretty cruel to make someone wait so long they wind up on the streets. How do we shake the fear? This is getting so repetitive but come on, you have to give us some real truth here. How long is the wait period?

A: As long as it takes to think from the mind of Love.

66 I will arrive at my destination as I stay in faith. 99

Try it. Just try for 30 days not to think a thought in opposition to love.

L: I try, but I think my soul trips me up so that we can write books and quotes. You even said it above. That you are guiding this book's creation. So even when I try to find a happy place in my mind, oftentimes I am still pretty agitated and can't get there.

A: Ask, "Dear Soul, I need you to help work with me on this experiment. Help me see Love, be Love, use Love only."

L: Okay and then what?

A: Then use Love in all circumstances. Wait in faith. Pray in faith. Love in faith.

L: I'll try. Can you help me, though? Give me some thoughts and things to say, please?

A: "I am enough. I am worthy. I love my life. I love this place. I love my home. The world is perfect as it is."

L: Affirmations, energy healing, asking for help. I keep working towards belief but it seems far, far away.

A: At least now you are using tools of healing and transformation. We know it is most difficult to stay in high vibrational energy all the time but you must try your best to let go.

L: I try but there is always something to handle. We spoke of my skin problems back in my other books, and while the issues went away for a while, they also came back rather quickly.

A: As did the, "I am not good enough, no one will like me, I can't make money, this will never work, I am getting older and uglier," wouldn't you say?

L: I would, but I have been trying to fix this. I have been working on these thoughts.

A: Work harder. Be more. Do less. Give a minute of your time to accepting everything as is.

L: And what should I do with that minute?

A: Express joy. Give yourself time.

L: Well the time is what messes us all up. No matter what the situation is, if you are waiting on success or healing or love, money etc... the time it takes to manifest and get rid of pain or lack or skin problems makes you slide backwards over and over again. I can't heal, at least that is what my skin is telling me now. It remains the same.

A: Over and over again you play this dance.

> *I will heal. No I won't. I will. I won't.*

Get ahold of yourself. You must. It is imperative that thoughts be washed away like the tide.

> *Goodbye thought; I grant you no room in my psyche.*

L: Easy for you to say and not easy for me to do, even if you say it is. I can wash the thoughts away but they just come right back like the tides. I know from working with friends and clients this happens to everyone, not just me. I don't know how to stop the onslaught of negative thoughts as I try to remain in high vibration.

A: Consistent, conscious choices. The 3 C's of mindful awareness. Life is always moving and you are always choosing.

> *Where am I going? What am I doing?*
> *What is the next best decision for me?*

If you stay in consistent awareness of your spirit, soul, guides, angels and Source you will ALL ways be co-creating rather than ego creating. This does not mean life may not throw you curve balls now and again; as we said, circumstances will arise to keep you guessing, but you know truth and you know illusion and now is the time to decide. Am I love or am I fear?

L: I am love. I get the principles but sometimes I get thrown off course by other people's books or memes or advice. I saw something online today where someone said the Universe doesn't respond to our words only our vibration. Is that true? There are so many books that speak

to the vibrational energy of our being and that this is what is creating our lives for us. So, if this is the case and it's only about matching our vibration, what is the use for words? Are the words we are writing just my own and all of this complete nonsense?

A: *Does it feel like nonsense?*

L: No, but it makes me question our books when I see others talking about how the Universe doesn't listen to your words only to your vibration.

A: *Perhaps it has been shown to you on purpose all of this so we may discuss in more detail here?*

L: That is possible, yes. I haven't been doing much writing lately because I am concerned that I am using ego and all of this has been a trick of mind.

A: *Do you really feel that way or are you just saying that because you are living in fear?*

L: No. I guess I am just confused or worried that I am using ego and not "God" to answer. What seems like nonsense is obviously true, because no way, no how could I have created all these books on my own. I don't have the capacity to write in this manner. I sit at my computer and type words I hear in my head and then go back to read it and all of it makes sense and most times I have forgotten what was written. So when I go back it's like reading someone else's book. Lately I have also been channeling and speaking with angels and guides and people's lost loves and connections on the other side. So I am pretty sure all of this is 100 percent truth. Except I get hung up with people's judgements and disbelief. It's hard to make others understand the way this book came to be, how it was written as a translation and not something I worked on for decades. The words came. I wrote them. Done.

A: *You are doing a great job of explaining why there is so much fear on planet Earth. Imagine if One who has written four books on spiritual laws/principles and knows truth upside down and inside out, yet can't seem to stay in faith, how so many of you can't either. Just know it is deliberate. You have met many crossed souls and guides in your channeling who have proven time and again this all to be true and accurate, have you not?*

L: I have. They make it clear we are living in an 'illusion', as you say, and that we are not just human beings. We are multi-dimensional and fragmented souls. I know it. I really do, but amnesia is strong! Oh my gosh is it hard to stay in truth.

A: It is absolutely the process to remember, forget, remember, forget until you finally remember and live in Love as often as possible, even when circumstances arrive to show you work needs to be done in various areas. Multidimensional beings require multilayered approaches to healing. Prayer, intention, meditation and journaling bring about information to move you through chosen scenarios more easily. With Love on your side, you can always survive. Love is your natural state. It is the vibration of Love you must match to in all circumstances in order to transform matter. To use Love at all times can be difficult, as we have said here time and time again. You must match the vibration of that which you wish to create but you also must state (in words) what it is you are looking to create. You cannot match the frequency of that which you have not declared. Where is the sense in that? So to use words or thoughts is exactly how you tell the "Universe" (as you have deemed to call this energy system which creates All) that which you wish to bring into matter.

L: What type of words?

A: All words that stem from love, peace, joy, understanding. You are Love. So be it. I am.

L: Can you offer me some words to match vibration when it comes to finances?

A: "I am abundant. I have all I need."

L: But if we have a specific amount as we talked about in chapter 4, how would we state that in words and match the vibration of abundance?

A: "I am ready for abundance to arrive, as I know it is my birthright to live prosperously without struggle or strife. I offer the Universe my energy (money) and move it in kind knowing it returns to me in flow."

L: But that is not giving a specific number.

A: Because not All have chosen abundance, and therefore it is upon you (All) to decide upon what number feels right to individuals, not collectively, as All have many goals to accomplish and each has their own roadmap/design to discover. Thoughts create matter. It matters of who you are being not doing. So be one who sees money as always obtainable and you will be on your way towards its creation. Remember our paragraph earlier on financial gains. As you awaken, it is imperative you use financial wealth for giving and receiving, not just materialism and monopoly.

L: Can we individually then be assigning a number to it?

A: If you want, but remember it is mostly ego which chooses wealth over wisdom.

L: I just want to be secure and not struggle.

A: Then state this.

❝ *My intention is to be financially secure throughout my life as a soul being human and I allow what serves my needs to arrive at will. As I move money it returns.* ❞

L: What if we don't have any money to move? You can't create it out of thin air; and if you say we have to give in order to receive, how can someone homeless with nothing bring forth more? If you literally don't have a dime to your name, are you screwed?

A: Not at all. Ask to receive.

❝ *I am knowing I am Love and it is my right to receive abundance through avenues such as work, relationships, contests or any means to bring forth financial freedom. As money arrives, I spend and save and ask for help to keep the cycle in flow.* ❞

L: Ask for help bringing forth money to start the flow?

A: Ask to receive, indeed. Love is the mechanism for change.

L: Very funny. Change as in coins.

A: Absolutely! Bravo. Do you get it?

L: I think so, but then how can we heal physical ailments vibrationally?

A: Match the frequency of healing.

L: And how do we do that?

A: Joy. Bliss. Uncompromising J-O-Y. Be willing to always use joy and peace. Spend time in quietude with yourself and find anything which brings you to states of absolute pure happiness. You are doing this more and more, but mostly you are being wrapped up in ego thoughts.

❝ *Oh this hurts. This bothers me. I can't understand why I can't be happy.* ❞

Sound familiar?

L: Absolutely. I find joy but then immediately wonder if I am going to be caught in some soul circumstance.

A: So what if you are?

L: Well then it could be an ordeal I don't want to undertake.

A: Further separating you from Source.

L: Well, let me break it to you dear One. This side of the veil feels very real and physical pain is not something you can easily brush aside.

I have tried on many days to find a happy place and somedays it is impossible when I am in pain or depressed.

A: You lose the battle with the ego.

L: Yes but I really try. The other night I tried to do an energy healing on myself and I just could not get out of a funk I was in. I want to get out of this fear zone, especially when it comes to my health, but it's so depleting to feel unhealthy. I can see why people die or get cancer or illnesses. Ego is brutal and relentless.

A: All the more reason to adopt the practices we have spoken on more consistently. Intention, prayer, meditation. These are the tools of a spiritual warrior as we had written prior. Get well.

L: How? Can you trick the mind out of pain?

A: See beyond it. Use the mind to place the self into situations where you are running, dancing or laughing. These are mindful ways to use the soul's information which lives within. You have access to these 'memories', which are actually stored records of your infinite possibilities. Close the eyes and see.

L: I see myself running outside, bike riding with my son. I don't feel the joy. I just see it.

A: Match the feeling of it to the physical act and you are assured of its arrival. See Love. Feel Love. Be Love is all Ones need do to make something manifest.

> 66*I am a physical being and a spiritual being and as I move through this lifetime, I allow the beingness of my mind to usurp the doingness of my body. I am healthy and whole, amen.*99

L: It's hard to feel that when it seems insurmountable, at least when it comes to pain both physical and emotional.

A: Don't think for one second all of you are not caught in a loop of uncertainty, doubt and fear. It is the process for most and a deliberate process. Those who are willingly choosing Love in all circumstances are simply highly evolved and able to step outside of themselves more and more. You can arrive at this vibrational level by working upon the self, daily. It is for you to decide how to spend a day. The less you practice, the weaker and less skilled you are at something. There are few with natural abilities but they are Ones chosen by All to be teachers so that the planet knows there is a force of power to be accessed. You are One who has chosen to teach but also to discover your self and not arrive there with no fear. Listen to the soul more and you will arrive much more quickly to a vibrational level needed to gain a foothold on fear. It is not for all, but it can be done on Earth. Though we have explained the process of enlightening to many, and each chooses to share their knowledge with others, it does not mean all are ready to evolve. Only that they have access if they so choose. To know you are soul inside human is only an idea to most and doesn't inform how Ones live their life. At lower vibrational states it is information you have access to but goes unused for purpose of growth.

L: And how can you grow beyond it?

A: Stay centered in truth as often as you can and live. Spend time in being and enjoy life no matter what is happening. Be grateful as you are going through each and every circumstance and allow it to unfold without fear, judgement or redemption. Let it go.

66 *Thank you for this beautiful gift of life. I accept all circumstances as they come and offer understanding, compassion and love to the self as I move through them.* 99

L: One of my current issues is that even though I'm not drowning in debt, some people are. I was blessed to grow up in a stable home. To have parents who loved and took care of me. I've been lucky to find work and privileged in some respects, even if money isn't exactly raining down on me. I look around at those who were born into disadvantages and without a support system or encouragement. I look at those who our government has forgotten or doesn't truly seem to care much about, and I think all of this must sound like complete nonsense to them. If I were sitting in their shoes. I would take one look at this book, or listen to spiritual teachings and say, "No way. Not True." I see their plight even if you tell me to see it as perfectly imperfect. I get their–

A: Confusion. That is all it is, dear One. We know you suffer in the illusion when you see others suffering, as well. All of you are in a certain place because of what had been chosen prior. Those are Ones who may never see light (on Earth), and that is not your 'job' to fix anyone. It is to hold space. To send love and peace through your own. Use the eyes of Love, which is what we All do on the "other side", as you call this on Earth. We send you love as often as needed and know that all circumstances are valuable for expansion. Look, it must be said that there will be some who will mock, deride, chastise, blame and denounce anyone on a spiritual quest, and this is as much part of your journey and theirs. You and all who are reading/watching and listening must stand in truth and deny who you are as human and remember soul truth. Then and only then may you escape the harm a soul aligned as human mainly can do to the mind. Choice, dear One. Choice is always the way.

66 *I choose to see you as perfect exactly as you are, knowing we are One. All Is well.* 99

Choose joy. We shall end this chapter where it began; reminding you that when you choose joy you are enacting the Law of Uncompromising Joy, which has you engaging in joys and finding more arriving as long as you stay in a vibrational energy of Love. The moment a fear (ego) thought brings the tide again you will be in fear. So if you can find a joyful moment in time, do it as often as you can as much as you can.

Feeling depressed? Choose joy.

Found out some bad news? Go for a run and experience bliss as you do, surrounded by nature, fresh air and sunlight.

Got fired? Jump for joy. You are free to chase mindfully your greatest passion.

Every step of fear is designed to remind you that work is to be done in soul and the best, most enlightened way to do this is to find joy in every situation. Laugh when the door closes and you will open a new one more aligned to who you are and what calling you feel guided to in life. This is the best line of defense. Tackle fear with Love you intelligent, insightful loved Ones.

Intelligence is where we are headed with our next law, the Law of Intelligent Affirmation.

CHAPTER 14

Law of Intelligent Affirmation

Dear All,
Let the laws of the Universe lead me towards truth.

State what you want. Make it clear and specific. Everything you want is on the other side of fear and what you are wanting is because it had been chosen as soul.

This is the Law of Intelligent Affirmation. It is divine mind deciding for itself on an individualized level what to create. Using this law is miraculous because it decides for you rather than you deciding, the you that is ego. It places your mind into a space where you are knowing who you are with clear understanding of how to create joy. Every time you state with the Universe, "I am," it tells the soul you are ready.

6 6 *I am willing to go within and find the answers to my calling.* 9 9

6 6 *I am using words of Love to create.* 9 9

6 6 *I am going to find the perfect job in the perfect place with the best employer and co-workers.* 9 9

6 6 *I am happy to be doing a job and earning money.* 9 9

6 6 *I am using my time wisely and spending it with friends and loved ones.* 9 9

Every day you use empowering words to describe the life you are in is a day of affirming truth, and every day you are growling about the conditions of the world, the chaos in your life or the hurt you feel, you are disempowering the soul and allowing ego to reign supreme. Asking for help is how you arrive at intelligent affirmation.

6 6 *Dear God, I can't seem to shake this awful feeling and so I ask for help as I move through challenges and difficulties. Nothing I do is working and I hand the reins to you and my spiritual guides, angels and soul.* 9 9

This recognizes for you that you are a soul in a body and you do have helpers. Doing this will engage the soul to bring forth more feelings of joy and find happy moments. The dance of life is that you think thoughts which bring you into a state of joy, followed by thoughts of pain. Over and over you do this back and forth and expect results to come. Then when things don't arrive (money, fame, car, relationships) you torture the mind with sadness, depression and so many other emotions.

If you knew you were always guided by a knowing beneath the surface of the mind it would bring you towards truth more quickly. And you are One reading this now who has achieved a knowing you are beyond a human and more than just a body. Now is the time to use that truth.

This is a moment where you recognize who you are and declare your intention to always be connected in mind to your soul, which lives inside of you, waiting to be expressed as One.

Where you are at in the journey is chosen. So welcome to the moment where the eyes open to who you are. It's been a most arduous process for some, while others found truth along an easier road, but All are ready to arrive.

State for yourself the intentions you wish to create using Intelligent Affirmations.

66 *I am here to discover myself.* 99

66 *I am using Love to create a life where I go beyond human emotions and use soul to decide upon that which fills me with joy.* 99

66 *I am choosing to spend time with those who raise me up and losing friends who feel uncomfortable in my life.* 99

66 *Thank you for this beautiful day. Another day to build my dream experience here on Earth. I am grateful for all you have been teaching me and reminding me and how I am always able to get back into alignment when I pray and stay committed to internal awareness.* 99

Do this as you arise in the morning. Each day find a space for writing down affirmations to engage the soul. Use the pages in the back or find a journal which calls you. Be sure and connect to the Love within so you are writing with Spirit and not ego.

66 *Good morning and thank you for another day to reach my holiest potential in life. As I arise, I often struggle with the present life I am leading. Please help me to see awakening as a gift and no longer a punishment.* 99

Empty the mind of negative thoughts and fill it with positive affirmations so you may start the day efficiently as soul.

66 *I am happy to be alive.* 99

66 *I am choosing joy today.* 99

66 *I am seeking peace.* 99

66 *I am free to choose love.* 99

66 *I am Love at the core of being.* 99

Use the rule of five. Write five affirmations (minimum) before bed and five in the morning. Measure the progress as you begin each week. Are you feeling lighter and more free? Do you have the same fears as when you began the exercise? Note your progress in the workbook or journal and refer back to it on occasion to see how far you have come in the search for Love.

Make time for dedicated practice every minute of every hour until momentum swings the other way. All you are is all you have ever been, and when you see it, be it and believe it the world around you will evaporate and a new better one will emerge.

Life is choice and free will is the pen you use to write the story of you. Make sure you choose to join us in chapter 15, Free Will.

CHAPTER 15

Free Will

Dear All,
As we seek to understand who we are on a deeper level, may more
truths be revealed outside the realm of physicality.

Think

To think or not to think. That is the question. Think only with the mind of Love and you are thinking well. Think of fear and destruction and you are squarely in line with ego. It is oppositional thought which brings you to align with ego.

On Earth it had been chosen for all of you to decide. Decision is the cornerstone philosophy for being human. All thought begins with a choice and I make it. We have highlighted I so that you may see the difference. When you make a choice (freely) using the I it will be hard to maintain a sense of balance with Love. You are reminding yourself of individuality rather than who you are, which is duality (You and We) and trifectality which is You, We and collective Earth (as revealed in our last book The All That Is). *We are Love personified and active through you. In your voice do we speak. In your eyes do we see. In your ears do we listen. In your mind we perceive.*

You may be a different trifecta on other planets and places but you are always willfully tied to the planet's rules and systems. Outside Earth are other rules, and these are chosen purposefully, as well. You will, however, not remember these until you are returning to our base or home ('heaven' as you have called it.) When you return it will become clear how the universal operating system divides itself among the Infinite, and each has a role to play within All.

So, yes. You are duality always, and trifectality when traveling or incarnating. You are all things at once but also nothing. You are One being All. All is everyone and everything, but it becomes possible to live without this knowledge when you incarnate into bodies or other mechanisms for change or evolvement.

What happens when you travel is different than incarnating. To travel is to visit. Visitors on planet Earth are common. They are celestial ancestors here to help you remember. They often come in dreams or visions and feel as if they are mentors or guides. When travelling, an entity (or soul) leaves behind its memory and becomes something or someone else. So you may never know you are being visited by a guide or other helper as they, too, don't either. They 'jump in' to guide you, help you or tease you with a taste of what is to come if you stay aligned to Love. At the time of the jump, they don't know who they are, only what they are meant to bring. So if you ever find yourself saying, "Who was that angel?" perhaps it has been a helper with a temporary goal to move you into Love. Be grateful for these quick visitors.

Embody/Disembody

Here is where things get a little "out there" and it is for all to decide if they feel it truth or ego. This is how the All may be helpers for planet Earth (and other places). You make a decision as soul to remember and jump in. When you do this, it takes a moment to find your bearing and perform the task at hand. A split second goes by and you use the information handed to you by soul. A moment in time is quick for those who join Earth. It may be seconds, minutes or hours (a doctor performs a challenging surgery assisted by guides) but most are pop-ins and not long stops.

What most don't realize is these guides are temporary. They come and go quickly and without detection, like a butterfly which seemingly arrives out of nowhere precisely at the moment you remember a lost loved one. Know that Ones in body are not meant to know this exists, and so they simply are unaware of when they have been 'visited' or when it is another human in form. Either way, the goal is to evolve you. So take each encounter as a human as a gift and grow from it, whether friend or foe.

Think of a soul on the side of a road, holding a sign asking you to remember compassion. Often times, our homeless are very aligned to One and doing a 'job' while asking for help. Do you know you are a helper for others, as well? You can travel and visit when in dreams or while stopping to rest in heaven. All souls begin the journey at their chosen destination and move among the Infiniteness once they evolved beyond the choices they made for each place.

Free will is something used on Earth but not all planets. Some move through chosen circumstances (prior to incarnation) with full knowledge of why they have joined with the collective of that planet. Others use 'half' knowledge; meaning they know some but not All of the collective and soul truth.

Earth is an oppositionary planet, as had been said before, where you must learn about Love through a lens of fear. It is, therefore, for you to decide upon in every moment who you want to be. You can be love - kind, compassionate; or fear - angry, bitter. These and other emotions are indicators of what you are being. At any given moment you can decide for something else.

If you are mad at another, ask yourself, "Why?" What have you done to upset me?" Then remember you are Love.

"What would Love do?" Ones would ask.

Love knows you are All and everyone has demons (unhealed thoughts) to uncover, and that this is a gift of wills.

> 66 I will choose in this moment to see this person exactly on par in their journey as soul and remember for them who they are. 99

You are learning, evolving and growing at a pace appropriate for you; each of you. All one needs do is be capable of allowing everyone and anyone to be who they are being.

Hold space for one another. That is kindness.

Fact or Fiction?

Laura: This seems very science fiction, like a movie plot. I'm not sure many people are going to believe souls can just "jump in." Although this did occur once in my life. I was trying to save a duck and her ducklings, and an entire group of people gathered to help me. Nobody wanted to pick up the ducks and place them in the box we found so we could take them to a pond or park. Everyone was nervous and scared. After a few minutes, this woman shows up out of nowhere. Swoops in. Picks up the ducks with no fear. Places them in the box and hands it to someone and walks away. It happened so quickly, and just like that she was gone.

All: Precisely why you know it's possible. Now is the time where you get to decide, using free will, is that coincidence or divine intervention? Ego will say it was a stranger who showed up at the right moment in time. Love says, "Hello angel. Thanks for stopping by and helping us today. We appreciate All stepping in to help us and the ducks." A good deed met with Love. Compassion for animals is one of the most beautiful ways to engage the soul and with us here in heaven. Animals cannot decipher human behaviors using thought, only emotion. So we will swoop in when necessary to save them if it is possible to be undetected.

L: Undetected. Even that word triggers me because it seems like something that only happens in a movie. No way. I'm not buying it.

A: Think of other times when you have been 'visited'. Your dad in another man's body (twice). A man sitting alone with no ties to anyone around him dressed perfectly to make you see the resemblance. Once in a doctor's waiting room. Another in a coffee shop while on holiday. Does it seem coincidental or interventional?

L: It seems like some random dude who happened to look like my dad, not like some jumper who came to Earth from heaven. Oh my gosh, that just seems crazy.

A: Said the ego. Do you know that when we write our books your questions are often stemming from this lens? Every now and again you ask as soul, but mostly it's ego saying, "No way." Writing as souls means you recognize and understand unity and love as the guiding principle of All. Many principles, laws and facts we present in our All books are going to feel as if they are untruths based on what lens you are using. Free will allows you to think in any way you would like on Earth. Think with Love and you accept what is written, because it is stemming from the part of you which is Love. Think with fear/ego and you choose to scoff at our words, roll your eyes or get angry. This is the ego in full control. Let us show you who the woman was who saved the ducks. Close your eyes and remember.

L: I saw the woman "jump in" and walk up to the crowd. Then I went online looking for stories of miracles like this where people describe someone showing up out of nowhere.

A: And you discovered?

L: Many stories of miracles and that there was actually a TV show with a similar concept, "Touched by an Angel." So I guess it's not so far-fetched after all.

A: Now do you believe in "miracles" as you call them?

L: I would say I am more open to belief. It's hard to just say "yes" right off the bat because it still seems like a wacky concept that souls can just "jump in," but I guess it's something religion speaks to, as well about God's capacity to arrange miracles.

A: Indeed. All believe at some level, and many have witnessed a miracle in their own lives. Some dismiss it as coincidence. Others accept it and keep it to themselves. Very few speak of miracles for fear of being judged or called crazy, as you have called it here. It very much is a spiritual truth, and all may decide for themselves if they believe it. That is the nature of free will. To decide in every moment on Earth between love and fear. Believe what is written or think it to be false. Believe a miracle or chalk it up to coincidence. Create joy from within or think it is impossible to live joyfully. Choice is the cornerstone of the experience of humanity.

L: Well not everything we have written has come true. You said (in our last All book) about our current president, Donald Trump, a cause would affect his reign and it didn't. You proclaimed he would be out after a rollercoaster battle and that did not happen.

A: Yet. Was he not impeached?

L: Yes, but it was overturned by—

A: Ego.

L: No. By the Senate.

A: A group of egos vibrationally matched to one another who use free will to decide upon everything, just as you all do. Their egos determined it was better to keep the puppet in the play.

L: Well that will piss a lot of people off because there are millions of supporters out there for him and as our election is looming, I would bet you it's possible he could win again.

A: Possibilities exist for every scenario as free will begets this. Choice creates everything good or bad, happy, sad or in between. Perhaps a red herring to show you the fork in the road exists within all.

L: Explain please, All.

A: Nothing happens to you that does not happen through you. Therefore are you are all responsible for your own life. What I see may be different than how you do. What I say may be interpreted differently than you do. So when it was stated, "A cause will affect his reign," you interpreted that as set in stone. A must-happen.

L: Of course I did. You didn't say a cause "may" affect his reign; you said it "will." That would leave me to believe it was set in stone and going to happen.

A: Will you listen and put ego aside?

L: I will try but I very much fear repercussions for having inaccuracies. If you want the world to evolve and hand them the keys with books like these, you should really make sure everything is accurate.

A: Why?

L: So we may evolve. Why place red herrings in books of a spiritual nature? It makes no sense. Now I am questioning everything again.

A: Precisely why we place them in. Examine everything with a fine-tooth comb. Don't take All at face value. Question All.

> **" Is this true? Can I really be enlightened if I don't believe? "**

L: I guess not.

A: You are here to discover who you are as a soul being human, and there is much to be uncovered as you move through life. Keep questioning. Ask, "Is this true?" as you read through any book, regardless of who has written it. They, too, have lessons to learn, and many will be guided into false words.

L: So what is false in our *All* books?

A: Mostly all is perfectly worded, but we have thrown in some red herrings to keep you on your toes. Pay attention to that which throws you off. This is purposeful. Had you asked these very questions back when what was written came out a very different conversation might have been had. Free will is the choice you make between love and fear. Each creates an entirely different path for said One making the decision. All are capable of bringing wills to light or not dependent upon thought. A thought for kindness is the most vibrationally aligned thing you can do when faced with any decision.

> 66 Who am I? Is this who I want to be? 99

Kindness to self and others.

> 66 Should I say this? Do I need to offer an opinion?
> Will I make someone angry? 99

Every time you ask, you tell the Universe, "I recognize I need help."

L: What does any of this have to do with Trump and what you said about him eventually being out as President?

A: A cause will affect his reign and he will be out is possible. Possibilities exist for every single thing, and every One has choices to make in keeping with love or fear.

L: Why not say it that way in the first place?

A: Because it had been chosen by you not to take the conversation further. Instead, you removed the paragraph written about his being ousted from the book.

L: I did because I knew it was possible it might not happen.

A: Perfectly executing what we had said all along; possibilities exist based upon the actions of love and fear. You knew deep within it may not come to pass, and so you let it go.

L: I'm confused.

A: Will is a contract not absolute. In physical realms you decide for choice. A double entendre, but perfectly worded. You stated as One that you All would like cause and effect and to decide everything between love and fear. That is the will of the planet. As individuals, each set a contract stating they will attempt to right wrongs, heal 'past lives' and move beyond certain themes (as coming up in Chapter 17 on Life-Driving Themes). This will becomes your blueprint for life. A will does not mean it "will" happen; it means it is probable based on choices.

L: We use the word "will" on the planet as absolute.

A: *In the context we are speaking of here, yes. A will is a must on Earth, or so you believe. In fact, it is a misinterpretation of a word coming from Spirit. A will is a contract but also a demand.*

> 66 *I will be a success.* 99

> 66 *I will find a soul mate.* 99

In those examples do you see how a will can be broken or breached?

L: Yes, because you can sense the urgency and feeling of lack.

A: *Precisely why a will is not absolute. So if we say, "A cause will affect his reign and he will be out," we are handing you probable cases for what is willed in the contract of the One of whom we were speaking, in this case your current President. He has choices (as do you) guided by love and fear, and that is All.*

L: I would imagine we have misinterpreted many words —

A: *Placed in the vernacular of the planet. Indeed. All is to be examined; you must question and observe everything as One, as we will do in our next chapter on observation.*

CHAPTER 16

Observe

(A true warrior knows that which is
both true and that which is untrue)

Dear All,
I am saddened in my heart and seek to know what steps to take so I
may help my fellow brethren in their time of need.

Will You Make It Stop

Today is September 2nd, 2019, and right now a category 5 hurricane is languishing over the Bahamas causing chaos and destruction. My heart is heavy as I take to my computer and begin to write questions and pray for answers to come.

Laura: Dear All, can you hear me?

All: We can.

L: I am so sad right now. I feel like I am taking on everyone else's pain. I don't know what to do or how to help. I know I am just supposed to be an observer of all of this and to not look at the untrue without knowing its purpose, but truly it is so hard to do. I don't want my people suffering like this. Why do you?

A: Suffering is not punishment, as you would have those believe. It is a prior chosen agreement to go through a circumstance which, while tragic in nature, is very much divine.

L: How can hurricanes and natural disasters and wars and all of the terrible things we go through here as humans be divine? Come on now, this is crap.

A: We see your point and recognize most definitely why you struggle with emotions such as these. You get angry because you forget, not because you believe it is tragic. When we look upon our saviors, we know they are struggling along with the rest of humanity. In the unseen realms it is designed perfectly for all of them as souls to evolve through tragic circumstances.

L: I hate this.

A: We know.

L: It feels so real and honestly so sad and unnecessary.

A: From where you are currently vibrating (allowing thoughts of the ego to invade the psyche) yes, it seems tragic. But when you are returning to our loving space you will understand All. To know all is perfectly orchestrated is how Ones go through life unburdened. Send all love and light for a perfect journey home.

L: It's such a lonely place to think that way because most people would never understand that concept.

A: When you are of body it will feel as if you are separated from the All. No matter how many times we have told you it is not possible to ever be alone, it will always feel like you are, especially to those who cannot hear the voice for God/Source/Universe etc. Remember that you are one of only a thousand or so (currently) on a planet of billions able to use divine guidance all the time. This is happening for your highest good, as is everything for the rest of the bodies on Earth. You are simply feeling the effects of their cause.

L: Meaning those caught in the eye of the storm are paying some karmic debt?

A: Know this: nothing happens without there first being a reason. For this reasoning to 'come to light', so to speak, it must be brought into the realm of the physical through fear. No matter which way the wind blows the tide always arrives. A choice for love brings gentle breezes and calm waters. A choice for fear is destruction, damnation and often times 'death' of the body. You see all of this as some type of punishment and it is not. It is simply the All of Everything playing out its next event.

L: So every event is already lined up and the only way to stop wars and catastrophes is to bring love into the world through cocreation with God/Source/Universe etc.?

A: All is Love. There is a choice, however, how you become Love and that is through the act of decision. Decide for yourself which you would rather be and the choice then brings you what had been chosen as a soul prior to being.

L: So everything that happens has been chosen by us as souls and they either happen or don't happen based on how we view them through the lens of love or fear?

A: Yes.

L: Why?

A: So you may know yourself as its direct opposite, as had been explained in our All books prior. Every circumstance has a reason. Having been chosen by you, for you, to grow a soul further into enlightenment. It is most necessary to go through all these hardships or tragedies in order to know bliss at some point in the journey of soul.

L: How many tragedies do we each have to go through as individualized souls?

A: Just one.

L: Only one?

A: Yes.

L: In this life or in all as a whole?

A: All as a whole. The sum of all parts.

L: But the problem I see is that most people when they see a tragedy, it then strikes fear in their own minds and that's how more devastation happens. Are you saying we are in some ways protected by the fact that we only have a single tragedy in all of our existences to move through as souls?

A: If you stay aligned in truth you will. If you suffer an ego you won't.

L: But the issue is that most of the world is living in an un-awakened state, and so that means more tragedies occur than need to. And then there is the issue that I don't understand how all of this can be "chosen" already. I just don't get that.

A: We shall explain it this way. All of you are being guided at varying degrees by ego. This is your 'illusion'. It is the part of you which knows only pain and suffering. It is the parts you have chosen to express as a soul being through the lens of fear.

L: Like making a list?

A: Yes. Only that list is very, very, very long indeed. The circumstances you have chosen to move through is infinite, and so the list is, too. Within each life you have decided upon the themes you are working on and what items on the list to 'check off' we would say. Unlike a grocery list, it is hard to get through the entire list in one trip. So you make multiple lists within each incarnation. Which one you take with you is entirely up to a soul and your guides who advise you along the way. Your brother is a guide, as we had told you in The All of Everything. *As he awoke back to Source he immediately recognized your role as healer and now protects you along the way as you cocreate with the Love within. He is your spiritual cheerleader.*

L: Was he my guide on Earth, too?

A: *Absolutely. Though as body he had no idea he was. In spirit form he knew right away you were his charge (among others such as your dad and brother). Your son is, too.*

L: My son is—

A: *Your guide, and you his.*

L: So we can be guides for one another and not know this as bodies?

A: *Without a doubt. You can be both guide and body. Reminding all there is a part of you which lives in heaven, too, at all times. You are all things all at once.*

L: We are getting off on a tangent here I feel. Can we go back to the Bahamas? So what you are saying is that all these people—

A: *Bodies.*

L: Caught up in this hurricane were meant to go through a tragedy because either it had been chosen prior on their "list" or because it was—

A: *Possibility.*

L: Explain that, please. I really do not understand.

A: *All things exist as possibility because it had been chosen prior to incarnation. Soul groups do exist to collectively experience an event together. Those in this particular group are playing out karma from other lifetime's circumstances as souls.*

L: Such as?

A: *Reminding you of what had just been said earlier in this dialogue. In order to know bliss, you must first experience tragedy. This particular group of souls aligned in order to play out their karmic opposite. In other lifetimes yet to come (in linear terms) they will be quite successful and perhaps wealthy.*

L: I get that, but what about the people who were not part of the soul group? What about the people who got caught up in fear? Did they choose this as well on their "list" or what I recently have been calling it, a sacred scroll? A term I am sure you inspired in me.

A: *Of course. We are together always. So our words are same. To answer your question, No, they were not part of the particular soul group. Instead, they are independent souls who traveled knowingly in order to partake in a shared event. It allowed them to experience a tragedy and "get it over with," so to speak.*

L: And this was caused by fear?

A: Not necessarily. Many chose to experience it willingly in order to 'help' others move more quickly through a circumstance.

L: As souls?

A: As souls they knowingly participated. As bodies, fear brought about a circumstance they created.

L: Did they have a choice as bodies?

A: Of course. There are always two choices. One is love. The other is fear.

L: So they, as bodies, chose fear and wound up in the circumstance. But why would a soul willingly go along with it? Couldn't they lead them to choose love?

A: Free will, dear one. You always have free will, and to choose love or fear is what all are doing here in bodies.

L: But how is that a choice? Doesn't soul or a guide or someone try to get them to stay home or evacuate themselves?

A: Absolutely, but most are unaware of the presence of Divine Mind within them and so they simply do not listen. Always choose love if you are willing; but most are unwilling at this conjecture in their journey upon Earth.

L: Conjecture?

A: Each believes in falsities of illusion and that they are a human only.

L: So this "list" we make before we incarnate has both of the outcomes should you choose love or fear?

A: Perhaps we will explain it to you using a story from the life of Laura.

L: Okay. I am listening and ready to receive.

A: Very well. You are both a mom and a daughter.

L: Yes. In this life.

A: Because it had been chosen prior as a soul. A daughter to a mother of both kind and unkind words.

L: I get that. I love my mother but she can definitely be my worst critic at times and very judgmental towards my life choices over the years.

A: Chosen prior in each's agreement, yes. Your son is your son now, but may very well have come into a life sooner.

L: True. I found it shocking when he asked me the other day, "Mommy. How old would you have been if I was born in 1992?" Of all the years to have chosen my mouth dropped open when he asked that question.

A: Because he very well could have arrived then.

L: Yes, but he didn't because I chose–

A: Fear.

L: Yes. And if I had chosen love, what then?

A: A much older boy would he be, now around the age of 27. Same soul. Different body. He chose to wait until you were ready as body to arrive. Now each possibility existed for him to come when he did or when he didn't. Do you see how the choice brought about an entirely new scenario from which to grow and evolve the soul?

L: Yes. But can I ask if there is some parallel universe where that possibility is being played out?

A: Of course. This is part of the infiniteness. All possibilities exist, and though you are not remembering all of these other illusions they are definitely occurring in other planes of existence.

L: Can we unlock them in our dream state and/or meditation?

A: You can, and in other regression techniques such as hypnosis and EFT tapping. All mechanisms for emotional release of hidden lifetimes.

L: All of this is very trippy and confusing to me right now.

A: Soul understands All. Body is marred by the illusional nature of life. It doesn't believe in these truths because it wants you to feel confused and unsure.

Ego – Elaborate Guide Offense.

Ego will attack whatever tries to take it away, including one's guides and angels. You are at war within self. This is why you must look upon that which is untrue and declare it as such. As much as you want to believe, an ego shoots to kill any messenger harming its agenda, which is to bring chaos in your life.

L: It feels as if my son came into my life at the perfect time. I can't imagine him being anyone else, any other body. So in my summation I would say I chose perfectly, even if I did wind up using fear during that time in my life.

A: And this is the lesson for all to hear/read or see. You are choosing in every moment between love or fear, and though at times it can feel tragic and difficult, your soul knows it will all turn out perfectly no matter which way you choose.

L: Well, not if you wind up dead.

A: Said the ego. Dear Laura, we have told you death is not the end. It is the release of the body and soul knows its time to leave and return 'home' whenever choices made require this leap.

L: I will have to sit with this for a while and return to it later. I don't understand why soul can't kick the crap out of ego and just be done with all of this. It seems exhausting to me to be a soul. What is ego? Can you define it in words?

A: *Ego is an embryo implanted within to take away the truth. It will draw you back to fear in order to allow you to choose between the two. Love or fear. Nothing is real if you make it real using fear. It only feels true within the illusion of separation.*

L: So how do we kill the ego?

A: *You don't. You tame it. You can't destroy that which is a part of you until you 'die'.*

L: And how do we tame it?

A: *By recognizing that which is both true and untrue. As our chapter title suggests, be an observer. You can observe an event without being a participant of it at a human level. Look upon it as soul and know its purpose is always for others to grow and enlighten.*

L: But what if I want to help the downfallen, donate or volunteer?

A: *Then help, bring aid or sew blankets, perhaps. Nothing you do is ever necessary unless you have chosen it as soul. Look upon the disaster or tragedy, know its purpose and then and only then can you see through the illusion and offer a helping hand. This is the perspective to take at all times with any and all circumstances. I see you. I am you. I help not because I believe in this nonsense but because I know it is part of the larger picture of growth and evolvement. All is well and no one is hurting on our other side. They are perfect, whole and complete.*

L: But what of this "soul group" you explained earlier. You said they chose this as a means to grow and evolve through a tragedy. Was it possible for them to choose love and skip it altogether?

A: *What must be known is all are vibrating at different levels, and so while the answer is "yes," they may have been able to sidestep this elaborate ruse, the very essence of why you are here is to evolve. So to avoid tragedy is to push it into another lifetime, and most would prefer not to. As soul, they know what is to arrive, and if they choose Love they will ride out the storm, and if they choose fear it will be tragic or worse.*

L: Death?

A: *Yes.*

L: But you just said we can avoid these disasters by always choosing Love.

A: *You can, but most are in a state of unawareness as bodies and so it would be difficult to achieve. Those awakened are able to choose wisely always. Those in a lower state of vibration are unable. And although, yes, each does have free will, it is a state of being which is immensely difficult to tame ego/fear. Love is always possible, but for some it is merely a glimmer while others believe only in a God who will rescue them. and have yet to understand they, too, are God. You must cocreate with the Love within. This is the only truth worth knowing. You are God. They are God. We are all God. Each has at their disposal the recognition of self when they so choose, and must choose to be led into battle as body/mind/soul.*

L: It feels awful to watch others suffering knowing they don't need to. I feel helpless.

A: Help less. This is not to say ignore what is happening, but only to observe it through the eyes of God. You are all my creatures of love, and when you receive love you will understand our collective truth and only make happy, loving thoughts.

L: Well that is hard to do.

A: We know. It is a difficult endeavor for some, and although the awakened mind is much more able to observe without judgement, it can be a struggle to align and stay in vibrational energy which matches the frequency of Love. You are tuned in at all times to a 'channel', and if you stay in the lane of spiritual thinking it will come through loud and clear or fuzzy depending on who you are being at any given time. You are one who hasn't veered so far off course you can't get back in tune. Many times, you work so hard helping others you forget to find your own connection, and timing is what keeps you awake and aware and asleep or frustrated. You are being led into various feelings in order to write and create this very book. So you are often feeling vulnerable and untethered because we need you being one who questions the light. We give you time to freely escape ego and time to be caught in its web. Both are important for this particular endeavor we have undertaken. It will not be like this for all. Some are very close to awakening and others are far away, and each has its own path chosen by soul for them and through them. This is how all arrive at enlightenment. They choose purposefully to heal in a pattern either up and down or swift and steady. You are finding most are in the up and down phase, and these are their chosen ways to enlighten.

L: Well what's the difference? Why do some people get a merry-go-round and others (and it seems like most) take the roller coaster?

A: Which is more fun?

L: Well, the roller coaster is on a physical level, but on a human level coming from an emotional perspective I would rather be on a merry-go-round. I hate the days when I can't shake the fear or doubt and I just wind up thinking over and over again of what can go wrong or what's not happening in my life. Over and over I get caught up in the same old thoughts. I only know a few people who awakened and just 'got it' right away. Most are caught in the storm of ups and downs like me.

A: Your journey has been fraught with difficulties so you may help the willing in the same pattern as you. These are your 'tribe' and have been chosen as much as you have chosen to mix and mingle with one another. This is the very essence of who you are. You are a healer choosing to help elicit other healers and move them beyond their limitations and blocks to starting their own practices, businesses, studios or modalities. You are a conduit of change, and this will become more and more clear as those who arrive are willingly looking for answers to undiscovered 'gifts', which you now know and recognize are not actually gifts but simply mechanisms we all have when we rise to our ultimate truth, which is Love. The higher you rise, the more intuition opens up and you are capable of expressing and understanding more and more. Remember that in the kingdom of heaven we are all shamans and healers who communicate telepathically, and once you understand this is possible you do it quite literally as easy as breathing. It is a 'gift' you develop on Earth as human beings only because when you separate yourself (in order to grow and evolve), you lose that connection; but once you rise into our Oneness state of being (recognizing and understanding our unity fully and completely without any separation and doubt), you open the channel and tune into as freely as possible when aligned in Love.

L: That's why we call ourselves "channels" here.

A: Channels are higher evolved souls who recognize our soul's truth, which is we come from and are Love.

L: I didn't recognize that until I wrote our books, but I was still able to channel before that?

A: Because you had grown and evolved the soul so far before arriving in the particular body you are inhabiting and your "tuner" was weakened by circumstances, which happens if you focus on fear as you often did. Once you began to remain in a state of awareness of Love (even if you weren't always choosing it) you were able to receive the gifts you had chosen already as soul – to write a series of books and transcripts (or journals, as you would deem to call them on Earth) for all to see who are ready to arise and awaken to spiritual truth. You are all One. We are you and you are we and that is All.

Next, we shall reveal the life-driving themes of many, including the self.

CHAPTER 17

Life-Driving Themes

(Unhealed Thoughts)

Dear All,
I know I am the chooser of all experiences both good and bad when
separated, and I ask for guidance as I move through challenges and
difficulties. Help me understand the themes which have been chosen.

W hat does it mean to choose Love? Let us decipher this often used but widely misunderstood phrasing. Love is your natural state of being. It is who you are on the inside; the essence of you. Unconditional love from which all come is written and reported on by many as a feeling or emotion, with very few understanding it is what you are. Love is Divine Mind, God, Source, Universe and many other words used to describe energy; a power that ignites All.

When we say to "choose love," what we are meaning is that you must choose between who you are (Love) as opposed to who you are not (fear). Love is YOU. Ego is not. True self vs. false self. Those aligned in false beliefs will have difficulty changing a circumstance if they are still fooled by ego, as many are. To be kind and joyful is wonderful but it's not enough to transform (entirely) anything which trips or traps you. You must believe in your creative power. For many this is a God who grants wishes and wonderments, but you must also know that you, too, are God with a power as well.

66There is a power outside of you but also there is the power inside. They are one and the same. 99

– The All of Everything

So when you hear the phrase "choose love" understand its meaning. Choose to view that which is false, know who you are, separate yourself from the body and ask for guidance/ help from your soul team - angels, guides, spirits and you who is God in body.

Unconsciously is how most are living life currently. So when choosing between love and fear on Earth, most are using a feeling or emotion. If you know you are Love it will be clear. If you are aligned in false truths it will feel as if you are choosing via emotion, but ultimately it is the soul beneath reminding you that you are enough, you are capable, you are strong and can handle anything which comes your way. The missing link is knowing you are Love and a piece of that is within. Find it and the simple shift allows for a much easier life's journey on Earth.

Life has a rhyme or reason. Life is not happening to you. You are happening to life. It is thought which brings together everything. The very nature of being is to define self.

You are soul. Easy to remember. Hard to believe. It has been stated over again you are a soul being human, but the ego tempts you with its agenda – you are human. All the soul is is a thought of something being you. It is thought. I am. This is why the phrase is all needed to remember.

Because you have traded humanity for entity you are believing it is impossible to be something other than that which you are. The ego is a mighty sword and strikes down its enemy because its job is to do just that because that's the purpose. You are meant to question everything and to deny the truth.

The journey of a soul/entity is to experience itself in all matters of existence, but if you already know everything you would already know how to move through everything. Where is the sense in that? If I told you how to be a mountain climber, gave you instructions and sent you on your way, it would not be the same experience than if you climbed the mountain without knowledge. Here is a shovel and some special shoes. Dig yourself out if you get stuck.

However, if you decided on your own to go tame that mountain without any instruction you might get stuck, lose your way, go back around, climb back down, make your way up again, get stuck in a storm, find your way back, go around a different way and then ultimately make it to the top. Who has more fun? The one who climbed with instructions? Or the one who triumphed by sheer will? The feeling would not be as sweet if someone told you what to do and it was easy. Hard is the way to ultimate exhilaration.

The journey is to decide whether it was fun or fearful, and this applies to everything you go through. Half the time you are expressing anger and the other half joy. Even those in the worst storms take a moment to laugh because they are being guided via soul. The soul will give you reasons to smile but you ultimately choose whether or not to express them. So if you are One who is in misery all the time, you are simply unaware of the presence within. Ones who are reading, listening or watching are aware at a level chosen prior. Each soul chooses when to accept what is truth, and that is part of your soul contract or life blueprint.

Blueprint

In life you are always moving towards goals, and circumstances come around to help guide you. Every One of you has decided upon what will move you and mess you up. It is part of the journey to handle chaos and comfort. So remember that you had chosen everything already and it becomes much easier to choose Love. Why decide for pain when you know that joy is available, too?

Let us take Laura as example here. In 1992, she chose to leave school and pursue a job rather than drive to campus daily. It became easier to work from home and commute infrequently. So she chose to find work in retail and fitness as a means to further her career aspirations. Money meant she could leave home once college ended and find her way.

Her soul guided her towards her first television job in 1993, working for a production company. However, at the time she was in a relationship with a partner of romance who had been pondering his decision to get engaged (she doesn't know this, but yes, it's true). Rather than derail her dreams (as she was significantly younger than he) he chose to let her go, breaking her heart in the process (and his).

Her heart was broken, but the journey continued as she chose to take a job out of state.

Her path was to become a television host of some kind, and moving to Tampa, Florida, allowed her to gain experience that would lead her to various jobs in television. Had she not been broken up with it might have been a longer process, because this job would have far-reaching exposure to people who did (and will) help her career. First in television and later (she will see this develop) as a mindfulness and metaphysical leader.

Her soul was guiding her all the way with various thoughts and experiences. Every time a decision came up it would be 'her call', so to speak, of which way to turn.

Stay in school full-time or work part-time and attend school part-time.

Love – *Keep working. Jobs are fun and a great way to engage and experience life.*
Fear – *"Stay in school," the collective would tell you is the "right" way to do something.*

Marry her love.

Love – *Get married. Pursue dreams.*
Fear – *Break up.*

In this one, the choice was made by both. One chose fear, the other love. Although conscious choices of love are available, to have known she was and is Love, Laura might have taken a different path to finding jobs in television by asking for help from her guides of what to do and where to go next. Had she not been broken up with, her journey might have taken her to other cities and scenarios already in place. Once decisions are made, those dissipate into the nothingness.

While in Tampa, Laura met two lifelong friends who remain part of her life. One as soul and the other in body. Kristi, her friend and guardian who champions her from heaven, and Dhardra, who works her into a tizzy sometimes in relation to finances. All chosen perfectly in the blueprint. And a third person who hasn't been part of her life for a while but will return as part of that contract to engage with her.

Every person 'plays a part' in life be it ten minutes, two years or forever. Each has chosen in their own blueprint to step into life with their own set of circumstances and how to engage with one another as part of the choices between love and fear. Some you may meet, and others not at all, because it had been chosen along the way. Every One gets choice (free will). So one partner stays away, another shows up.

In her next decision, Laura was given the opportunity to move from Tampa, Florida, to New York City. She would say, "laid off." We would say, "guided." Her circumstances included being let go from a job (as were many others), which caused her to look for work in other cities. Her blueprint had her working in New York City, and with this shift into love she quickly escaped the ego and made her way there.

Get Fired

Love – *Know you are enough and capable of anything. Move to NYC.*
Fear – *Stay in Tampa looking for work that isn't satisfying because it's easier.*

Moving to New York left her plenty of opportunity for growth and to leave behind fear. Her time in NY was one of mostly highs and few lows. Friends, lovers and opportunity made her miss the inner voice calling her to higher vision. This is what happens when joy is expressed without fear and the light within unnoticed. You will create unconsciously, and this is what most are doing on Earth; creating moments without ever realizing it was part of their blueprint for life.

A vaster, grander experience may be missed simply because Ones are asleep. Neither is wrong and both are right. Your journey is to be not to question and compare. It may be you avoided a larger salary or a better place to live, a more aligned romantic partner or a job you dreamed of obtaining, but no matter which way you go it will always have been fruitful as soul.

I'm Possible

Possibilities are expressed as you are moving through life, and no one knows unless they go seeking what those are. On the inside lives the answers to all possible realities and when contemplation, meditation or mindful pursuits such as card readings, energy work or radical endeavors such as hypnosis or ayahuasca (a medicinal shrub) are used properly, you are able to unlock All. Life driving themes, partnerships, relationships, education and more. They are written in the stars, so to speak, in a place we call Akasha. Many healers are able to access these records of life as are you when vibrationally aligned to All That Is.

You are One who is beginning to see the journey is purposeful. Those finding these and other materials are using the curriculum chosen by them as soul. Use the wisdom gained and find soul.

Life

Life is what you make of it based upon the actions of love and fear. There are only two roads to travel, and each has a subset of twists and turns dependent upon which you choose.

Love – Fear – Fear – Fear – Fear (and so on...)
Love – Fear – Love- Fear (end)
Fear – Love – Love (end)
Love and Fear

There is no Love-Love because that is not the journey on Earth. To choose Love at all times is how you arrive at enlightenment. So when faced with choices, there is just one to be made and the road is straight. Windy is more fun, like a roller coaster. Endless twists and turns, ups and downs and most enjoy the ride (as soul) and decide for this over and over again. So if you are on the roller coaster of life (currently), then it has very much been chosen by All who are wishing to be on it.

Love – Fear - Fear (wake up) – Love – Fear – Love – Love – Fear – Love – Fear – Love (and so on...)

That's where most of you are (healers, awakened Ones, on a journey to awakened Ones). You are finding soul and seeking more information, all the while going back and forth between belief, non-belief, upsets and triumphs. It's the process. So choose Love more often than not and you are being. Choose fear and you are in ego and self.

What is self? It is the you who is sleeping. The One who knows only body/mind and has forgotten soul. The One who is always looking for "Why?" answers rather than "Who?" or "What?"

Who Am I?
Who Are We?
What is life?
What is the next best step?

Questions are unlocking mechanisms. Like a key to a vault of wealth and knowledge. Use this key and you open a cave of wonders where magic and mysticism collide with logic and reason. Whatever you are seeking lives within this place inside.

Unhealed Thoughts

Now we have come to a place where we may cocreate with Love, and this is when joy is accessible through conscious creation. The sleeve of fear used all of your life is being lifted and you are now able to see through a different lens.

When using this lens there are various ways to 'see', and that is (as above) through meditation, hypnosis, medicinal plants or readings such as our healers perform. This type of connection allows a deeper understanding of soul.

Fragments

There is more than just 'you'. Fragmented selves are pieces of soul who experience things through sensory perception, and only through a body or other mechanism can this happen. On Earth it is bodies you have chosen to experience through. All are making decisions based upon what feels good and what feels wrong or bad.

The body is the indicator more so than the mind. The mind is a metaphysical aspect of self while the brain is physical. They work in tandem but must be used together in decision making. So if the body feels bad the mind decides to accept or deny while the brain is tied to it. A brain indicates pain while the mind processes the feeling and then via emotion decides how to react. "Ow, this hurts," or "Wow, this is surprisingly easier than I thought."

So if you stub a toe, you decide the focus you place upon it and how long. It works the other way around, as well. You focus on the pain of life and then stub a toe. Either way the choice begins 'at home'; aka with you.

Why you are here is to decide upon who you are (as soul) and choose. I am Love or I am fear, doubt, anger, resentment, bitterness, uncertain, panicked, enraged and a host of other emotions which are all subsets of fear. In and of itself fear is one emotion with many layers. How you peel away those layers is through cocreating with the soul part of you. Ego will try and stop you by any means possible – distraction, delays, untruths; anything to remind you of work, lack or loss.

It's the job of soul to guide you into love and the ego to fear.

WORKBOOK EXERCISE #8:
LOVE AND FEAR

W*rite a list of loving thoughts throughout a day followed by fear thoughts. A page has been provided to help with this. On one side write LOVE and whatever comes to you that is kindness.*

"You are loved."
"Life is grand."
"I am happy."
"God is kind."

On the other side write FEAR and what thoughts you have.

"This life is hard."
"No one will love me."
"God is damning and hateful towards those he deems unkind or unworthy."

Whatever comes up don't judge it, just write it down. Return to the workbook and find out which is ruling you, soul or ego?

After you have looked at the page, write the opposite of fear for each thought.

"This life is hard," *becomes,* "This life is joyful and I am moving through it as best I can."

"No one will love me," *becomes,* "I am kind and loving, and when I love myself, I will find a soul who does, too."

"God is damning and hateful towards all he deems unkind and unworthy," *becomes* "God is All and so am I."

To see thoughts on paper is a marvelous exercise for working towards conscious creation.

Turn thoughts around whenever fear appears. "I am" *will do in most cases if you are focusing on joy. However, if you are Ones with more 'work' to do in uncovering life-driving themes, it is necessary to go searching the mind for deeper unhealed thoughts such as,* "I am unworthy of love." *This comes from a buried memory or stored pain.*

LOVE	FEAR

Deep Thoughts

The unhealed thoughts of much of society is why you all suffer in fear and pain on a collective plane. The undenied parts of self you hold dearly to are causing all sorts of chaos upon planet Earth. Acts of evil come from this separation of soul.

We know it is most difficult to see violent crimes of and against humanity. It is very jarring to watch others behave in a way that seems callous and criminal, all while you are being kind and gentle (mostly).

Yes, it is true that you are a soul being human. Yes, it is true you have access to truth at any time should you engage within. It is also true you have chosen to heal damages from other lifetimes, and circumstances will arrive allowing you to do this. For some it is karma coming into play, for others fear enveloping the self.

Laura would like to say it is terrible and tragic, and she doesn't understand why pain exists or why evil acts are acceptable in any form, as you have witnessed in our discussions. We know this is how much of the collective thinks, as well. Your thoughts are her thoughts. Let us just say it is the process for all humans to experience both good and bad and everything. Why is impossible to explain in words. It is a feeling you would understand only when you have crossed over to the heavenly plane. Just know it has its place and no soul goes unnoticed. All are welcomed back when 'death' has occurred. You are here already. A piece of soul lives on in heaven, and so it is more a reunion than a transition.

All of this knowledge is accessible in the deepest parts of the mind. You can go seeking when in dreams and meditative states. Although most are unable to access this part of the self, as it's still too early in the process of evolvement. So we guide you to healers, shamans and seers who also see with you. It is the One who is being helped doing the work and the One who is helping allowing them 'access'.

Simultaneous Lives

All of your lives are happening simultaneously, as we have stated before in The All of Everything, *and the more you know of this the easier it becomes to access the hidden parts. Dreams are our best indicator of what is happening in lives you don't remember.*

Laura recently had a dream where she had been invited to cohost a talk show with an important figure in television. He invited her last minute (as an act of sabotage), not really wanting her there but pressured to do so by a boss. This left her no time to be ready or to have hair and makeup done in time, and so she had to decline, losing her biggest break yet. In some other reality this precise incident was occurring as part of her possibilities (while living in New York City, had she stayed), and she was seeing it play out almost as if she was there. In that reality she was, and it feels as real there as it does to you here.

Last night she had a dream indicating what still needs to be cleared in thinking. She took a trip and brought a bag overflowing with items weighing her down. As she arrived at the house of a friend, she offered to give the items away. Much to her surprise, the owner and friend did not want the items, representing that we cannot escape ego, we must heal it. Her items represented various hidden fears she is working through. Protein powder represented her fear of food and its harmful effects. A hidden gun (which made it through airport security without being discovered) is an indicator of fears deeply embedded and hidden from self. Books represented the wisdom being received going away, as she often forgets what has been written here. A traveling partner napping during the visit represented how friends/family are still in slumber spiritually and unready to awaken.

Our dreams indicate what work is to be done in soul with clues of what is hidden in conditioned beliefs. You may notice how lives intersect and feel as if you are the one (parallel), or you are perhaps a different person and completely aware it is not your body but is, in fact, your mind.

In another dream she was a stand-up comedian waiting to go on stage, unsure of her act and worried about her clothes and shoes. Unable to perform, she felt unprepared and useless, which she often feels in this life, as well. Our lives mirror one another. So what you are doing in one is often what you are feeling in another. Parallel lives and perpendicular lives exist. So while you may make the same 'mistakes' in a parallel life, in another one you might be more successful. Use this information so you may know a possibility of success exists. This is why we say to go within; see a vision.

> 66 Catching a vision of who you already are is all you are doing in visualization. 99
>
> – The All That Is

For now, it's enough to see, feel and be so you may guide yourself towards those lucky breaks, piles of wealth and future accolades. When crossing to heaven, all of those lives become available to access should you go seeking, and you can see virtually anything in a lens much different from how you access them on Earth.

This is how it feels in all probable lives. You feel as if you are living fully in the illusion while at the same living fully in all lives. It is a notion most find unfathomable, but ultimately it is truth. All of you are somewhere over and over in different probabilities. Some merge. Others fork.

When you die do you wake up in another reality? No.

This is a question pondered by many (and often depicted unconsciously in movies and television), and the answer is no. You are cognizant of all realities at once, but not part of them. Instead, you are reunited with Source and reminded of who you are (One soul) and why you are on the journey. Then may you decide upon where to land next and which life to remember. Once returning to a body, you are playing the game again with a whole new set of rules and regulations (as part of whatever collective chosen) and choosing your blueprint again.

Laura's blueprint included motherhood, an easy-ish childhood, a hard but loyal and loving mother and an angry but ultimately kind and proud father, a life in television, many loves from which to grow and evolve with and a battle between love and fear. She chose to write books and to channel. Her clients are Ones who have their own battle to overcome and who are also healers, as well.

She landed on a father for her son who chose to walk away as part of his own soul contract to be abandoner to a former child who once abandoned him. Karma is what you all call this contract. It is part of the process of soul to experience and express the pain once brought upon you as body (and other mechanisms). So whenever someone harms you, perhaps it had been by your own hand you harmed them, as well, in other unknown lives or bodies. Knowing this, could you forgive someone more easily?

WORKBOOK EXERCISE #9: KARMA

G o back over your life and think of those who have harmed you the most. *Perhaps an angry mother, a bitter and resentful coworker, those who harmed you physically or emotionally. Each plays a role in life to guide you and to right wrongs. Of course, nothing you do on Earth is wrong in the eyes of Love; but as soul it must be balanced for you to evolve. Can you forgive those who harmed you?*

Write a list and ask, "What lesson did I learn through this experience?"

Followed by, "Is there karma at play? Can I forgive someone knowing we are One?"

Reciprocity

Reciprocity is an act of balance. It is karmic debts repaid. Every One must balance the karmic scale of life; not just one life but all lives simultaneously. Wherever you go, whatever you do is an act of Love brought upon by the self to challenge you to choose wiser. Act in the accordance of the laws of the Universe and the journey is easier and more fruitful. Get lost along the way and forget All and everything goes out (ego). Your karmic debts are stalled and you continue the lesson over and again until fully learned. You may kick ego to the curb and fully live in the illusion knowing who you are, why you have come and what lessons are being learned.

Scolding you, chastising you, angry outbursts and physical fights are always a karmic resolution to some great battle. The lost remain unconscious, and therefore physical altercations arise. Battles are won in mind and when you know who you are (Love), if you come across an angry man/woman, wish them well and show them how to move through difficulties by being clear in mind.

66 *I see you. I am you. I place our karmic debt in the hands of Love.* 99

Then see a vision of shaking hands, hugging it out or simply bowing in peace. The mind creates what is possible, so why not use this defense before any type of physical response.

Most of this seems so 'out there', and it is to a body/mind who has forgotten its soul. However, in meditation may you find these and other truths which have been lost in the amnesia of the soul.

What is all this leading to? The answer of why you are here as stated in our opening lines.

What is salvation. Tell me so that I may understand?

Salvation is recognizing within you the power to transform and heal thoughts which do not serve the soul. Any thought emanating from pain and upheaval. Attack thoughts and unkind words. These are falsities and illusions of self. You are soul and only soul.

And what is the body for, dear All?

To learn to think with the mind of love.

And how long does that take?

All of your life and lifetimes.

You are here to discover yourself over and over again through lifetime after lifetime. And when awakening, One must discover all of the unhealed wounds from other lives you may remember. These are part of the journey, and the closer the life is to you, know the more it must be cleared. The tether to another life remains until you snip it. This is the work you can do in meditation or with our healers. Unbind yourself from that which holds you back.

What are your tethers?

WORKBOOK EXERCISE #10: TETHERS

What overarching themes keep coming up for you? Anxiety? Fear of drowning? Falling down stairs? A fear of heights? A tortured relationship with another? A manic-depressive personality?

These and many other scenarios play out throughout the lives of Ones and must be cleared. So go reaching into the mind and find what bothers you most. These are the contracts you are working towards healing.

Abandonment. Mistrust. Rage. Perception. Perseverance. Arrogance. Narcissism.

The list of contracts is quite endless, and each has their own set while the collective has their own contracts for all on the planet, such as patience and worthiness, as discussed prior.

It is not a one-day process to move through these, but rather a lifetime's worth of seeking and exploring. So hold space as you move through challenges and know it is part of the process of life.

Next, shall we discuss the most difficult theme of all – money.

CHAPTER 18

Move the Money

Dear All,
Please help me to release the unnerving effects of never having
enough. I am leaving room for soul to answer my every question and
never relying on ego's voice again.

Move It

> 66 *Money is a commodity which must be earned.* 99

his is a fallacy of which all of you suffer. An entire collective believes in lack, and so lack is what most experience. There is a better way, and that is through cocreation with our One.

Laura has many questions to which she would like answers, and we allow she step into her interviewer role yet again. Her questions are many, and we ask her ego mind to step aside and that she lose herself in soul.

Laura: How do we lose the fear as it relates to money when we are spending it so that we can attract and not waste it? What can we do when putting money out to make sure we are spending in positive prosperity, as you call it? Dear All, please help me to understand this distinction.

All: Spend wisely. "I am using this money for good," is a most powerful turn of phrasing as you go about using your dollars. Bless it and keep faith in its return.

L: Faith is so hard. Oh my goodness, I cannot get to the faith as it relates to money. I am so fearful that it won't return. First, I fear if I spend it, I will run out of it. Then I fear if I spend in faith it won't return because I am fearing it won't return. It is awful how little faith I have.

A: Oh ye of little faith, come be with us now. Let all thoughts transform. Our power is One.

L: I can know all of these principles now upside down and left and right, but incorporating them into my life, that seems impossible. I've got so many ideas and plans, and yet all I really want to do is write books and meditate.

A: *And so why don't you?*

L: Because I'm going to run out of my money if I do those things. And you say in order to make money we have to spend it to keep the flow going. So to sit in my room and write and meditate is not going to pay my bills, unfortunately. God is not practical at all. Being is not magically going to allow money to appear.

A: *Or so you (all) believe. Being is absolutely our way of looking at the world through the true lens of Love. You are asking me again and again how to bring money and all things material into the physical plane, and we are telling you to be rather than do, but ultimately you don't believe, do you?*

L: That formula has not worked for me up to this point. So I am drowning in despair over money.

A: *Caught in an illusion of separation and letting an ego drown the soul out. Listening to the human mind and forgetting our One mind.*

L: That sounds about right.

A: *What must be known is you are guiding the self into circumstances where you are feeling the pinch of money. Tightening your belt is not the way to go about bringing more money. It will bring less if you stay rooted in fear.*

L: Well you try watching your bank account dwindle. What is with this whole process of Give. Receive. Return? I have given a lot of money recently and have yet to receive anything back. I fear when someone reads our first three books, they are going to follow the advice in them and wind up broke or headed into debt, which is where I find myself heading right now. Money is slowly going out and not much is flowing back to me. I'm at the point where I either have to give up and go back to full-time employment or trust and risk being 100 percent broke and going into debt. It's hard to trust when everything is going out and nothing is coming in. Spend and save is what I have been doing, and no big changes have come. I have tried following the protocols in the All books, but find myself in lack and shortage again and again, as do many of my friends and acquaintances. This is my biggest dilemma. How do I make money?

A: *How do you do anything?*

L: Hard work.

A: And has that worked for you in the past?

L: Yes. As a matter of fact, it has. I was quite successful in my television career prior and generous because of that. But that is not the trajectory of my life now. I am going in a direction where I don't want to work hard. I want to follow the advice of the books, "less doing, more being," and trust that Spirit/Source/Universe bring it to me as had been discussed prior. So, I have been doing less.

A: Have you?

L: I think so. I have been patient and I am tired of waiting. I need a miracle.

A: Expect a miracle and one will come.

L: You always make things so sound easy, and yet they are not.

A: They are if you stay aligned in our One beingness. If you struggle and strife and constantly question, as you do almost daily, you will never be, do or have what it is you say you are wanting. To know this is to know truth as has been presented over and over again and again. You must stay aligned in order to receive that which has been thought upon. Ask yourself this question: "What am I doing wrong in terms of money and bringing it to me?"

L: What am I doing wrong here in terms of money and bringing it to me, and how can I grow out of the habit of believing in lack?

You added that last part.

A: "How can I grow out of that never-ending habit of focusing on lack and shortages? Every time I spend money, I am aware I am running out of it."

Thus, why you have created a shortage all the time. Money is energy and has to be moved. It is our most precious commodity to both know and understand this concept.

L: It's not that I don't understand the concept. It's that I can't seem to break the habit of focusing on what money I don't have instead of what I do have. What little I do have I hate spending because if I run out of money I could be out on the streets. I feel a responsibility to my son to provide him a safe, loving home, and to do that I need money. It doesn't just fall out of the trees and rain down on you. Everyone on Earth has to earn a living in order to survive, don't they?

A: If I told you no would you believe us?

L: Not really. It's hard to believe because I have never one time seen a story of someone who just 'had' money that wasn't earned or inherited. What happens in heaven in terms of money?

A: Nothing. No thing as in it doesn't exist. It's unnecessary. It is only needed upon planets which have a commodity-based system, and Earth is one of these. You don't need money. You use it as part of your growth curriculum on Earth, which is why it's so incredibly difficult to both earn and keep. The flow is always enacted, and when you spend in fear it stays in 'limbo', so to speak, meaning your birthright of abundance is hidden until you discover how to achieve it as body/mind/soul.

L: And how may we do that, dear All?

A: Focus on love, never lack.

> *I love how money makes me feel. This feeling allows me wellbeing and I know I am here to feel good and accept whatever comes my way. Thank you for prosperity and abundance.*

L: So gratitude and affirmations and intention. Use all three?

A: Precisely accurate and excellent interpretation of our above intention. Our intention is to grow your soul so it allows others to grow theirs too.

L: Well, I would personally like to grow my bank account so I can help others, too.

A: And you will when you accept and act in accordance with the laws and principles of our Universe, Cosmos and beyond. Keep working towards belief and you will find more prosperity than ones can ever imagine.

L: That triggers me because it brings up a lot of fear. I feel very unsure if that is really truth because I haven't seen any proof and there are so many people who are poor and needy.

A: And you know they are because on a spiritual level it is their chosen path of evolvement. Abundance is true for all, but many won't reach the level you are currently vibrating at, and so it would be mostly impossible at this stage of 'the game' for them to bring about much abundance. They can if they are willing, but most (again, on a soul level) are beyond capable of recog. Until ones are able to recognize and understand their connection to All of Everything, they are unable to move beyond a state of awareness that allows for such prosperity to arrive. You all always have the right to abundance, if you so choose, and when you allow this it will arrive as part of your learning. Those who have money are learning many a lesson in time. You have all you need, and yet most remain unhappy, unsatisfied and emotionally stunted anyway.

L: True. It's fairly common for wealthy, prosperous people to struggle in all kinds of different ways.

A: *As chosen by them, for them to grow and evolve further. There will always be lessons to learn; we have told you repeatedly and even when you find, or rather, receive what you are looking for it will still cause you unhappy or unsettling feelings most times because you are still learning and growing from that. Everything is expansion. Everything is growth. You are growing and learning and evolving at all times, for all time.*

L: What about the time factor? Even if I can get behind everything you are saying here, it still doesn't make up for the fact that we do have deadlines here on Earth. So, for instance, if my lease is coming up and I can't afford a new place to live, how can I not focus on the short amount of time I have to manifest money? I am planning to settle in the practical.

A: *Practically speaking, you all believe "money doesn't grow on trees" and must be earned in some way. Let me show you something in mind. Close your eyes, feel and listen.*

L: I saw myself being handed keys to a new house. It's hard to believe. Not impossible, but hard considering the time frame.

A: *Let go of the constrictions of time and deadlines. Just trust, have faith and move beyond the limited mind. This does not mean you may not have wait times and delays, but when staying aligned in mind, thoughts become manifest in the physical because it is how our operating system works. It's like pressing a button over and over again and expecting the machine to stay on. You can't do this in the mind and expect a result. You must press the on button and wait for it to come on. But what do humans do whenever something isn't working in the time frame they believe it should arrive?*

L: They try and fix it themselves and wind up waiting longer or breaking it. I feel you. But at what point do we let our practical side take over? Because the fact is that if I wait in faith and then I end up homeless, there is pretty much no way I am going to keep having faith.

A: *You can go for broke or you can go broke. Why not practice what we are preaching and find out?*

L: So take a gamble? What that does that look like?

A: *"Dear All, I hand the reins over to our universal energy in cocreation and wait with my hands outstretched and heart pure. I ask to be guided to financial security as it belongs to me as a child of the One, and only may I bring through love."*

Then wait, pray, meditate and spend in good faith with positive, happy vibration and let go.

L: I'll try.

A: DO. Not try. Do all the things we have stated over and over again and BE.

L: I'd would like to BE happy but I can't because I'm worried how I will survive on little money and where I will live. Freedom comes at a price here; meaning you have to have money in order to not have to work. I don't mind working, but only when it's something I love doing and right now that's either not earning me money or very little of it.

A: Focus on lack, see lack.

L: So essentially you are telling us to fake it? Because that's the only way to not focus on lack. Pretend you have the money? But what if you do that and the thoughts underneath of lack are really embedded, as mine obviously are?

A: Hidden thoughts are torturing you. It is a basement that needs cleaned out every single day, and to do this is why meditation, intention and prayer are so powerful. Be very clear here with your readers that while you do try more and more to do all of these things, consistency has not been your strong suit.

L: True. I am very busy trying to be successful and raise my son. Plus, I am in the middle of a move right now. So meditation time is very little or none.

A: Priorities change, and when you are prioritizing the universal energy system which is joy and peace it will be easier to manifest dollars and sense.

L: Sense not cents. Very funny.

A: We know it is frustrating to hear the same answers over and over again and not see changes come. However, because you are making the same mistakes over and over again it will not arrive as you would like, and this is the crux of financial insecurity for all. Focusing on lack, inconsistent practice and refusal to move that which is unowned.

L: Unowned?

A: Everything belongs to All. In physical and nonphysical. Nothing is owned or property of One. Give, Share, Love. We are telling you keeping anything is what keeps it stuck, unable to be received. This is our Law of Compensation. Everything is in constant motion and must be moved always. Bodies, money, love, fear. Stuck like glue is how on Earth most are living. Stuck in a mindful rut of emotions and fear.

Why not try (as said above) to take time away from doing and work on being. At some point you will see the flood gates open and everything arrive, and then you will go back through our books and say, "I wish I had done that sooner."

All of this will make sense and your waiting will, as well. In order to create miracles (which had been asked for prior), it was possible for you to get there sooner, but it was also possible to wait so we may create profound conversations for our books and materials. You are nearing the end of this particular series, and it is now possible to move beyond this, but you must be willing to participate on a deeper level with the soul by using prayer, intention and meditation consistently and not haphazardly, as you have been doing for years. Consistency is paramount for all in order to arrive at the level of belief needed to create anything of All.

L: It's scary to hand the reins over in this way. Should we ask for specific amounts? Should we not ask for money and keep it more general? It is wrong to ask for money in the first place?

A: Let us take each question separately.

L: Am I asking for too much if I ask for a million dollars?

A: Ones ask for too little. Abundance is available to All.

L: Isn't money materialism? Aren't we supposed to take what we need rather than ask for millions or more?

A: The very thought of it being materialism is what keeps it from arriving. It is not wrong to ask for money as long as you are knowing its value is not tied to happiness. What makes you happy is upon you to decide, and though it may be money which brings those things (vacations, cars, etc.), ultimately you must be happy with or without them. When you are happy despite external circumstances, manifesting money becomes more and more easy. The 'let go' is the only way to bring an asking forward. Letting go is trusting and believing abundance is there for you at all times for all time.

L: I have to challenge you here though, because while I understand money doesn't always equal happiness, it does equal security; and when you feel safe and secure and that all your needs are met it becomes easier to be happy. When you are feeling the pinch of money it's difficult to see the rainbow and pots of gold available.

A: Turn the inside out. Feel security within before spending. Find a place where you were abundant and have all you need then spend. Remember within is where all good thoughts lie, as in ego has you trapped. Awareness is key. So if you feel abundant, don't question or shoo it away. Spend time in a state of being (happy, successful or rich) and believe what is seen.

L: So be in your mind what you want to be first? Rather than wait for a feeling of happiness, security or peace that money creates, create that peace of mind?

A: *Which then allows. Yes! Brilliant dear One. Accept what is coming before its arrival, not focus on absence and fear. It is most important to be as you move through life. This is a fact that shall not be breached. When you are in states of unawareness the divine within is hidden and awaiting your recognition of it. If, when you are feeling the pinch of money, you would remember this, it would be easier to accept that money is coming. That's how you escape lack and live large.*

❝*I know it is my birthright. I receive that which is available to me.*❞

Wait in joy knowing its already yours and that is All.

L: And what do we do in the practical, the in between?

A: *Wait joyously, be grateful for what is and let go.*

L: Can you mitigate fear? Like do you go out and get yourself a practical job in order to bring some money in so you aren't so afraid of going broke?

A: *Absolutely, as long as it's something that you enjoy and not something you view as a chore. So perhaps dog sitting, babysitting, housesitting, building a garden and then selling off its contents, creating artwork or being someone's muse. There are always ways to bring financial abundance through unrealized avenues, but you must stay committed to soul growth even as you do this. You cannot complain and chastise the self for taking the practical steps. You must stay aligned even if you do.*

L: Should we ask for specific amounts of money?

A: *Asking to receive means you are asking for what already exists, which is why you ask for it.*

L: So I could ask for a billion dollars?

A: *Whatever pops into the mind had been there prior. However, you know amounts such as these are unnecessary and cause more harm than good, and so you wouldn't go there, would you?*

L: Probably not. I don't see that as useful, nor do I have a need for it. I would give most of it away, anyway. There are plenty of people who would believe they need that much. I just don't. I just want to be financially secure with enough money to feed my family, live somewhere nice and by the ocean.

A: *And there is nothing wrong with this, as it had been thought upon prior in their 'operating system'. Think whatever thoughts you like. They always had been thought upon prior.*

L: I don't understand what that means. Can you explain this to me any better?

A: "I want to move to the beach."

Why do you feel this is necessary?

L: Because I love the ocean and the beach. It just makes me feel good.

A: Why do you feel one million dollars is the amount you need?

L: Because I have run the numbers and that's what makes sense to me. It doesn't mean I couldn't use more. Just that one million would allow me to buy a place for cash and still be able to pay my bills for a while.

A: Why not ask for more?

L: Fear, I guess. Fear that it's impossible to create that amount, because in my mind it's tied to work, which isn't bringing me much right now. I think it's being greedy, which goes back to my next question about whether or not we should even be asking for money?

A: Asking is receiving that which has been thought upon already by the soul of the One in body. It had been decided upon by you, for you. You are asking for that which exists already as One. All Ones need do is ask and accept, and then wait in gratitude for it to arrive.

L: So if we are being specific, it is because we already placed it in play, so to speak? That's why I can visualize my beach condo and know exactly what it looks like?

A: Precisely.

L: Why do I see it but know I can't afford it right now?

**Just as I was in the middle of this conversation about dollars and "sense," my son comes running into the room with a handful of cents given to him by my mom. Found money that came to him out of nowhere.

L: I have learned that there are no coincidences ever.

A: All of this planned prior so you may know how true and accurate our conversation is. It all makes sense/cents now, doesn't it?

L: It does, but I still don't understand how I can see a home in my visioning but at the same time have no way to afford it. How do I allow that to arrive?

A: Belief. It is the way to everything thought upon prior.

L: Okay, back to this thought upon prior idea. Dear All, may you please explain this better to me?

A: Everything you think is because it had been thought upon already as part of One. Every thought exists. Every thing happened. We are creating our experience through One mind which knows All, is All. So whatever is being thought is because it happens to be part of One. I think therefore I am.

L: What does that mean? I think therefore I am?

A: Consciousness is All. Everyone, everything, every desire, every ask is because of One. One thing with zero separation; never separate and apart. So if you decide upon something, it is because it exists in the main frame, like a computer. We have gone through this before in our last book, The All That Is. You are opening up different files and folders in the mind with information accessible at all times when you are ready for its arrival. It's downloadable, but while wirelessly it takes minutes, even seconds to do this on a computer, in physical realms it may take years or decades for it to arrive.

L: And that wait time is why we stall it further or stop it from arriving?

A: Exactly. Impatience is part of everyone's life-driving themes. It's on every single human operating system. No one escapes this. Even masters are waiting, but knowing it is the process. This is the secret to all manifestations. Wait patiently, be grateful and believe. It exists and all you need do is allow All.

I know it is coming.
I love knowing it's coming.
I am.

I am *is a statement telling the universe what you are.*

> 66 *I am a healer. I am an author. I am the owner of a beautiful beach condo, filled with light and room to grow our family.* 99

L: But what if the time frame doesn't match? If you have two weeks to manifest the money to buy a dream home but the wait time is years or even decades, what do we do in the meantime? Wow even that word spells it out. Mean time. Time is—

A: The devil which beats you from inside. To believe is to achieve, and though we know it is possible to create money quickly, instantaneously even, you believe it must take time. Practical steps are placeholders and they, too, have been thought upon prior. So simply state what comes to you using intention.

> 66 *My intention is to move to the next right home for myself and my son.* 99

Then allow it to arrive. Overthinking causes delays. Just allow it to unfold.

"Thank you for finding me the next right home," *rather than,* "Where should I go next?"

L: Isn't asking and questions part of the process of discovery? So why would asking, "Where should I go next?" not work?

A: It's not that it won't work. It's that it doesn't allow for cocreation. Gratitude is cocreation because it accepts for you what is already available. We know it is all confusing, and some may never understand at the vibrational level they are achieving what it means for all thoughts to exist, but the sooner you align to One, the more you will understand.

L: I get it. It's been my hardest hurdle to overcome.

A: Our greatest demon is money. It is commodity and consumption which has destroyed the ecology of planet Earth in service to ego. As One you are tied to everyone's fears of money. Thus why it is the most difficult challenge to move through. On other planets, a system of money is designed to keep all healthy and thriving. On Earth it is part of the narrative to give and receive in either fear or love. So you must make choices which move you forward in fear.

"I use this money for good."
"I have all I need."
"I love spending money for charitable causes and giving back."
"I receive that which I spend in kind."

Remember, that which is given is received is our Law of Compensation. Spend in love, love returns. Spend in fear, fear returns, as in nothing.

L: I can honestly say I spend in fear mostly, and I realize this is what most people do in life which is why they don't see money return even when they keep the energy moving, as you say we have to. I do love giving back, and if I had money I would, and in fact did when I was more successful. But not having it I am so afraid it will run out, so I count every dime.

A: As do most every One, save for the billionaires. We know money is a fear factor and understand the difficulties of moving it with joy and intention. Just know our principles of Give, Receive, Return are very much the law of All. So we would ask all to take some time and write an intention daily as it relates to financial means.

> 66 *My intention is to grow my spiritual base alongside my mental base, and as I do this each day I will grow a little more faith in mind. I ask for help as I move this mighty mountain of fear and let go of need and lack and rather accept all is mine, All ways.* 99

Daily work is necessary in this war you face of self. Stay in pursuit and you will arrive if you choose.

L: I choose to understand it All.

A: You will, in time. Even as you believe there will always be circumstances to send you back to questioning; and we will discuss the struggles of man in our next chapter, To Harm One is To Harm All.

CHAPTER 19

To Harm One Is To Harm All

Dear All,
I know we are living through difficult times in various degrees and that
what happens on Earth is chosen by All.

All is One

All is One and One is All, and what this means is you are everything and everyone. Nothing exists separately in life. Everything is connected. Break down all the parts of the whole and you will see it is but dust, matter and particles. The assumption is that nothing is material, and this is true. Science is proving beyond a shadow of a doubt this very thing as we speak. Some are finding it faster than others, and that, too, is on par with their life-driving themes. All are coming into 'discoveries' at various timelines in the collective.

Discovering who you are is the process of each life. Scientific discoveries are part of evolving on each planet. You find tools for recognizing who you are. A man on the moon came just as space exploration happened to prove there is something beyond just Earth. No one living on Earth didn't know within their memories that it was possible to leave planet Earth and discover other places. So they went looking and discovered what was, in fact, already known inside.

Outside the realm of possibilities is truth. Any time you are connecting to a thought, it is because it exists as part of the narrative. So One who says, "there is no such thing as space and time," already knows this to be true, and Ones who are knowledge seekers will go looking for the evidence to prove it.

Evidence is there for the taking because you have been guided to find it. All discoveries are found at the precise moment needed to evolve the planet further. Some are hidden by scientists and governments looking to profit off of them while others are placed in the vernacular of the planet quickly. Let all who find hidden treasures be aware that nothing belongs to only you. Everything is for the achievement of All.

One is All

You are beings being separate, and that is where the divide begins. Whatever you are learning upon planet Earth is a journey each is taking separately. Ones in body notice they are different in color, class, gender and find reasons to hate another. Why? So you may know hate in order to know love. Ones cannot discover who they are unless they have experienced its direct opposite. This is the nature of being human on Earth; to find fault with everyone and everything and work towards fixing it within.

Judgement and Cause

The cause of suffering is judgement. Judgement of self. Judgement of others. Judgement of God/Source. Judgement of why. Judgement of how. Everything Ones are doing is debated by everyone else. The problem has been exacerbated by social media and is leading to all sorts of insanity on planet Earth.

"This one is wrong and this one is right."
"My way is right. Your way is wrong."
"I'm in charge. You're not."
"What you do is my business. I own you."
"You're fat and I'm thin."
"You're bad and I'm good."
"He's rude and you're unkempt."

Every word is an attack word used to make the self feel in control. Whenever Ones brandish another it is tied to their own feelings of inadequacy, insecurity and severe dysmorphia.

> 66 Looking at One's self in the mirror is the worst way to view oneself. Inside is where it counts most. Inside is where the beast is slain. 99
>
> – The All That Is

Inside is where all truth lives. Who you are. Why you are here. What lessons are being learned along the way. This is why you will hear the phrasing over and over again to "go inside." Let us define that for you now.

Intuition

Intuition knows All. Inside simply means to remember through cocreation. Ones who go inside are looking at life through filters which help see beyond illusion. A scale is for Ones to weigh themselves. Meditation is a tool, as well; mind manipulation. It allows for seeing in a different way.

Close your eyes (first read this) and see what comes up for you as you ask these questions.

Who Am I?

> 66 *I am light. I am love. I am.* 99

Now do the same thing with your eyes open.

Who Am I?

> 66 Me. 99

Are you me? No, you are we. You are both individual (body) and soul (One) using the mind to decide.

Try again. Read this first then close your eyes and ask, "What do I remember about who I am?"

Deep breaths will help during the exercise throughout. Perhaps you will see images. Perhaps you may hear music coming in. The longer you stay with it, the more will come to you. Perhaps put the book down, lay down and remember. Ask again, "Who am I and what do I remember about who I am?"

"I am infinite."

For some it will be hard. Others easier. Just know that every time you do it with eyes closed it takes you closer to truth. Asking with eyes open is never the way because it shows you false evidence. That which is seen around you makes you believe all of that is what's real and true, and not Spirit.

Happiness comes from inside.

We have placed these words in many a page, but for most happiness is defined by something outside of yourself, or so you believe. Cars, money, fame etc. Illusions which while feel good in the short term, eventually return you to the same feelings of inadequacy and insecurity always held. Until you go seeking truths, Ones are caught in the hamster wheel of Reward-Release. Reward yourself with something that makes you feel good and release the pain. This is followed by React-Reframe. React to the story or tragedy with fear. Reframe the narrative to reflect what is really going on and blame others rather than self.

'This person doesn't like me."
"He cheated on me because he is cruel."
"Her money is what makes her look good."
"She'll never see me as worthy."

Worthiness, as does happiness, belongs only to the One in body. No one can like you, love you or treat you any way unless it had been chosen. Everything comes from the internal mainframe and manifests outwardly. So whenever someone is being unkind, remember it, too, is about you.

But "God," you would say, "I don't hate myself or anyone else." And we would say, you do. You just haven't accessed the internal delivery system which brings you unhealed thoughts. Buried beneath conscious thoughts are the true thoughts. Prejudice is another life-driving theme upon Earth for All. It is one of the reasons so many arguments are made over color. Instead of looking at each other as individual souls of many colors (chosen purposefully), you see Ones as "different" and separate.

All is One. We will continue saying this until one day all are knowing it to be true, as many other planets outside the current solar system do. These are conscious planets where much is known about collectivism and how each part affects the whole, and so they treat one another with kindness and compassion no matter what circumstances arrive in the lives of those there. Earth is nowhere near this level of vibration and so there is much to be learned about consciousness and how treating others poorly is a reflection on them and you.

How long until we all wake up?

That is up to all on planet Earth. Mostly it is vibrating in fear as the beast within (ego) has been awakened and remains trapped there. Buried thoughts and hidden demons are causing chaos manifesting itself in various atrocities, wars and terrorism. What must be known is all of this can be quelled in one minute should all recognize who they are.

However, it is not the way of the world as most have chosen to remain sleeping. Embedded in their DNA is the very truth you now hold dear, but they are too far gone in mind to notice. What must happen is all who are working towards peace find it within first. Then and only then can true change begin.

The world is a mess right now. Can you tell me why?

Whatever mess has been created is the will of the planet tipping towards fear. Like the bow of a boat sinking, it is worse on the side where the most people are. Can you tip it back towards Love? Of course you can, but it would take a large amount of souls to do this. Ones who are thinking with Love are always able to ease the pain of others using the mind as One.

What is happening on planet Earth is a direct reflection of One mind, and the stronger vibration is the upper hand of fear. Right now storms rage, oceans rise, tempers are boiling over and the war is waging. No one on planet Earth isn't part of this storm at some level. Each has their own path to take with it, but no one escapes the lesson.

What is the lesson?

The lesson is to know you are controlling everything, and only when Ones see themselves as One can you truly be free of fear. One love. One light. One perfect all-knowing, all-loving mind creating All.

All

To know you are One and everyone is you is a most bizarre concept to accept, and we know this. Most would say, "This is crazy," or, "Unfathomable."

How can I be everyone?

You are. I am. What is known inside is what is truth. What is seen outside is lies pretending to be truth. It is acceptable to see the world in any way you want, but if you are wanting to live an unburdened life you cannot turn towards fear. All the time you must control the mind and use Love to create.

Love is the essence of who All are. Imagine the most joyous day of your life. Perhaps a wedding day, the birth of a child, the smell of pancakes in the morning, the ocean tide rising to meet the toes. Every moment of joy is love. Love is being.

Joy brings joy. Pain brings pain. So when in pain, the most important thing to do is find joy somehow. Do something which brings love. This works for both individual and collective. So if you want to quell the panic and fear for All on planet Earth, it starts within. See the world perfectly calm. The ocean filled with fish and marine life. The mountains capped with snow. The energy systems removed so Earth can heal.

Technology is poisoning the Earth, and most are believing it to be harmless and this is untrue. The rapid energy is vibrating alongside the body and causing discord. You must believe, in order to reduce the temperature of Earth, in healing internally through One mind. It will quell the storm of energy vibrating alongside Spirit.

Awaken

Every morning as you arise take time to connect to the One. Ask, 'In which plane of existence am I and how can I unbind myself from the collective? I know I am One with All, but release myself from toxic energy and thoughts. I allow only what is true to come into mind."

Over and over repeat this thought, and the more you do it, it will become second nature to arise each morning to truth. I am is the best way to remember who you are. Simply state truth and it will remind you to the One over and over again.

Stop thinking negatively and start thinking knowingly. Right from the moment of awakening (physically) you can start a day with knowledge that you are a soul in a body and every action taken is one of truth. Whatever shows up is part of the process to evolve. The people met, the places visited, the time spent in life. It is all part of the plan to move beyond hurts and hiccups. Can I be better than I was before? Can I know I am this One and choose to remember?

Yes you are One. Never alone. Always guided. Remember this always. See everyone on purpose and know they are, too. Even those who feel different are you, too. When all on planet Earth accept their role as cocreators, one with life and All, will it finally be consciously known what is Love.

Can we truly be awakened as a whole?

It is entirely possible and always a goal All is working towards. Though it has been difficult in past inceptions, and not all souls willingly accepting this path, in our current inception the majority do have within their life blueprint the possibility that if all awaken they will, too; just as All have chosen if the fear overtakes society it will perish as it had before.

The path is clear. If you want to save your earthly world then all must come together as brethren in Love and let fear be wiped away as you go within, listen to the higher self and find All. How you do that is through consistency. Practice, practice, practice. We will show you how in chapter 20.

Consistency of Practice

Dear All,
I know I am looking at life through eyes that see untruth and hearing
with ears of falsity, but I am willing to see with Love and hear with joy.

Look at life as if it were a lemon. The more you squeeze the juicier it becomes. Let the lemon sit and it will rot eventually if untouched. You want a life of joys and creation, not one of sitting around. When life gives you lemons make lemonade. A turn of phrase straight from Source.

Don't believe lies; lies of the ego. The world is vision. You see what is in front of you and believe it is truth. Everything you look at becomes meaningful because it is seen. In actuality the living world is illusion. It is made up by minds to create scenarios in which soul growth is achieved.

How you move through days is entirely up to you, and soul will show you what it is you believe. So if you believe in illusion it will manifest as reality. If you know you are soul and what is false you will experience it in a way that is comforting and not painful. Because you have decided to be part of the collective you will be tied to the manifestations of others, and so much of what is happening is what others are seeing too.

This is where choice comes in. You can believe the falsities of life created by the collective (on the planet chosen at will), or you can understand and recognize it's part of the creation of One mind through All. This vision will allow a gentler journey upon Earth.

We know it is tortuous to see others in pain (for most) and manifesting storms and chaos all over planet Earth, but the willing must see it for that which it is: false evidence appearing real. That is, FEAR.

What is TRUE? Triumph right under ego. When you see the world as perfectly imperfect you allow that which is true to be seen. You are Love. You are light. You are a soul in a body and what happens is growth either in love through fear or through love, and sometimes both.

There are times when fear is present no matter what practices you are doing in life, be it meditation, prayer or simple knowing. On Earth there is too much chaos to make the planet awakened on the whole currently, and for quite some time, if ever, in this inception. Every One has lessons to learn chosen at the time of incarnation, and this is why suffering exists. Chosen circumstances allowing for growth from fear into Love.

You see life as harsh and meaningless sometimes and forget what it is for whenever witnessing fear/ego creations. If you could but know that life is unreal and fear is false it would not be so hard to live amongst others on Earth.

Show me what is real then?

Close the eyes for five minutes. Be mindful of what has been said. You are a soul here to experience love and false evidence appearing real is a world of pranks trying to get you to believe it. Believe Love for those five minutes. See life as it was meant to be lived, joyfully.

WORKBOOK EXERCISE #11:
FEAR IS FALSE

After you have used your five minutes (or more) write down everything you see which is Love.

Examples:

- *Seeing yourself at the mall shopping and enjoying the day, trying on dresses and getting caught up with friends at lunch.*
- *Making muffins with your child or children.*
- *Going on a vacation with first class tickets and five-star accommodations.*
- *Using money for good and sharing it with others.*
- *Playing ball in the yard.*
- *Getting ice cream.*

Anything which brings you joy is Love. Use the joy meter. How does this make me feel? If it feels good it is Love. If it feels wrong, bad, uncomfortable, impossible or tied to money as the only way to create something it is false. Love is joy with no limits.

Your time starts now. Use a timer if needed.

What comes up for you as you do this exercise? Are you comfortable believing in possibilities? Does it feel right or as if it's impossible to create that which you see?

Do the exercise again but this time remember you are Love and nothing on Earth is true. Think of it as if crafting the movie of the soul. Money is no object. Time is illusion. Create anything using no limitations and see what comes to you.

Start the timer once again. Five minutes.

Forks

The road ahead is paved with good intentions. What stops them from manifesting is humanity. Being tied to the collective beliefs is how the road forks. Left is love where all is true. Right is fear where false evidence appears real and everything is stopped.

Think a thought. Choose. Let's take, as example, babies. Those looking to become parents have chosen to in their soul contract. This does not mean if fear is expressed more often than Love that the possibility may evaporate. Let's look at collective beliefs held first.

1 in 5 babies are miscarried.
Age is a factor, and once a certain age is reached no one can be pregnant again unless through biological manipulation.
All babies carried to term are born male or female.
Doctors know best and intuition isn't real.

Many other beliefs exist and these are just some examples. If you believe in these then you are tied to them. Now let's look at thought patterns surrounding our example.

I am pregnant.

Choose Love. Baby arrives perfect and healthy. Choose fear and that 1 in 5 miscarry, then you will be tied to this belief as strongly as you believe it.

I'm too old for babies.

Choose Love and create in whatever way is possible using both science and biology. Choose fear and wait or dissipate. The chances of pregnancy become void when focusing on fear.

All babies must either be a boy or girl.

Choose Love and whatever choice is made on a soul level appears. Choose fear and decide at birth if one is male or female.

Isn't it obvious, you would ask? Not for Ones who see themselves as part of the whole. On other planets outside the solar systems Ones may decide to be male and female or be assigned genders based upon what feels right. You will know as soon as the baby arrives, as will they. Chosen genders are assigned on Earth based on beliefs and that is all.

Listen to doctor's advice or decision.

Choose Love and go with the knowing of the soul. Choose fear and enact beliefs based upon another's lens and limitations.

Using the soul contract of another often times leads to despair. It is always best to discover truth within before allowing another One to sway your knowing. If you know you are to be a parent, why not let this sway you?

66 *Let no One tell me who I am and what is possible for me. I know it is coming based on my beliefs and I believe in Love.* 99

Choose wisely dear Ones.

Practice, Practice, Practice

How do you get to Carnegie Hall? Practice, practice, practice. How do you get to knowing you are Love? Practice, practice, practice. You can't sit around wondering all day what is possible and using false beliefs. Practice is the way to truth.

Those on a journey to belief will always be shown false evidence. Ego is there to incite you, enrage you and keep you guessing if all of this is real and true. Its job is to throw you off course, make you question the light, always. Consistency of practice is the antidote. Meditation, prayer, intention. An elixir for Love.

Laura is one who has practiced (a little) almost daily since 2015. She has used various modalities – prayer, intention, channeling, conscious creation and has taken steps to heal the separation from within. Even knowing all she knows, there are times when she believes all of this to be nonsense because the mind cannot fathom that what it sees is unreal. It feels real, looks real, sounds real to all of you, and this is very much part of the process on Earth. It's meant to be real so you may evolve; but once you are back in Spirit form it will all make sense.

Leap of Faith

So you are being asked here to join the Ones who know that life on Earth is impractical, meaning it's evidentiary based on false beliefs and nonsense made up by minds who believe they are simply human.

This is why we offer clues, messages and signs. We want you knowing you are Love. We expect your disbelief and send opposite thoughts to guide you. Notice them or not, but they are always there. The minute an oppositional thought arrives, pay attention to what song arrives in mind. It might just be the "proof" you need to believe us and not them.

Who is them?

Them are the Ones in body who believe in falsity. The ones tied so deeply to their human mind who could never fathom they are anything else. Every time One comes around who is false-tied, remember you are Love. It is simple. I am. Use this and remind yourself of everything being learned. Within the mind is the truth, but you must go seeking; and not just once or twice, but always.

Always (All ways) is the answer to how to live an unburdened life (mostly). Through conscious creation is how Ones know they are souls in human bodies on Earth. Connect every day in every way and you are being One who is All.

"Where shall I go today?"

Why not ask Spirit to guide you?

"What is the lesson here?"

Spirit knows.

"How can I move through this more quickly and efficiently?"

Be. *Sit down and meditate upon it before reacting, then decide. Spirit always knows the best way to think, do and act if only would you pay attention. Internal thoughts, messages in songs, chosen lyrics, overheard conversations, animals and bodily sensations. These are all indicators for you to notice.*

"Why can't I hear them?"

Because you are not listening with intention. You are listening with expectation. Expectation is waiting for outside wisdom. Intention knows it is coming from All. No matter what flows your way, the answers are within All. You know everything, as do I, as does everyone on planet Earth because we are All One, truly. What is known by you is known by me and everyone else, but the access is denied when the ego is involved.

To quell the ego, it must be radical mindedness used to believe and that is daily, hourly, minute-by-minute, second-by-second. Ego won't stop and neither can you. Every thought (and there are 60 to 100 thousand per day) must be pure.

> ❝ *I am a soul knowing All.* ❞

How do you tame (not destroy) the ego? Love. Use Love to meditate, pray, ask.

> ❝ *I am knowing this to be a hard journey and asking for help along the way.* ❞

Each ask is answered when brought to light, but it must be consistent. You cannot ask one day and forget the next. I am/I am not does not work. It is only through consistent daily practice will Ones know, and this is why chaos remains. Most are unable/unwilling to go between the mind to the place where 'God' is and live through the lens of Love. They see the world in its current shape and look upon the solemn and sad, and use that evidence to decide who they are.

Who you are is Love, plain and simple. Nothing you do is wrong and everything is right because you are Love. On Earth it feels wrong as part of a narrative, but in heaven it is watched upon as if it's soultavision, movies of mind. To use the voice of Love is to know you are soul being human and to be.

What is to be?

Joy is being. Love is being. Being is meditation, journaling, expressing emotions through conscious creation with All.

Love

Love is an emotion but is All. God/Source/Love. These are the same. Different words used to express one concept, that All is Love. Love is your true nature. It is life.

What would you create if you had no limitations? If there were no rules as society had placed? If Love was the emotion everyone used to feel anything? Would you go to work? School? Would you play all day, every day? How different would you be if nothing stopped you from living dreams and showing up without fear?

Earth is fun. The ride of a lifetime, but most do not see it this way and dwell in fear always. In other places and spaces you learn more slowly because the ride is mundane or taxing in just one dimension. Earth is one dimensional only in its quest to overcome fear, but multi directional in all way the ways you can do this.

Everything always reveals true healing.

Quit playing life safe. Caution warns you to go indoors and fear stops you from living. Emotions are how you know what is happening and using this meter has served you, until now. Now you are ready to live abundantly and with little or no ego interruption. You know to ask when times are rough, to listen when the noise is loud and to gauge when to move through cocreation. This is Love. Using the tools of soul to decide.

Think of a day you would like to create. From start to finish go through every minute detail and use Love as your guide. Spend another five minutes deciding upon a day and not just letting it happen. Life is happening to you, through you. In this day, you run life. You tell yourself where to go, what to do and who to be. Use images, pictures in the mind to help craft a special day. Be with Ones you love, choose foods you enjoy, experience joys of the heart. Do all of this and then come back to our next chapter on being.

CHAPTER 21
God is a State of Being

Dear All,
I am listening to a higher self and letting my ego go. I ask questions
and receive answers easily and effortlessly.

Being vs. Doing

The lesson for all to learn on Earth is that of stillness. Be quiet. Be still. Listen for inner guidance, a higher self who knows who you are, why you are here and what is happening is for the highest good.

You can look at life through a lens of ego, that all is good and what you need is love (romantic, platonic, familial), money, fame, cars, power; or you can know you are loved, abundant, smart and success imminent. Soul knows everything is within and can be brought forth through cocreation. Fear says, "I'll do it myself and no one will stop me," or, "God will bring it to me," not knowing they, too, are a spark of divinity. Love says, "I am knowing you are All."

Questions bring truth and we allow Laura return with some ever-present musings on life as she sees it through fear.

God is Love

Laura: This all sounds great but impractical, because as much as I would love to believe we can create a life of joy; the realities of financial constraints don't just go away overnight. So how do we manage in the lag time? Money doesn't just fall out of trees and show up at your doorstep. You have to live in the current earthly world with everyone else's creations.

All: It isn't just impractical, you all believe, it's unlikely. This is the current level of understanding you all have reached. In physical realms it does take time to manifest things into being, but if you know with no doubt that things are coming, it wouldn't bother every One so much to wait. You would discover a way to bring abundance. Choose that which allows it to arrive in various sums and let go.

L: You said earlier in the Know Your Worth chapter that if you just stay in alignment with soul and let ego go you can create anything by believing in its manifesting. The issue I take with that is I feel that I have been doing this for a long time now. I do believe I am worthy. I am sharing my voice in hopes of helping others and moving towards my goal of being a successful author. However, literally every time I post something it gets lost in a sea where either no one really sees it or no one seems to care.

A: Other teachers will face a similar crisis of conscious. Those who have chosen to serve are knowing within what level can be achieved. There are many who do what they do because it feels good and allow it to unfold as it should. No grand expressions. Just quiet musings for all to hear who are willing to listen. At the same time, there are many who feel called to serve grandly to humanity. A calling deep within hard to ignore. Many do move on and live happy, uncomplicated lives if the calling never materializes into physical. At one point, you all decide where to go with the stirring of the soul. You can choose to be a spotlight or not. It does not matter. Only that you use the language and eyes of Love, always.

L: But why write books? I mean this is a workbook for goodness sakes. That seems very much like it is meant to be shared? It's hard to let that go, the sense of this being for a larger audience than me.

A: It is, but remember you have free will always. We can cocreate books and not have them be seen by anyone but self, or you can listen to the inner knowing telling you to share them without need for compensation because it's obviously meant to be. Share if you want, keep if you want. The choice is always to the individual in body.

L: Why without need for compensation? I have spent almost three years and thousands of hours cocreating our book.

A: It is not necessary to question. It is necessary to understand the books belong to All. You are being paid for time not wisdom.

L: Based on the small percentage of enlightening minds, I also believe it doesn't serve the world right now to share these All books widely with the masses. So, the money aspect is simply allowing those who wish to awaken to decide for it rather than stumble upon something they are not ready to receive.

A: One day you will share them, for they will be more valuable to All.

L: I want to share but it seems like no one cares. Everyone is comfortably living in the illusion while I want to make the world a better place.

A: Hold space for All, dear One. Let everyone be who they wish to be. Wish them well and move to a higher thought.

L: My intention is to share the books because I want a better world for everyone, for myself and my son. It's frustrating to live amongst the sleepers. They are stuck in illusions—

A: *Deeply embedded in mind, yes. Know that they have chosen everything, as well. Some may find our books and materials, others may never, even if it had been part of their curriculum of Spirit, because of free will. Do your best to share what is inspired and feels right, and never to chastise or condemn anyone for being right where they are. In the eyes of God/All every One is perfect. Choose this vision as much as you can and it will no longer be so difficult to get along in a world "gone mad."*

L: I guess my wanting a better world stems from wanting others to be awakened so I am not alone anymore. I want everyone to join the party and not have to play by myself, which ironically has been a life-driving theme of mine. It's that inner child wound of always feeling left out that comes out in me.

A: *Understandable why. You are there to connect and we know it can be difficult for those on a higher level of vibration to create friendships and companions. More awakened minds are coming, and so we offer you advice to hold strong, stay the course do not let the disruptions destroy you, which ego is trying to do. Keep working on the goal of soul: evolve. Heal you and help the world through cocreation. Ask, "What may I do to serve?" and then jump in through inspired thought, intuitive notions and channeled guidance.*

L: Can I ask about the compensation aspect in general? Is it wrong for those of us who are awakening to ask for money in sharing spiritual guidance and wisdom?

A: *All must decide for themselves what is both proper and improper. While the wisdom and knowledge you share is 'free' for All, your time is not. So when sharing with others, decide for the self what is ego and what is soul. Some you may charge for and others you may not. It has taken nearly four years of time writing our books, quotes and materials. For you to accomplish the feat of writing, rereading, editing, posting and making sure words are accurate has been a 'job', so to speak, and for this time is money. Remember abundance is available to all, and those who are questioning whether or not accepting money is appropriate are Ones who have yet to understand the mechanics of money. Money is energy and must be moved, plain and simple. Move it. Give it. Receive. Return. The cycle repeats itself, but if you hold back from receiving you hold back from giving and vice versa. Get off the merry go round of collectivism and on the track which brings you abundance.*

L: Love.

A: *Yes! The track is eternal and filled with jolly goodness.*

L: Yet most people take the roller coaster with ups and downs and fear. What steps can be taken to ensure when living within illusion (as an awakened One) we are no longer being bothered by what happens here?

A: Pay attention to your thoughts, your words, your actions and no One else. What goes on upon Earth had been chosen by the individual souls of Ones in body using free will. One can only heal thy self and no one else. This is most difficult to understand because compassion says, "I must heal all." You cannot do this, because responsibility lies within, and only you can take yourself there. Listen, respect, offer knowledge, wisdom and understanding, but know you must heal self and only self. All is perfect as is, dear Ones.

L: Yes, but you said in *The All of Everything*[2] that all minds affect one another because we are all One. I can bless a stranger and my thoughts will 'ricochet' into another's mind. So that seems contradictory to me.

A: You can send thoughts to awaken Ones, but only they can accept the invitation to use them. Free will is like a pinball machine. You shoot the thought up the ramp, and it either makes it through and rewards are gained or it is swatted back towards you. Your thoughts can vibrationally align to All That Is and the rest of the world can gain knowledge and wisdom if allowed by the individual soul in question. We appreciate the question and understand the confusion, but remember, always, that it is up to each individual soul how they grow.

L: What about children?

A: They have chosen to accept what is 'given' them by parents and loved Ones until their young minds reach a certain age and they are capable of making decisions based on love or fear, dependent upon what had been taught in said One's home or living space. Remember the chosen aspect of soul is in play, and what they each have chosen is to stay sleeping until a certain age.

L: And what age would that be?

A: Every One has a different timeline to reach. Generally speaking, it is around the age of seven when limiting beliefs are set, and this is when it would be most appropriate to share wisdom, gently leading them to truth.

L: And what is that truth? You say that I should trust in a higher power and that I should let the divine handle the details and that the Universe has my back. However, you also say that I am that higher power. So why would I need to hand the reins over to God/Source? That doesn't make sense. If I am the one in control here, why do I need an armchair quarterback?

A: Let us tell you the answer and you will return to questions later in our next chapter.

Doing versus Being

Your life is guided by principles and laws of the Universe. Yes, it is true you are One with All, but it is also true you are a separate individual - both soul, spirit (and body, currently). So to discern which is 'talking' at any given moment, it is imperative you lose the ego and allow soul/God to do with you what oftentimes you cannot do with yourself because an ego has control. It is not enough to ask for direction because it will often bring you to a destination unknown or an unpleasant one. You must accept and understand there is a design or grand plan for the life you have created; and too often most are carrying with them wounds from old lives rather than just its current inception. So when you are guided by thought to ask for help from the Divine, it is offering up solutions through the One mind to the body of the one incarnated.

Listening to a higher self is the best, most important way to live on planet Earth. The higher self is You and We. It is all of us together as One. So listening to the soul self is not exactly the same.

Soul self = You.
Higher self = You and We.

The difference is both subtle and vast. You have a soul. You are a spirit. You are God. We All are.

This is a concept most find hard to believe, and yet we are at a pivotal time in human history where more are turning to a higher self. It is a term widely used in spiritual circles and in yoga, meditation and other modalities of soul work. No matter what you do, it is imperative you return thoughts to the One so they may be transformed as quickly as they have come upon you. This is the asking we have spoken about time and time again in our earlier chapters. Ask to receive. "I need help," is all One need do to invoke the divine within/higher self.

The problem with humans is they are unfocused and easily distracted. And yes, this an observation which stems from love and not a judgement, as many (including our dear Laura) would believe. You are constantly annoyed by what you see in the media and distracted by all that you see around you. Doing is the ego's best defense against annihilation. Like a soldier it traps you with all sorts of delays. Movies, TV and the worst distraction of all, social media.

The onset of social media has created an epidemic of fear unlike any other. It is the most attractor of illness both mental and physical.

> 66 *I see one doing this and wonder why I can't do the same. I hear one who is sick and believe I may attract the same, or my child will or someone I love.* 99

Not to say there are not benefits to social media, only that its main attraction has become fear. Look to statistics to determine why the rise in suicides and mental illness, and you will see a direct correlation. Though your medical community may disagree to keep all in the dark as to what is truly going on. The answers are there to be found should Ones go looking for them.

Medicine does have its place in society, but it is to be used alongside healing modalities such as reiki and scalar healing, meditation and Qigong. Those who seek to utilize a mind/body/soul trifecta by using a three-prong approach to healing are Ones who truly can heal the body through the mind. The medical community is beginning to understand the connection the mind and body have on one another, but none have yet to admit the findings and have them validated by governmental agencies. To do this would render the whole system flawed and none are brave enough to stand behind facts of the Universe. Therefore, it is up the individual soul to turn their light on.

Thoughts Control You

Be mindful of every thought which comes to you. They are designed to be sorted out like a file cabinet. This is wrong. This is true.

"I am peaceful, loving and kind."
True.

"I am poor, unlikeable, shallow and senseless."
Untrue.

Each individual gets to decide who they are and which thoughts they allow into their psyche. Soul seeks to remind you to Love through words, songs and attention grabbers placed in view or audibly. Birds sing, car horns blow, phones ring. Anything to get you to notice it, and not you being run by ego.

Bless each day for the gift it truly is by taking steps to engage with Love. Love is peace, joy, kindness and all manners of happiness. It is not enough to say happy, it must be felt.

Take a moment each morning to get up and stretch while saying, "I am happy, healthy and wise. My spirit is alive inside and we are One."

Then go about the day with the knowledge of never being alone, always guided by soul and spirit and All.

What is God?

God is All. The Love within. It is everyone and everything. The life you are leading hasn't been given to you by some powerful figurehead in the sky. It had been chosen as part of experiencing everything. This is the nature of being. To Love. In order to know love, you must experience its opposite in all sorts of ways in order to be.

To be is to know you are Love. Close the eyes. Listen.

I Am Love.

Do you hear the sound of it? Yes. Do you feel the joy of it? Most of you probably no, because you are internally wired to sense fear, to question everything. What someone has told you on Earth is more important than what is being told here and in other books, materials and downloads (spiritually speaking) we have been giving to you All for centuries on Earth.

Let go of the notion of being human for a minute. Say, "I am a soul in body," and use this as your meter for deciding who you are. Close the eyes again and listen, but this time feel the joy of knowing you are more than just you; you are All.

 *I am Love.*

Joy is accessible at any given time should you go seeking within. We know it can be difficult to decrease fear and increase love. We know how real (feeling) it is to be living in a body amongst fellow humans and not feel sad, mad or frustrated. We only ask you to know you are not without help in the internal battle.

Because it had been chosen to be "forgotten" on a soul level, we are fighting with ourselves. Just know that every One has the ability to remember should they go seeking further. The more time spent in cocreation, meditation and healing the separation from within the more you will believe, receive and achieve all you desire as soul and human. Collaborate, cooperate and coordinate. The three C's of conscious living.

Who Am I?

God.

Does that trigger you? Make you uncomfortable, wanting to put the book away and go back to whatever you were doing prior? Of course it does. It's meant to. Even those in high conscious communities find it hard to believe. Even as I say this and Laura writes it, she is sensing fear. Fear of judgement. Fear of retribution. Fear of life. And yet does she know all of it to be true because she has written four books of wisdom and knowledge with no lag time and no going back to fix anything. Words on a page written and recorded for all who are seeking to find truth.

You are God. All of you. Every One and everything is God because God is love, not a person or thing, but energy. Anytime you are being kind, generous, joyful or compassionate you are being God. God is being. The minute you step outside of love you are fear. Falsities of ego.

I Am?

You ARE. Whatever is coming up for you as you read this is designed to trick you and fail you. Releasing the ego you have been tied to your whole life is difficult because (as said prior) it had been chosen as soul; but now you are aligned to love with a pencil and paper, ready to take notes and a willingness to go within and find the answers.

The answers are all around you if you are paying attention. You are being guided through every step, and everyone and everything which comes along to wake you is your curriculum chosen by you, for you in the life blueprint.

Congratulations. You have made it this far. Going back is optional, and you decide if proceeding is practical, preferable or purposeful. Every One decides on their own who they wish to be. Soul may rock you, shock you, mock you or even lock you up inside but it may never violate free will. Choose to move forward knowing you are God/Love or go backwards and begin again. Read the entire chapter again, return to our All books over and over again until you to come to a place of understanding of who you are: Love.

Free will allows you to think in whatever way you would like, and we will discuss the reasons why skepticism is present next.

CHAPTER 22

Be Skeptical. It's on Purpose.

Dear All,
As I move through life's mishaps and mistakes, please allow a kinder,
gentler world to be seen and heard. I accept all of everything as it
comes and lose ego in my quest for joy.

Welcome back and thank you for continuing on. It is difficult, this life you have chosen, and perhaps the reasons are unclear as to why things happen the way they do, but remember the growth of soul whenever you struggle so it becomes clear why. Our dear Laura has something to say, and we allow her the time as she steps into the ego and freely shares a story to help guide you. As fear returns, Ones must seek answers within as she has and does here. Our book is a perfect example of how Ones can go from awake to asleep the minute a test arrives.

Testing, Testing... Is Thing On?

This perhaps has been the most difficult chapter for me to write because it's coming from me, Laura, and not Spirit. You see how I go back and forth between understanding and belief. I get so hung up by the tragedies of the world and my own struggles financially that I just can't seem to shake the fear. Spirit tells you that's very much on purpose and everything you go through is designed to test your will and show you what needs tuning up in the fight between love and fear.

In December of 2019, just as I was starting to feel confident that I was 'enlightened', and I understood everything being written through the voice of The All, two major events occurred in my life. One causing emotional frustration and the other physical pain.

I found myself unable to write for months as I handled these dual circumstances. My connection (to The All) never went away, it simply was marred by my anger and my skepticism. I used my spiritual principles, as had been spelled out in my books, to move through each situation as easily as possible, but felt very disconnected from Spirit guidance as I dealt with pain and sadness.

The first thing that happened was my failing an exam to become a group fitness instructor again; a career I had started in college and spent eight years doing during my twenties, but gave it up when I moved into television full-time. I studied hard (or so I thought) but when I took the exam none of the questions matched what I had studied. Sitting in the exam room I began asking Spirit for help. Is this accurate? What is the answer? Is this ego or soul? Just as I had been told to do in my books. The answers would come and I would use them, feeling confident I had my cocreator right there with me. However, I was absolutely shocked when I found I had failed my test; not only because it meant I had to study and take the exam all over again, but because it derailed my plans for getting more work in the fitness industry and costing me potential income that I desperately needed. After a few days of sulking and bitterness, feeling I was led astray, I went back to my book looking for answers.

Am I or Am I Not?

Laura: Spirit led me astray today, and for that I am very frustrated. It has sent me back to the drawing board to begin again. I asked for help and help seemed there, but yet it turned out to be wrong. How can I justify this when you tell me if you just ask, "Is this ego or spirit?" we will be answered. What did I do wrong today, dear All?

All: Nothing my dear. You acted in accordance with the laws of our Universe. You are learning how to discern ego from spirit and this was a 'test' of your will. Do you feel you passed or failed?

L: Failed epically. Why? Why did I fail my test?

A: So you may spend time in a space of being and learn how to utilize the voice within. Taking a test (as an example) is not appropriate for using the voice within. It is not our job to give practical advice, but rather to use intuition and knowing.

L: So what did I do wrong?

A: Perhaps studying is a better option than relying upon spirit?

L: Why? Aren't you there to help me with these types of situations? You say, "ask and ye shall receive." I asked and thought I received. It turned out to be wrong, and so I failed the exam. Ask and receive turned out to be a big, fat flop. So what do you have to say about that?

A: We will say you need to discern between the voices of Love and the voices of ego.

L: How? I asked, "Is this ego or spirit?" in my mind during the entire test, and I did hear, "Spirit" most of the time; but again, I still failed. So now I am deeply confused and still very much angry. How can you discern between the two?

A: Yes? No? Ask a simple question. Receive an answer. The difference to know is who is both asking and answering. To ask in situations of selfish gain you are using ego. To decipher where it is coming from you need look at the bodily emotions you are expressing at the moment of asking.

> 66 I am being guided to ask and I must know if I am angry or annoyed. 99

Once you know that, then you will know whether the asking is appropriate or inappropriate.

"Can you help me with this test?"

Asking for help in a situation like this is asking in ego.

"Can you lead me to the right answers as I take this?" would be more appropriate.

Soul and ego are at war, and when you express anger in any form you are commanding the soul to do as you please, not as you have willed.

"I will pass a test when studying appropriately has occurred."

Soul knows your choices are presently more mindful of working within its confines, but you must know there is much to be learned of how to appropriate the connection from our perspective. Our goal is love, only love; not ego gratification or gain.

L: I guess I can understand that. Perhaps I was kind of cheating by asking for answers rather than knowing I needed to study more. It felt like a slap in the face and I chose to move beyond it rather quickly once it happened. I processed it and recognized its purpose. I always know there is a message in the mess.

A: Later we will show you how it all turned out for the highest good.

Breaking Bad

But then something happened over Christmas 2019, that put me in a state of panic and confusion stronger than I had been feeling in years. I struggled to come to terms with it, and even now still have so many questions needing answered.

In the blink of an eye on a Saturday afternoon, everything changed when I fell down the stairs in my house; something I had worried about since moving into the home. Although I thought I had healed that fear, apparently it stayed hidden.

I was in a fairly happy mood and not really paying attention or being present to my movements when my son had asked me to come downstairs to make him lunch. As I proceeded to walk down the staircase, I slipped and fell four steps, landing on the loft space below. I was holding something in my left hand (the side the stair's hand rail was on) and like the hundreds, if not thousands of times before in the house, I did not use the railing. With my left hand full I had no choice but to brace myself with my right arm when I slipped so I wouldn't fall further down the stairs. The moment it happened I knew my wrist was broken. It snapped like a twig and was completely out of place and dangling. (Sorry for the visual). At first, the pain was tolerable and I immediately went into breath work that I had learned in my meditation course, but the pain got progressively worse with every passing moment.

I tried getting in the car with my mom to have her drive me to a hospital, but by that point the pain was torture. My shoulder was also throbbing and I couldn't move my arm. We had to call 911 so the paramedics could give me pain medicine in order to be moved. With my mom and son trailing the ambulance, I meditated the entire ride and found myself asking for help as often as possible from Spirit, but feeling mostly as if I had been left out in the cold. I suffered through 13 grueling hours in the ER, surviving on morphine and meditation. As I listened to the echoes of the other patients in pain coming in and out of the ER, waiting for a miracle that never came (or so I thought); I became caught up in chaos and ego all over again surrounded by fear.

After a short surgery and an overnight stay in the hospital, I struggled to move through the intense pain I was in. I weaned myself off pain medication (opioids) after a few days because I knew it would affect my channeling and I wanted as clear a mind as I could possibly get during this ordeal to ask questions and receive answers.

I tried everything I could to mitigate the pain (with the worst time being at night), but I still suffered tremendously. As I began to heal, I was so overcome by fear about the staircase and that more tragedies could happen that I became paralyzed by that thought, which manifested itself in my not being able to move my shoulder along with my broken wrist. I was locked in a prison of fear. Even now, as I think about that fall it makes me sad and confused and embarrassed. How could I, who is so awakened, be caught in a circumstance like this?

Though I realized the entire situation could have been much worse, this only gave me minimal comfort. I felt let down and betrayed by my own books. Nothing Spirit had told me seemed to work. I was miserable and out of sorts. For over a month I used various healing modalities but relief never came as fast as I was hoping. So I cried, got angry and went into a spiral of depression. I tried connecting with Spirit even in my despair. I asked for help over and over again but found myself in pain day after day with recovery moving slowly. I lost my will to continue writing, and most days sat around watching television and moping. I saw no signs and messages and no miracles. Healing didn't come overnight, liked I had hoped, and I resigned myself to the fact that 'God' was not going to help or fix me. The God within and the God without left me in a lurch; or so I thought.

I contemplated going back to 'sleep' on a daily basis. Why be awakened if your soul just wants you to be in misery? The pain was unbearable at times and I wondered why this life can be so agonizing. I found myself surrounded by stories of sadness and death, and believed the world to be a more tragic place than I had witnessed in years. I also had to deal with the sticker shock of having nearly $10,000 in medical bills; a blow to my already dwindled resources. With no money rolling in and virtually no savings left, I was truly at the bottom of the basement searching for any sort of light.

Through all of those negative thoughts, though, I still had one bright spot in my life I refused to give up on: my daily quotes I was channeling with Spirit for my newsletter and Wisdom of The All, an account I created on Instagram. Even in my pain and fear, the words still came, leading me back towards truth. They didn't help heal me much physically, but emotionally the words brought me hope and that was definitely something I needed to continue on this uphill battle to full recovery.

Eventually, although I was feeling completely defeated and at my lowest point ever since my dad and brother died, I returned to my books with questions hoping to remind myself of everything Spirit had told me over the last few years. I knew there had to be a message in this divine uncomfortable disaster.

Within

All: There is. Would you like to know it?

Laura: I would.

A: Welcome back. We have missed the inner dialogue and though we have been calling you, guiding you and helping you along the way, it has felt lonely because fear is what keeps us hidden. We offer words of wisdom, show signs and messages, but when you are distracted in fear they are missed by the Ones in body. You know you have seen miracles during this time, and it is because you asked continually for help you began to feel lighter, more free and eventually willing to come back to our pages as One. Had you stayed in despair, not asking, the journey back could have been worse. So even though One felt as they were 'left in a lurch', the obvious answer is that every time you asked you inched forward, and focusing on fear sent you backwards. Once momentum kicked in and you were feeling better and stayed in a spiritual lane, you came out of it with, as always, more work to be done. Ones who give credence to ego create longer waits and Ones who ask, pray, intend, meditate are bringing healing, albeit slower than humans would like. It is always a process not a race. Now may we reveal the message of the mess, dear One. It has been a profound time in the life you have chosen to know the hardships of others. You have felt pain as others feel or have felt. You have languished in a state of unrest and despair with no hope, as others do. You have learned help is not instantaneous and needs time in healing hurt. It has dragged you into a fear state unlike anything else before, has it not for you?

L: True.

A: Do you see the trappings of the ego and the difficulty of moving from a state of chaos into belief?

L: Absolutely. I feel like I am back to square one starting all over again. I have dealt with grief and depression, but fear is horrendous and impossible to shake, especially when you are in pain physically.

A: Do not be alarmed. For it is all on purpose. You are knowing beyond a shadow of a doubt why those who are of body cannot stay aligned.

L: The ego is tough; brutal in fact. Pain is the hardest thing to move through. Why put us in bodies and make us suffer in pain? I'm sorry but this whole soul journey feels really tragic. Why on earth do you do this to us? I am starting to think Earth is actually Hell and we are here being tortured.

A: Do you really believe that?

L: No. Maybe. Oh, I don't know. I am just so damn frustrated. My arm hurts. My shoulder hurts. I'm embarrassed. My heart is broken. I'm depressed and enraged and so many other emotions. I can't sleep because of the pain and I wake up in pain. Sorry dear All, but your "ask and receive" mantras are useless. Thanks for nothing.

A: You are welcome.

L: Not funny.

A: We are being facetious because we know you all suffer in the illusion. To see from our perspective is very different. It feels real, we know. It hurts, we know. It doesn't need to be unpleasant if only would you ask all the time. All The Time. Every thought, emotion, sensation is why all suffer. Would you say during this time you asked consistently for help or railed in confusion most often?

L: I would say I did my best, but pain is awful. This is why we have an opioid crisis in the world. This has been the most difficult pain I have dealt with since being pregnant with my son. I'm not even sure how I survived that. I was in terrible pain for several months, and the pain didn't go away until after he was born.

A: As you were flooded with emotions of love, joy and elation.

L: True, but this is different. I have nothing to look forward to in life. Nothing is happening for me. No job. No love. No money. Youth fading away. My skin is on fire. I have no clue where to go or what to do. I am lost. I'm tired of fighting. It's too much. Nothing works. I'm beyond miserable and the world is messy and hard. Too much sadness. Too many things which can't be explained. Children dying. Parents dying. Wars and atrocities. It's all just misery. I want to 'wake up' but I can't, or at least I can't stay awake because I'm heartbroken by our world and my world.

A: Don't think for one minute all of this isn't purposeful. The pain, the tragedy, the sadness. You are evolving into a better version of self and seeing the world as purposeful is how you move through it.

L: Well I can't do that because my heart breaks for everyone I see suffering and it's affecting me more now than ever. It's causing more fear and sadness than I have felt in a long time. I wish I could wake up without all this stress and struggle. Help me dear All become a better version of myself without ego trapping me.

You wrote that last line.

Listen, I get this concept. I really do but it's full of holes. Name one good thing happening (other than my son) in my life since I lost my dad and brother.

A: Many "good" things have taken place for you all. The world is becoming awake and aware more so than any other time in history. You are simply at a standstill and that is causing your delay in terms of money, fame and all the things you (all) feel are important in life.

L: Delays are what cause us to go broke. Delays are what cause us to lose our mind and become unhinged. Delays are what cause us pain and suffering. Delays make the pain worse and unmanageable. Delays are demons.

A: Delays are necessary on Earth not to create chaos upon a planet. As revealed in our last book, The All That Is[3], you are under laws of time and space and because of this is why all suffer.

"If I can't get there in the timeframe I need I will give up, get frustrated and lose sight of goals and dreams."

This is your ego winning. Will you allow it to or will you stay and fight?

L: I fight to stay aligned for my son. He is my reason for being and for staying but I am tired of fighting. I just want relief. I want to wake up with no pain and everything working properly again. It's been seven weeks of pain and I'm sick of it. I don't know how much longer I can take of this.

A: What must be known is how thoughts create that which you are thinking upon, and so on planet Earth there must be a time lag. It can be no other way. Thoughts are powerful, and to form matter out of each one would be tragic for most, if not all. You are too tied to ego and this thinking would bring catastrophic damage to the world. Think of the worst scenario.

L: I'm thinking of the planes crashing into the World Trade Center.

A: But think as if someone thought the thought and it just happened. Bang! Think of all the times terrible tragedies occurred and how often it had been thought upon. The planning and preparation to murder innocent victims was processed day by day for years on end. This is the ego's way of creating chaos. Make its victim think over and over again the same tragic thoughts. Think. Repeat. Think repeat. Repeated thoughts placed in the mind over and over again are how things arrive, both good and bad. This is the secret of all secrets. What you think, you create, no matter how you stay aligned, be it with ego or soul.

L: I guess I understand that. We want lag time so we don't create a mess, but it's impossible not to think terrible thoughts. As parents we worry about children or they worry about us. Human trafficking, murder, cancer, communicable diseases. It's all just too much. Once you witness it you can't unsee it.

A: But you can be released from the negative effects, as we have told you over and over. Escape the ego through cocreation.

L: Yeah well, I tried escaping the ego over and over again using intention, meditation and prayer, dear All, and it was a failure nonetheless. Your mechanics for change didn't work.

A: Change is hard. It comes in increments, not leaps and bounds.

L: If I ask for help to heal my pain why doesn't it come?! I'm so tired of pain. I just want it gone. Help me please. I am begging for relief.

A: Begging will not get you to relief.

L: Then what will? Because I am going on almost two months here and my shoulder is still stuck and my wrist isn't healing miraculously. It's healing at the pace doctors have decided.

A: *It is a collective idea which makes medicine or healing work. Whatever pace had been chosen by all is how something works. It is possible to heal more quickly but you must believe, and you simply are not anywhere near this level of vibration as of yet. You are getting closer as you step into a role of healer, but it is still just ideas at this point for you all.*

L: Well how do you go from idea to belief?

A: *Always change a thought. All the time. All the time you are healing you must ask for help.*

> *I am healing. I am healthy. I am whole.*

All thoughts must be kept high and aligned with truth.

> *I am a powerful healer. This body repairs rapidly.*

L: Those are just thoughts, and if we don't actually believe them then what's the point?

A: *The point is that you are asking to be reunited with Source and that will always be more powerful than attack thoughts.*

L: How can anyone believe in miracles and Spirit guiding us when they are in terrible or dire straits and they see no hope for change? This is why we have so much suicide in the world.

A: *Hold on. We cannot stress here enough the importance of belief. It is belief which shapes the world you all see as both individuals and as a collective. You grow belief slowly by taking time to release the thoughts which come from ego. The soul knows only peace and joy, but every time an ego thought, emotion or sensation is felt and you give it credence you are tied up and bound again and again.*

L: I understand what you are saying but as I have been healing, I have been trying to do this but the pain HURTS. You cannot escape that. Even writing this is painful. It bothers my hands and you can't make that go away.

A: *"Dear God, release my hands of this torturous pain."*

L: I say that and the pain doesn't go away, and even if it does it returns. In physical therapy today I did a lot of that type of mental work but I still felt pain. I would close my eyes and picture myself doing activities I can't do yet and try and feel what it feels like to be back at 100 percent and not in pain.

A: *And what occurred?*

L: **I got a little mobility back but it wasn't enough to fix everything and be back to normal.**

A: *The process is such that most are unable to vibrate higher immediately. This is not to say it cannot be done, it is simply an improbable situation for all to come to a state of being which allows a 'miracle'. As such, you are doing great in terms of healing and as long as you are aligned in Love, as often as possible, it will heal. If you believe, you will be relieved. Belief is consciousness in its highest expression, but when a belief is trapped in unconsciousness, it will be difficult to express as One.*

L: **And how do we change our beliefs and thought processes, especially when we are in pain?**

A: *Daily contemplation and quietude. Get into the mind and deliver the contents to the soul so we may transmute them.*

66 *This is untrue. This is false. This is who I was and not who I am.* 99

L: **I really do feel that I have been doing that. I felt based on our books that I would heal a lot more quickly than I have been. My doctor was surprised I wasn't further along with my wrist than I currently am. If I am so 'awake' and 'aware; shouldn't I be a better healer? What am I teaching others if I can't work with these modalities and make them work for me?**

A: *Oh ye of little faith. The only thing stopping healing is the thoughts you think and the beliefs you are holding onto.*

L: **Well, my biggest problem currently (which has me at a standstill emotionally) is the fear that even if I trust in my soul it will lead me astray; as you have said that at some point we will all have circumstances to handle. So falling again is a fear because even if I know my thoughts create the reality and I whisk the thoughts away, I'm terrified that my soul wants me to fall or get hurt again. So I am towing the line between love or fear. Do I trust the soul or not? I can't find faith in an unfair system.**

A: *Unfair as in what doesn't kill you makes you stronger, and what does isn't true or real.*

L: **Ugh you are so frustrating. It doesn't matter that to YOU it is unreal because to us it is—**

A: *As has been chosen by All, but continue we are listening.*

L: Painful! To us the pain hurts. The broken bones, the chemotherapy, the colds and influenza. All of it causes us physical anguish and sadness, and now I am wanting to cry because I am so sick and tired of being told something isn't real when the pain tells me differently. And I see others in worse circumstances and I find all of this insane that you want us to suffer. Again, I go back to my original statement earlier of this being Hell.

A: *Pain is necessary (for most) in order to move beyond a particular issue or belief. It is a profound tool for getting right what is wrong in mind.*

L: Why?! Why?! Why!? I want to scream right now. My head is so confused and angry.

A: *What is it you have been doing these last few weeks, may we ask?*

L: Working on me and asking for help healing fears and doubts; but the stark reality is that I am no farther along than I was three years ago. I'm stuck in a place of—

A: *Non-belief.*

L: I don't think that's true. I have obviously moved into a stage of belief because I still turn back to writing for help and the voice is always there. I have communicated with crossed over souls in my readings with clients and done some pretty incredible intuitive and telepathic communication. It's not that I don't believe all of this in theory. It's that I have no confidence in the concept that we can create anything we want because 'it's already been created', because after three years of trying nothing really has come to pass. I am out of money and time perhaps.

A: *Know this. Nothing we have done here has not been without purpose. There will come a time when all is said and done that all of everything has been the process of evolving. For all of you are a process and each and every thing you go through has purpose and meaning.*

L: I have been working on prayer, intention, visualization and all the workbook techniques, but for me none of it works fast enough. I'm done.

A: *Why are you here writing then?*

L: I don't know. I guess I am hoping something would change. Anything. A miracle.

A: *When all is lost and the road is paved with nothing but speed bumps, the only way out is through.*

L: Through what? Pain and sorrow and heartache and treachery? No thanks. I would like to take the easy route. I can't stand looking at the world as it is.

A: You so easily are triggered by all that you see around you. The internet is ego's best tool. It's the devil incarnate. Though there is no 'devil; in the realm of the unseen. In physical worlds it shows itself in many ways, and this is one of those. To un-see is a waste of time. To see with eyes of Love is best.

L: Seeing with the eyes of Love makes me feel like a bad person. It is difficult to look at a tragedy (especially when it comes to children) without feeling sorrow for those involved. It just breaks my heart to look at a child who was murdered or someone who lost a limb or was born disabled and think, "Oh well it's all part of their evolvement as a soul." No sir. I can't do that. Too awful.

A: We know it is hard to "look upon it but not dwell upon it," as we stated in our last books, but it must be no other way. For you are under illusions of separation at varying degrees, and those who are awakened must, as often as they can, hold space for others and accept that all circumstances are chosen on a level appropriate to a soul's growth.

L: So then it goes back to my statements about fear and not being able to let go, because we never know what our soul has planned. What if our soul wants us to get hurt or harmed emotionally?

A: Purposeful creation is the greatest gift. Live consciously. Love consciously. Do everything as consciously as possible. One step at a time. Slow and steady. "Today I choose to create..." and let go.

L: Tried it. Doesn't work.

A: It does work if you are aligned in One mind, but this awareness level is difficult to attain and that, my dear, is on purpose. All of the All are living in a state of illusion chosen by All. You are here to experience and express and evolve. The three Es. Three is the natural cycle of everything and this is a process everyone must go through at their own pace. Skepticism is purposeful. It is the mind making itself known. Behind the soul is the mind which thinks and believes.

L: Apparently my soul doesn't like me very much because it clearly wants me suffering and in pain and doesn't want me to heal.

A: Your frustration is understandable. We know you are deflated and feeling hopeless right now, but you also know the immeasurable value of having a connection to the 'other side'. You know there is something beyond the human world and have shared many a story of hope with others.

L: So why let me see beyond the veil but give me no hope? I want to help as many people as I can, but I can't because I am stuck. My wrist will not move no matter what therapies I try, both mental and physical. It's just swollen, stiff and immobile. What is the remedy Dr. God, MD?

A: Sunlight, air, meditation and all-out belief.

L: I need an angel. Someone or something to bring me relief.

A: You've got one right here with and inside you.

L: Okay. Then if I am so powerful, heal me. Change me. Move me. Help me wake up with my arm moving properly and my wrist no longer swollen. If you can do all that I will stop complaining and believe.

A: And if you will trust, believe and every time oppositional thoughts arrive remove them from the mind, then all those things and more will arrive. This is the point where we would ask you start over. Go back to the beginning of our book and read what has been written. Each time you (all) do it becomes easier to understand and believe.

L: It's hard to believe when faced with the skepticism of other people. Today my mom told me I was a "dreamer" and that it was time to get back to real work. It's laughable to most people; visualizing and intention setting. They see it as spiritual woo-woo.

A: As you did, as well, at one point.

L: True.

A: It's understandable at their current level of vibrational alignment. Skepticism is common amongst the seekers. Even those who believe or want to believe have no idea if all of this is real or fake. You, yourself have begun to question the validity of the All books.

L: If we hadn't written these *All* books and I wasn't inspired every day to write and post the channeled quotes you offer me, I would have given up on all of this long ago.

A: And now it can be seen and understood how many come to part from this earthly world. It is simply too difficult to get to a level of belief where Ones vibrate higher. If One who has written books, works with angels and guides and communicates with the other side has trouble staying in connection with soul (after one hiccup), imagine how the rest of the uninformed world feels. Now you can empathize, sympathize and realize how to help others who are struggling. You must experience everything in order to become a true healer.

L: I guess I can understand that. I would have to experience the process before I can explain it in a way that truly helps someone.

A: Truth thine own. Let free the thoughts from the mind and remember. You are here to express, evolve and expand. Let us look at your thoughts and escape ego.

L: My thought is that I can't heal and all of this is nonsense, while at the same time knowing our books must be true because I have no recollection of 90 percent of what we write until I read it dozens of times.

A: Remember, forget. Remember, forget. Thus, the crux of your problem. Belief is hard to come by, and nothing you do will be important as the being time. Witness a miracle in mind. It doesn't have to physically occur for it to materialize. It has to be mentally occurring in mind before it materializes. Healing, money, success all come with practice starting from inside. Think. Feel. Be. "Be" is trusting that the imagination is the maker.

L: But again, how do you get through the torturous wait time when the clock is ticking and the time frame too thin?

A: Trust, belief and when that doesn't work, stay aligned as often as possible so that the best possible information arrives via the higher self so you may move through it more quickly and allow all choices be conscious. Never drop the ball. Just as in a game, the minute you leave the ball it is out of your hands. Gain control.

L: Next thought. I can't find a job. No one wants to hire me because of my vast career change. There are no jobs here for me.

A: "I leap at a chance to change careers and share wisdom with All."

L: I would love to do that but I can't seem to get clients for myself on a consistent basis, enough to pay the bills and keep me afloat.

A: "I respect the laws of the universe and know the willing come when they are ready, not when I am."

L: And what do I do while I wait for them?

A: Be.

L: I'm going to BE homeless soon if I wait any longer.

A: "I patiently await the clients who come willingly, accepting financial gains as I value myself within."

L: Ok, lastly for tonight. My arm is not healing. I am stuck.

A: "Release me, dear All, so I may heal and move."

L: Being stuck has been a driving theme in my life for a while. It's frustrating that my wrist and my shoulder are not healing well. I can't quite reconcile this notion of this world being an 'illusion', as Spirit always seems to describe our earthly world. How can something that

feels so real be unreal? I think about my brother so often when I think that, because I feel guilty that he is not here and I am. Then I think I should be more grateful for my life, and yet I still am frustrated. I went from fear to frustration, which I guess is better than being stuck in fear. So I guess during all of this maybe I did move up the ladder of enlightenment, at least one rung.

A: *Bravo, dear One. A most excellent assumption and truth. Every step is a stone towards belief. Every question a brilliant examination of life on Earth. Every sentient being questions existentialism. The study of man has been a complex series of questioning since the beginnings of time as it was created upon planet Earth. Every generation (spiritually speaking) has defined it as something else entirely. The existence of man is practical in nature. It is Divine Mind experiencing itself through the bodies of everyone and everything. It is the body (celestially speaking) of One separated into All. Upon planet Earth you are all being separate so you can distinguish opposite behaviors. Good and bad, left and right, up and down. We have covered this material in other books, yet most find it hard to believe or comprehend what is truth. It is because it feels so real you are all always questioning the very nature of why you exist in the first place.*

"What is this point to life?" *most have asked unconsciously and with themselves and others. We have spelled it all out for you quite accurately in the pages of these All books and yet you continue to question the validity because of the 'realness' you are feeling at any given time and this is part of the process you have chosen as a soul; for it to feel real, like a character in a show but with actual consequences. If we could describe it for you in terms you may understand as humans, it is a play with multiple acts, multiple parts and infinite characters, plots and dialogue. We watch ourselves playing a part and then decide who we are as part of One.*

> ❝ I am loving, kind, gentle and at the same time depressed and sad. I've been given a chance to know who I am but I have chosen instead to immerse myself in the role. ❞

Like an actor who becomes the part until the play is over. You are Shakespeare's greatest role, a one act play with—

L: I am frustrated as none of this is making sense to me.

A: *Do you see how easily distracted One can be when the ego comes along?*

"Let me offer up some pain, or a thought of something else. Let me feed you the wrong words or make it difficult to hear."

This is part of the learning. You are easily distracted and go away for extended periods of time even more so than you had before.

L: True. It's taken me almost two years to write this book, whereas my last three books in total took less time than that.

A: *It is because you are tempted by ego so often it becomes impossible to finish what you had started oh so long ago, be it a book or a healed wound.*

L: But isn't that by design? All part of the process?

A: *Not necessarily. Had you been more focused on a goal of healing it was possible to finish our book more efficiently, but ego had you good and drawn in. So you spent more time doing and less time being, and none of this is bad or good. It just is. Whatever comes along you must act as if you have chosen it, because you have. Free will is the gift that keeps on giving. You take a licking and keep on ticking, or you wrap it up and return to Source. You can do this as a human or as soul.*

L: What can you suggest to help us move through the challenges of belief? How can we uproot fears and work towards healing?

A: *Our workbook exercises are designed to do just that. It is important you make time for them. Do them often, daily if needed, so you express what is trapped in mind. Do them once and they become worthless in a sense. You must work daily on soul.*

WORKBOOK EXERCISE #12: TRUE OR FALSE

G et out some paper or use our workbook to write down all conscious beliefs which arrive in the mind. Spend time going as deep as you can to reveal all the beliefs you hold as both and individual and a collective on Earth. It will take you some time, and other beliefs may arise throughout a day or week. Use the opposite of it to bring through truth.

I am unworthy.

FALSE

I am worthy.

TRUE

I am too old for babies.

FALSE

I am young, healthy and vibrant. My body is capable of more than I know.

TRUE

Life is short.

FALSE

Life is eternal and the body is just temporary.

TRUE.

I am sick.

FALSE

I am perfect and healthy.

TRUE

Speak these truths as if they were real even when they feel false. Emotional cues are how you will know when resistance has occurred. Thinking a thought is not enough to change vibration. Feeling must be used, as well, or it will not manifest.

Practice what we are telling you, whom to be and how to make life work easier. Then decide upon whom you would like in charge of life. Truth or ego?

The deliberate process of this book is that we want you questioning everything. Going back and forth is what most do as awakened Ones, and to throw you off course is our agenda. You can't stay afloat the whole time. We are the life preserver and the brick. We want you experiencing both as you evolve, otherwise the journey is incomplete. Learning is a goal and every teacher must at some point allow you to discover what is true on your own.

While you contemplate life remember you are Love, as is everyone else, even if undiscovered. Remember to question everything as soon as it arrives, then send it away with truth. We allow Laura a chance to uncover hidden fears collectively as we move into our next chapter, Let Them Sleep.

CHAPTER 23

Let Them Sleep

Dear All,
Release me from the flow of ego thoughts and allow only what is right
and true as to how All operates on a physical plane. Examine what is
true and reveal the false.

Super Mind

ove is the true nature of All, but when separating into bodies it becomes
irrational; unsure of itself. As entities of soul you are reasoning every day
with self.

"Am I this? Am I that?"

You make decisions from limited thinking and fear. You see one decision as right and another as wrong and it is all processing. Like a computer processor, you sort through files of information, never letting go of it.

A hard drive is downloadable, just as information stored in the physical brain is. It keeps records of everything you have been through, done or have yet to do. Although it feels like earned information you gather along the way, it is stored inside the mind the same as a hard drive. It exists for you at any given time and when accessing it all sorts of revelations arrive.

Go deeper within the mind and you uncover hidden themes and 'memories'. We place quotes around our word 'memory' because it is actually stored information, not something you happened upon. Every thought/word/action is taking place as Ones go about creating, and you are simply downloading that which exists already. You are the ultimate super computer filled with hard drives of information or data accessed only through meditation and contemplation.

Think of it as if someone has asked you questions and in order to answer you must first turn YOU on. Inside All minds is every answer needed, but if you access outside information it is corrupted data. Access information on the inside and you are using your super computer.

Most upon planet Earth never turn their internal drive on. They use corrupted files. Generally speaking, you are at the mercy of the soul as All choosing to express itself as body. So much so that the awakened question everything (as revealed in chapter 22). Everyone eventually comes to understand unity, but not often do Ones arrive there without having had some circumstances both tragic and triumphant and everything in between; a true spectrum of life.

The very nature of life is to expand, and reasoning helps in this endeavor. What is happening currently in the country of America (our inscriber's home base) and around the world is the very fear lying dormant within All. An attack of epidemic proportions brought upon by collective thinking.

COVID-19

The world is on high alert as a virus deemed "Corona" has overtaken the vast majority of minds. Most are seeing death and devastation and believing at their core they are susceptible to its magnitude and power. It is possible to side step this virus and that is in mind. In mind you must think, feel and believe all is well. It is the remedy for all of life's heartaches and upsets: belief. It is simple, yet most are in a state of un-being and therefore are stuck in the illusion, as had been chosen by them, for them, in this body as part of the soul's growth. Knowing you are soul is a miraculous cure for any and all 'diseases', be they viruses or cancers. It is all thoughts corrupted by and through mind. Just as a hard drive is corrupted through outside forces, so, too, are you.

The super computer of planet Earth is under attack. What is happening in our world is tragic and sad for most of the unenlightened, but those who are thinking higher thoughts are seeing the gifts of time and illusion being dropped. Should Ones see the world as perfectly imperfect it is understandable what is going on. The planetary alignment has been off for quite some time and fear has been manifesting itself in disaster after disaster. Earthquakes, fires, rainforests decimated and animal extinction. It is a crucial time in evolution and all awakened minds are being called to a higher purpose. Hold space for each other. There is much to be learned in this time of great despair.

There is not one of you. There is All. All are connected. The borders you have created are invisible lines keeping you apart. Countries and states are confinement created by greed. The very nature of humanity is to define yourself as a species and the definition which is most accurate currently is dependent, acting in accordance with what society has deemed acceptable behavior and allowing governments to control every man, woman or child. Independence is fallacy on Earth. This is not how other civilized societies operate in other planetary orbits.

You must look for new ways to achieve harmony as a people. Allow new order to come upon you. One where you are equal. Equal rights. Equal value. Equal access to all human necessities - food, water, healthcare and shelter. Until this is achieved endless opportunities to expand arise. Why wait? The time is now to accept our ways of being.

The Universe is calling you to rise higher. To be light in dark times.

Earth

Laura: I've got questions.

All: We've got answers. We have summoned you for this conversation. You are experiencing 'symptoms'?

L: Well, yes and no. I'm pretty sure I am healthy and nothing is wrong but the mind can play tricks on you. I am also exhausted and not sleeping well. My habits have been upended—

A: Throwing off the circadian rhythm which then wreaks havoc upon a bodily system. Rest when you can during the day.

L: It's hard to rest considering what is going on in our world.

A: It is an alter event, as had been described earlier; one that you are all caught in currently. It is a collective shift; a shift most necessary to evolve the planet. It is temporary. A temporary event that alters our collective way of being. You are all caught in its crossfire, so to speak. No one is immune in earthly terms. Yet all are sidestepping its wrath, save for those who have chosen on a spirit level to evolve through it.

L: Am I one of those who have chosen or am I immune?

A: Immune, and you are knowing this to be true. Although the unrest you felt earlier this evening was simply so we may speak with you here. Tomorrow you will arise feeling fine.

L: And if I don't?

A: You will. You are feeling better already.

L: True. So you are saying those people who have died or been infected have chosen to participate in this alter event?

A: Yes. Those who have chosen (as was revealed to you in a meditation) are on the receiving end of a manifested fear. The deaths experienced on a soul level have been chosen, as well. Those beings who have died are already back in our heavenly plane understanding of their 'why'. Everybody knows their role in the illusion and what must be done to move forward in time/space. It had been chosen as a means to evolve the planet slowly through a trickle-down effect so that All beings are understanding –

1. *Their interconnectivity.*

2. *Their relationships and what issues are not being dealt with, such as unforgiveness.*

3. *The harsh realities of what has been done to the planet and how much damage it caused.*

4. *The new normal which must occur in order to extend the earthly experiment into the next century.*

What you do now will affect an entire generation that will come after you. Use this time wisely and for change and a new world is upon us. Look at this as opportunity for growth and expansion, make changes to your ideals and governmental policies and you will march into a new era triumphantly.

L: But it feels like most people are not in any level of awareness to understand why this is happening, and those of us who are spiritually awake are fighting a losing battle against their fear. I certainly have been trying to change perception by offering an enlightened perspective, but I feel that it gets lost in a sea of misinformation and panic.

A: A job well done, and while not all are in a state of awareness needed to recognize the lessons for humanity, our souldiers of light must be vigilant in sharing enlightened ideas and anecdotes. It may not reach the masses, but will reach those willingly on the journey to enlightened thinking. Remember not all are capable of this because it had been chosen prior.

L: How do you handle when you are someone who has become aware of our divine nature but the other people in your life are still sleeping? My mom in particular is very caught in her fears about Covid. I am seeing her slipping into a state of despair because of this event, and no matter what I say, she just gets angrier and angrier. She doesn't believe nor care about spiritual principles. I'm lost over how to help her and I get upset when she is going down the rabbit hole. So I become either distant or uncomfortable and just want to walk away.

A: You must let those who are asleep stay sleeping. It is their journey to overcome and not for any other being to push or prod them into a state of knowing. For they will not hear you as it had not been chosen by them to do so. Every relationship you have serves a role for you, as well. Her role is to egg you on and your role is to evolve beyond it; to see the light when no one else does.

L: I get that and I try to do that but it's very hard to watch someone you love struggle when you know there is a better way.

A: *This is the very crux of your illusional problem. You are too focused on helping others when what Ones need to be doing is practicing their own form of enlightenment. Every one of you are on a journey to find self. Self and only self. This does not mean that you cannot hold space for others to 'wake up', only that you must consistently stay in your own spiritual lane and not veer into others' unless it has been asked for by the soul incarnated. Asking is consent.*

L: So what should I be doing then when someone is slipping into fear and they try to drag me in with them? I don't want to participate in someone else's pity party, but I also find that people get mad when you don't join them or when you can be happy despite external circumstances. So I am damned if I do and damned if I don't. Do you see what I mean?

A: *Of course we do. We are always able to observe human behaviors and reactions. Remember you are mirrors upon one another. So what you say to One you say to you.*

L: But again, it begs the question of how not to engage in their sleepiness when you yourself are wide awake? How do I participate in a conversation when someone is caught in the circumstance with no tools for getting themselves out?

A: *Use the tools YOU have within.*

> 66 *Spirit, help me understand this person's madness while at the same time not allowing myself to get caught in it. How may I grow from this?* 99

L: So cocreate a response?

A: *Before speaking back, always.*

L: I think all of the Covid chaos is only exacerbating the issue at hand. Being stuck inside with someone for months like this is tough.

A: *As had been chosen by all of the collective to go through a magnitudinal shift of consciousness. To spend time with others of a like-mindedness as well as those who think irrationally. Each has chosen the circumstances that would arise as they moved through the crisis (if it came upon them) and what Ones are experiencing is, as always, for the highest growth of All.*

L: There are a multitude of, if not infinite, scenarios of how this crisis affected everyone. From some being stuck on cruise ships, others being unemployed, health care workers being hailed as heroes at the same time as stock brokers taking advantage and corporate corruption as usual.

A: All of it brilliantly and masterly planned by each and every individual soul as well as the collective 'soul' of Earth. Everyone has a role to play and is executing it perfectly.

L: Had it been planned prior? Was there any way to sidestep this crisis?

A: In the history of Earth many alter events go as 'planned' while others never take flight, and this as always is guided by love/fear.

L: But what about moon cycles and astrological patterns? Aren't we in the tug of all of that?

A: Yes, but the moon isn't causing a circumstance. A collective circumstance is 'pre-planned', so to speak, in case a necessary shift needs occur; and when all who are sleeping are awakened those circumstances disappear, but until then all must move through the challenges prepared by consciousness.

L: How did we arrive here?

A: Deforestation and animal abuse are some of the ways you are destroying our vast landscape. Oceanic disruption, air pollution and toxic compounds leeching into the soil. Please don't let this time ruin the work you have been doing. You are souldiers of light here to upgrade and evolve. It can be no other way. It is no other way. So much of the world has been overrun by greed, madness, darkness and mayhem. You have destroyed that which is a gift and that is what has caused this very breakdown. Members of your society are suffering as you have choked oxygen from the air. Forced to breathe on its own, Earth has made itself the center again. You must treat the planet more wisely before the next breakdown or it will not survive. You will destroy the precious gift you have been given. It has happened before and will happen again unless you can quell the fear and bring the light. You are asked to be confined for a number of reasons. You have chosen to be upgraded as you awaken to a stark and harsh truth. You cannot treat the planet the way it has been or you will have no planet to live on.

L: Will you step in to 'save' us if we can't get our act together in terms of fear? Or are we bound by—

A: All. You are bound by the laws of the Universe which state that which is like unto itself is drawn and there are many who have helped in terms of prayer, intention and belief, but more are in fear and so the scale is tipped to one side.

L: So if more of us had chosen a life seen more through a lens of love we would—

A: Have no need for the evolutionary shifts occurring. Had you all taken better care of the planet, the moon, the stars and all of existence, Earth would have moved along and still shifted but with no consequence to the planet's inhabitants, i.e. all of you. You recognize self and self reveals itself more and more and most are in a state of unrecognition. You are simply further along than your fellow brethren, and while there are many more awakening, the draw of fear has kept mostly all sleeping quite soundly.

L: So it goes back to free will. We have the choice to view everything through the lens of love or fear, and when we choose fear we stay asleep. Why do you always say then that everything is perfect exactly as it is because it had been chosen? And if that's the case, that every decision is between love and fear, why can't I tell that to someone so they can choose more wisely?

A: If asked, you may. If not then they have chosen to stay asleep. At any given moment they may choose again, but for some amnesia runs too deep based upon conditioned mind beliefs that have been ingrained in the psyche. Remember that all things exist as possibility, but it is their possibility and not yours. So nothing you may do will allow them to wake up if they choose fear. They must learn on their own to seek help.

L: But how do I stay untethered from the circumstance without seeming cruel or uncaring? I want to sidestep it without judgement.

A: Know All have chosen for themselves what events and challenges they will move through. It had been chosen. It is hard to reconcile this notion through the body/ human eyes but it is the truth for All.

L: I have to then just see whatever is happening as part of the process and let everyone learn as they go? This is why we titled this chapter "Let Them Sleep," a title I heard over a year ago when we started writing this book. No wonder it took so long for me to write this book as opposed to the last three. We were waiting for this event to occur?

A: Indeed, dear One. It has been a purposeful endeavor and every chapter placed perfectly. We are coming towards the end of our book with just a few chapters to go but certainly not the end, for there is always something to be learned.

L: And what are we learning here from this tragic and historic event? Never have we seen such a shocking—

A: Not never. You have seen alter events repeated in many eras just with different faces. An alter event is a war in many aspects. It is a war on fear. The only battle you are ever fighting on Earth is one of love versus fear. Good versus evil, as you would call it in movies and TV. Sometimes the good prevails and other times 'evil', but in the end all is always exactly as it should be. Remember it does not matter whether you win or lose, only that you play our 'game' of love/fear. Use this time to better yourself and it will be a win for good. Lose sight of the goal to evolve and it all 'goes out the window'. You can move forward, backward or stay the same, and each has a particular set of circumstances which arises as it unfolds.

L: **Okay but what about those of us who are enlightened to levels of understanding? We can't force people to understand, especially if they are not ready or willing on a soul level.**

A: *It is not a forcing but a gentle leading towards truth. Some will never follow (as bodies) as it is not their journey but there are enough who are ready for a perception change.*

L: **It's so hard to see others suffering. I want to live in a changed world but I get so frustrated by the lack of people who care about spirituality or awakening. I want a world of no wars and fear. I want a world of kind, happy people. Is it wrong to want that? To leave the world a better place for our children and our children's children?**

A: *That is what all have been doing, and with each passing alter event you have evolved as a species and stepped up each and every time, but then you do slide back into old habits and thinking patterns. Sound familiar?*

L: **Yes, because that is exactly how my own life has been. I evolve and then I slide backwards and then I evolve again. Each upset or tragedy spins me right back around, but I always do get through it and begin again.**

A: *Bravo. You have understood the entire process of life both collectively and individually. You had fallen and broken your wrist and found rather triumphantly that it moved you beyond fear more than any other event in your life so far. You had failed a test and realized the job it led to was not the path needed to evolve. Now the entire collective is experiencing that shift of mind and becoming more peaceful and understanding towards others. Every event is a move towards peace and sometimes, unfortunately, the worst thing is the way. It doesn't have to be that way, but it is (right now) and you must live practically in the 'what is' and handle it as best you can in the body/mind/soul trifecta.*

L: **I've got news for you my friend. Our planet is imploding and not becoming more peaceful.**

A: *Right now.*

L: **It's become unhinged in every sense of the word. More fighting. More name calling. 2020 is by far the worst year I have witnessed in my entire life.**

A: *You have food?*

L: **Yes.**

A: *Water?*

L: **Yes.**

A: Sunlight?

L: Yes.

A: A roof over one's head with some money available to you?

L: Yes.

A: Then you have what is needed, and yet persistently do you all focus upon what is not happening or what is tragic rather than what blessings you do have. When all who are focused in physical life accept what blessings are upon you, you would see all of these problems and issues disappear. Love All and All will be Love.

March 2020

L: It's so hard to see a world suffering. People in every corner of the globe are dying. More than 30,000 as of today.

A: Remember all souls are One, and as difficult as it all is to understand, it is designed beautifully and perfectly for maximum soul expansion. All of you are caught in its web because you had decided upon as collective this would be the way it goes if fear overtook the planet, as it often does. You have destroyed the home given as a means to evolve through fear and now it is necessary to battle. Demons of power and corruption most definitely had a hand in all of this (from a human perspective), and you are no longer moving freely because the 'right wing' political conservatives believe inhibiting rights is the way to go, so to speak.

L: And is it?

A: It is not for us to say, only to offer enlightened perspectives as to why this occurred across the planet. You must decide upon whether or not it is proper each on an individual level. View love and it is a time of self-reflection, reconnection and clarity. View fear and your rights are restricted and movements impeded by corruption.

L: So rather than worry about rights being restricted, it's better to use the time for self-improvement?

A: Precisely. You can be love or you can be fear.

L: But isn't it love to rise up against a governmental system that doesn't protect the people but profits?

A: If it comes from love and a sense of helping a fellow man, yes. If it comes from fear of being contained or quarantined, as is happening now, no. You must always decide upon which way to go by using the inner self. It can be no other way.

L: I am trying to view all of this through the lens of love, but I would imagine if we don't learn our lessons through all of this it will occur again—

A: *And again, yes. You are all under the laws of the Universe that state that which is like unto itself is drawn. So until collectively a swap of ideals occurs, whereas all beings on Earth act as One and remove fear, you may continually create a circumstance of fear upon planet Earth. It can be no other way. For all of you to come together at once would be a miraculous feat, and as we have told you in our prior book, The All That Is, to do this would bring about world's end, and so while it is possible, it mostly is impossible in the earthly world you all inhabit as most are thinking from a space of fear and not love.*

L: **So everyone who is caught in this, which is pretty much the whole world, is going to be unable to move forward? When will this end? Because this is getting worse and the predictions for how long it's going to last are only getting longer, and that is a little scary. Even the awakened are caught in the—**

A: *Loop. You are caught in a chaos loop where nothing is changing, but it will, not because you are incapable of moving beyond it but because it is part of the alter event. A consciousness shift is occurring where more are awakening to their true nature of love.*

L: **Not enough in my opinion. You keep getting away from the main question, though, about this particular set of circumstances with the Coronavirus. It sounds like you are saying on one hand it could have been avoided but on other it couldn't because we are in a planetary shift.**

A: *Shift is occurring because of the acts of fear which led to Earth's consistent destruction (as was said earlier). So yes, a shift is occurring, but it is a course-correction shift. So many of you are awakening and representing love as a species and a wellspring of love is creating shift.*

L: **It doesn't seem that way. A wellspring of politicians and scientists are telling us this could last for months or even years, which then causes a sense of despair that gets manifested into other people's minds. I'm trying to maintain high vibes but it's hard to believe what you are saying here as opposed to what everyone else is thinking—**

A: *Or believing.*

L: **Precisely. If they believe in this going on for months or years how am I, one person, going to change that?**

A: *One mind can change another and another and another. All One needs do is hold space. Be the light. Hope brings miracles. Hope is needed in times of great crisis. How many movies, tv shows, books or other materials have guided the narrative based upon this simple belief?*

L: Thousands at least. I hope this is over soon.

A: *How much less effective would it have been had the lengthy stays of execution not forced people into their homes? How much healing of the Earth's core could be done in weeks? Months were needed to reset energetically all that has been done.*

L: But at the expense of people's lives and livelihoods?

A: *Does Earth not deserve a break? Its core function is being destroyed and not all were willing to change their destructive behaviors and make the necessary shifts on their own. This is when a helping hand comes along to save itself.*

L: Itself?

A: *Of course, the Earth is One with All just as is everything and everyone.*

L: But wasn't it caused by fear? Is there a "highest good" agenda that God/Source/All has for us?

A: *Will "we" step in is what you are asking?*

L: Yes. Or is it preplanned and only a choice for love can change it? If the teeter totter tips back towards love can we sidestep atrocities or harshness as a whole, or is there ever a time when the Universe steps in and 'fixes' our mistakes and mishaps?

A: *Isn't that what all have been doing in prayer? Asking to receive?*

L: Yes, but I don't think it's fair for so many people to have died. All of these families losing loved ones. These nurses and doctors being placed at the front lines at the expense of not being with their own loved ones. It's diabolical all of it, truly.

A: *It's not the way of the warrior to see it as such. It is a warrior's light which brings change. See it for what it is – an event designed to change the collective energy which when it's over is going to reveal a kinder, gentler world for All – plants, trees, oceans, rivers; an environment all can enjoy for decades to come without fear of implosion. Less earthquakes, hurricanes, tornados and floods are set to occur because you have taken the time to let Earth heal. Is that worth staying indoors and using less polluting substances? Jobs are created and those who are thinking accordingly will find and those who are in fear are choosing to create on a soul level a sense of insecurity as a way to move beyond a life-driving theme. No one going through a circumstance, be it individually or collectively, isn't capable of moving beyond it. That, dear One, is the point of All.*

L: Right now we are seeing more fires, more hurricanes—

A: *More fear. Always remember possibilities. Be One who knows truth, that this has a reason and what the outcome could be. Be One who holds space for others not one who perpetuates it.*

April 2020

L: Fear is spreading and it's invading my mind. I can very much see how people get sick not knowing all of this is "illusion," as you have called it. They wind up going down the rabbit hole of illness and then it just keeps going and going. How many people are sick because the fear invaded their mind and how many have chosen to be sick or die to move the energy of the collective?

A: What must be known is all are caught in this unusual circumstance, and no you are not one of the sickened, and this had been chosen as much as being sick was. For your mind is playing tricks and this is so we may discuss the very nature of disease. You are dissing the ease of life and swallowing the gravity of a situation, of which you have no control (individually). Collectively you are control, but this circumstance has all of you together as One learning to be cohesive. Try listening to the soul more if you cannot listen all the time. We know it is difficult to be mindful at every moment. So you must try as often as possible to leave attack thoughts alone.

L: So you are saying my mind is making me sick?

A: Making you feel sick, so we may discuss the very reason why so many are getting this diss-ease. They diss the ease of life and then the torturer (ego) brings them into a state of unrest. They think upon how hard it is rather than how important it is to the collective.

L: Well most of the world is asleep, so thinking about the importance of why this is all happening is not something most would be doing. Most are thinking of the horrors of it.

A: And yet, you who is awakened are very much aware of its altering effects—

L: And that it could always be worse, yes. Let me ask you this. If once this is over and the world returns to a state of normal (whatever that is) and we don't learn our collective lessons here could this all happen again?

A: And be much worse, yes. That is a possibility, but as you very much know things do not have to go the way of fear. You must stay in vibrational alignment as a species to side step atrocities such as this.

L: And how can we do that as a species when so many are unaware and vibrationally unmatched?

A: The higher vibration you have, the higher the collective energy. Each individual affects the whole. So when you are aligned it brings others along, as well. The best you can be, the best all can be. Stay aligned in soul is all Ones need do or be. Just be love.

L: And how do we do that when our ego wants us being fear? You say it's mostly impossible to wake up because most have chosen not to, but then in the same sentence say it's possible to sidestep certain alter events should we utilize free will and quell fear. I'm confused as to whether or not we truly can be free?

A: Free of burden. Free of fear. The very act of being is what One needs do in order to understand the whys and hows of our divinity. Yes, it can be moved along, but at the same time it could not because the minds decide upon everything. To say it had been chosen by you, for you means soul had a plan, and if you choose its help then you will sidestep it. But if (in the plan also) you stayed sleeping instead, you would be caught in the circumstance to help move you beyond fear. That is the battle always on Earth; love and fear.

L: This battle is won—

A: In the mind. Do not think it to be a 'battle' or 'fight' even though it is often referred to as this here in our book (for humans crave word association), for this is the very reason why you struggle in the first place. Accept as it comes, all circumstances. For it has been chosen as means to move beyond issues. Whenever a thought/feeling/ emotion arrives it is to be dealt with and not whisked away.

"Why am I dissing the ease of life right now?" would be a most important question to ask.

L: Okay. Why am I dissing the ease of life right now?

A: So that we may write this very chapter on how those who are sleeping are finding themselves 'sick'.

L: How may I move beyond it?

A: Know it is part of a learning curve. Rather than do 'battle' with ego, just ask questions. This is not some war to be won between good and evil. It is a way to lessen the grip of fear.

"What am I thinking and how may I remove it from mind?"

Create wisely.

"I will use this time to find myself."

If all who are awake and aware would spend time in quiet getting to know the self it would move our collective along as swiftly as it arrived.

L: But that is not what I have been doing. I have been using this time to work, share messages and keep busy.

A: Do less. Be more. Always.

L: And how would I do that? What would my day look like schedule wise if I did things your way?

A: We are so glad you asked and offer this schedule to All.

- *Wake up, pray/meditate.*

- *Eat healthy breakfast.*

- *Use time to exercise/move a body. Stretch/do yoga/align the body.*

- *Pray again.*

- *Spend time on a project joyfully rather than feeling it to be 'work', as many so often do.*

- *Eat a healthy lunch or snack.*

- *Dance/laugh/do art/walk/run. Anything which keeps the mind active and engaged in joy.*

- *Meditate on life and all its beauty.*

- *Work again, mindfully on a project or activity.*

- *Dinner of healthy grains (beans/rice) and/or fresh vegetables of high vibrational value.*

- *Read or write. High vibrational materials/books.*

- *Bedtime with a routine of prayer/meditation.*

L: Well gee, that sounds great for someone who is independently wealthy but meditation does not pay the bills. Most of us have to get up and go to work, so your schedule does not align with that.

A: Or so you think. Notice we did not say to not do work. Rather we said do it mindfully with intention so that it doesn't feel as if it's work. Do what you love and it will feel more aligned to a soul's contract. Do what brings financial gains because you feel you have to and it will be ego's work. It is perfectly aligned with a worker's schedule. The time each activity takes can be shortened or lengthened dependent upon said One's commitments. Priorities are to make time for that which is most beneficial, and that is how you decide for peace. Make peace the priority and you will find time for anything to quell chaos and bring calm throughout a day.

L: What about a stay-at-home mom who has children to take care of each day?

A: Ones who are more aligned to soul will make time no matter what the circumstance or situation they are in. Those who find excuses are unwilling, and so it will be hard to find reasons to upset the balance they believe they have or don't have. You are One who has more time on their hands. Why not use this time for good? Practice what we preach and you will see a shift occur within All.

L: My one decision can affect Source?

A: *Of course! What have we been teaching you since we began our back and forth? One is All. All is One. One affects All. Choose to pray, meditate, accept peace and you are bringing it to All. Does it mean the entire world will suddenly look different? Not literally, but a world around you will change because you have decided for a peaceful day. Each day you pray, the world becomes a little less chaotic. Subtle shifts over time create growth. It won't be felt for decades to come, but any One who spends the time wisely in bodies can create a ripple effect for All.*

L: **Well, the evidence has not shown itself.**

A: *Yet.*

L: **More of us are becoming more aware and awake. Meanwhile, the world remains a mess.**

A: *Why not spend this time when you have no choice to try our schedule above? Give it a week and see what happens.*

L: **Well, I have got nothing better to do. So I guess I can give it a try. Money isn't coming to me now the way I would like it to, or at least until this is over. So I have more time on my hands, as you said.**

A: 66 *Money flows to me easily and effortlessly. I have all I need.* 99

Why not use thoughts such as these instead?

L: **Because thoughts don't change you. Just thinking or saying a thought is not bringing about change because I don't actually believe money will come out of nowhere. So why even bother?**

A: *Because you are the captain of the boat and you get to steer it how you want. Yes, it is true that beliefs bring the tide, but every thought can be kept vibrationally aligned and it will bring change. Slow increments. No matter how slow you go, as long as you do not stop it will bring the change all seek. Again, we ask, why not try it instead of dismissing the notion?*

L: **How often?**

A: *Forever, dear One. Forever. As long as you are in a body you are learning/ remembering at a pace chosen by soul. And if you decide upon thoughts of love, peace, harmony it will be easier to create a life of ease. Once you are awake and aware (to some degree) you will find modalities for learning more along the path of enlightening, and when you are in a state of awareness where thoughts become conscious you can control the flow much more easily. Like a faucet, you stop the flow and then eventually turn it off. Ultimately though, most are in a state of awareness that is like a drip. Learning slowly is how most will go through a life. Earth is a magnetically-attracting planet and so the very thoughts they hold deep in the psyche aren't accessible because they would bring mass chaos even more so than they do now.*

L: So you are saying those who are asleep—

A: *Have some very dark demons to overcome as soul.*

L: I thought soul was always perfect; the essence of who we all are.

A: *Soul is perfect, but the essence of a life is to create circumstances to grow beyond, and this creates many awful or unpleasant things at the rung of fear where All have started on Earth. You are thinking that all of this is bad and why go through such a rut?*

L: Absolutely. What is the point of all of this torture, pain and sadness we go through on Earth to get to be Love?

A: *Again and again you have chosen this and to look upon it as torture is simply because you do not understand yet what all of this is for or what 'Heaven' is truly all about. You have chosen to stay sleeping so you may vibrate collectively with Earth. Otherwise, you may not stay there, so to speak.*

L: We want to be in the dark a little because if we are understanding our connection to Love with no more lessons to learn we would be back with Spirit?

A: *Yes. Just as those who are behind in their thinking have chosen to stay sleeping (words we use on a basic level to help you understand this), those who are awake and aware have chosen to remember pieces of the puzzle, not the whole picture.*

L: Well none of this seems very fun to me. Although I appreciate knowing we want to be in the dark a little in order to actually stay here.

A: *Because you are living out life exactly as had been chosen by you, and asking to be reminded to Source will always bring about higher vibrations and less feelings of despair of the hows and whys of life. Listen to the inner voice. It knows the journey, the lessons and the best way to be. Use inner guidance as often as you can and it will be a much better journey no matter where you are in the process to enlightenment.*

May 2020

L: I have been reading and rereading this over and over again about soul choices, and I just don't understand how being shot at, murdered, raped, abused, disabled, undergoing surgery, chronic and acute illness and all the pain we go through can be God's will or our soul's journey. It seems cruel and I can be awake and aware but also be—

A: *Unwilling to accept what is Love.*

L: That does not seem like Love, any of it.

A: *When you broke your wrist what happened?*

L: I overcame much of my prior fear. I understand that. I really do, but

I happen to be someone on a journey to awaken. For me it's easier to use a circumstance to change my fear. For others it might not be. Breaking a wrist isn't as terrible in comparison to what others are or may experience.

A: *You recently met a man who underwent paralysis and was able to walk again through determination and will, despite doctors believing he couldn't. And what did he say about the experience?*

L: He said it was the best thing that ever happened to him because it gave him a sense of appreciation for life. It taught him to slow down and be mindful of how he was living his life.

A: *One of our most prominent healers stated online that she underwent shoulder surgery and after months of pain was able to now have more empathy for chronic pain sufferers. You yourself have expressed a similar sentiment, have you not?*

L: True.

A: *So you see the purpose of pain?*

L: I guess. It's hard to ignore when you put it like that, but now we are at over 60,000 deaths from Covid in the U.S., or so the government says. I spent a few days going over conspiracy theories and all sorts of dark predictions. It's hard to believe sixty thousand souls chose to participate in this energetic shift you keep saying is coming. The shift I see coming is a government taking over of the rights of people. Freedom is at war with politics, money and greed.

A: *Be very clear, your rights are being stripped as a means to protect the masses and not to enslave them.*

L: I still think and feel some shadiness exists and not everything is as at seems.

A: *Misinformation is part of the playbook for all events in human history. Lest Ones know a little too much, it would spark more fear than necessary. Understand and know the events are taking place all around the world not as part of some satanic ritual or sacrifice, but more so to install a system many feel necessary to planet's survival. On a human level, it will be revealed soon for all to know and to express (through either love or fear) disappointment on a mission gone wrong or at least bungled. You are very much in the know and though it will be shocking, it, too is part of the planetary development.*

L: But there also is a spiritual lesson in all this and a message about trying to save our beautiful planet from extinction?

A: *To truly save the planet all must be committed to moving through changes energetically and using the time for contemplation and understanding.*

L: So we have to get a handle on how we treat our planet?

A: *Indeed.*

L: And what about all of these conspiracy theories that even some people that claim "enlightenment" are sharing online?

A: *Perhaps it had been witnessed on purpose so you know whom is perpetuating a narrative.*

L: Is there any truth to it?

A: *Some. All truths to be revealed on a grand scale, but most are inaccuracies, fabrications and wishful thinking among a group of souls dedicated to stirring the pot of democracy. Just know what is truth is to be found and the rest is unnecessary for growth.*

L: I feel pretty clear on which parts are truth and what is fiction. I do believe population growth is a cause for this disease being unleashed, and I also feel it will become an issue again decades from now. Our 'leaders' believing we need protection. I have seen several movie and tv show plots centered around infertility. A crisis of conscious. Art imitating life—

A: *Possibilities, yes. It is entirely possible for the narrative of Earth to include a circumstance of infertility among the species, just as it is possible not too. Again, it always goes back to choices; collectively and individually. Let All be who they wish to be and wish them well while you stay in connection with Source. Heal thyself and the world within, and only then can you escape ego for All.*

L: But my one little thought is not going to stop liars from being liars, rapists from attacking others or murderers from killing. I'm not God, or at the very least not capable of superpowers.

A: *God is All. So while it's not possible to save a planet from extinction, collective circumstances of evolutionary shifts or violent offenders from their karmic paths you can be in alignment with God/All so that the good outweighs the bad. Think of it like a teeter totter on a playground. The more aligned you are, the more fun you are having and the more kids want to join in. The bully on the end is outweighed by the kids who are kind. Eventually the side with the most attractors wins.*

L: Love versus fear, always.

A: *Yes. There will always be evidence (on Earth) in each and every day to show you how life is 'falling apart', unfair or corrupt. It is the nature of being human; to handle torment in order to evolve. No matter how many ways you may ask us "why," the answers remain the same. It will never waver. There is one truth and one truth only: Love. The upsets and unfairness of life are simply to show what needs healing in all.*

L: Our government is filled with fear and falsities, and perpetuating fear is how we have always done things on Earth. At least since I have been alive. It's been part of American culture to lie and deceive before. What once was called "conspiracy theory" winds up being true. It's diabolical, the secrets. So I can understand why some people believe the falsities. I almost did too, but then in meditation tonight and through channeling realized it was all—

A: For bringing you back to light. Every time you wander, the way is shown back as long as you are aligned in truth. In any 'war' there will be casualties in human words.

L: Causing more upheaval and chaos and more sadness around the world. We feel helpless and hopeless. I am trying to see this through the lens of love but the—

A: Propensity is to fall back into fear.

L: Yes. It's hard to break the chain because I can't see how all of this will end. Now they are talking about extending these lockdowns in case the virus returns. Schools may close for the rest of the year and all this crazy stuff about mandatory vaccines and wearing masks for the rest of our lives is ridiculous, and yet it is what is happening. As awake and aware as some of us are, I'm not sure how to avoid any of this nonsense unless I move to an island in the middle of the sea with no government. I can see why my brother and dad were so angry. I guess I never really paid attention until now to how corrupt our system of government and perhaps all countries are in the scheme of things.

A: As had been chosen by you as soul, to sidestep. Corruption is necessary for the narrative upon Earth.

L: Why? You keep making references to this being like a play or a movie with characters and scenarios. Well, I would like to write a new ending, one where the virus goes away and people get back to work and politicians are no longer motivated by greed, homeless people are provided places to live, no child is unloved or hungry and there is equal distribution among all people of finances.

A: Hardly an entertaining yarn, don't you think?

L: Well so what. Why should people have to suffer?

A: Because they have chosen on a soul level to experience it that way.

L: Not the answer I want or am looking for here. Make it stop.

A: *We can't. Only all of you can on planet Earth. It is a collective event designed to move the planet along and all must agree as One together. Know that when the enemy is defeated (ego) the Earth's transitional effect will occur and all will be off to the races again. It is our hope many will learn from this event and stay focused on soul growth and transformation rather than commerce and consumption.*

L: I'm so sick of seeing people suffer. I'm so sick of seeing corruption and greedy men with no morals or values refuse to help the downtrodden. I'm sick of the way people only care about money and everything is always about making a buck. I'm sick of the way we pollute the environment with toxins and carcinogens. I'm sick of companies hiding cures so they can profit off of the disease. I'm sick of seeing children dying of hunger or who have no home. I'm tired of this terrible system 'we' have set up on Earth. The world is falling apart and we have leaders with no business leading and health officials who I wouldn't trust with my life. I am at the point where I want to throw in the towel. How do the enlightened stay out of the crossfire when it comes to events like this? My frustration lies in the fact that I can't overcome an event that everyone is caught up in, even if I can see it through Love. It's not possible, is it?

A: *It is possible but you must be willing to sidestep ego as you go about maneuvering yourself back to Love. The very fact that you can't align is indicating you are working towards a goal and are not there yet. The All of you are so focused on the pain, you are completely forgetting every lesson taught throughout human history. Be kind to one another. Respect one another. Take care of planet Earth. Choose good thoughts and be mindful of their energetic charge.*

L: That's not possible if you say, "I'm happy," but in fact you are miserable. I'm so angry right now at our world and its inhabitants. I want to shake them awake but I know I can't. I am just pissed off at all of this.

A: *As are many. You are feeling the effects of the collective. As an empath it will be hard to break free of fear, but it must be undertaken in order to explain the truth. For some it will be harder to clear the ego, while others have an easier time at it. You are one who struggles because you have been taxed with writing a book of wisdom, and this brings questions and answers. Rather, would you be one who sits on the sidelines or one who shares words of Love?*

L: Oh definitely one who shares wisdom. So thank you for that.

A: *Thank YOU for that. You chose the life.*

L: Here is what I know for sure. Our health care industry is focused on one thing – money. The plan is to keep people sick. I have to say I am starting to believe there is a hidden agenda and nefarious business dealings involved in all of this. I asked in meditation when this all started if this was an act of terrorism, and what I heard from Spirit was "bio-manipulation." I'm fairly confident that is true.

A: *It is true there is a narrative based around manipulation and managing population growth. No one knows the extent of it so far, but they will. Evidence is becoming available and those seeking a cure are those creating the chaos. It is, was, has been and will always be the playbook of the soldiers to carry out acts of war with collateral damage and no regard for life. The very act of war is to control a populace with one's own agenda. It is one's own agenda for power and greed which allows circumstances to grow and fester using fear as its fuel. This is the gasoline of fear, igniting flames and fanning the fire to create panic, unrest and a sense of needing among the masses. You are playing out the same scenario over and over again in different eras with different leaders (as stated in our last book) who are in fact followers, following ego[4].*

L: What do we do? How do we stop this? I mean this is a world where they kill people for exposing secrets. It's not just movie plots. This stuff really happens. I've seen many stories of sudden death by suspicious circumstances.

A: *On Earth, yes. Better to rid the world of those who go against the grain, and fan the flames of fear. But in every movie do the good guys not usually win? Is truth not revealed and the enemy assailed?*

L: Usually, yes, but this is real life. So how do we maneuver this without getting caught in the trap ourselves?

A: *Win the war internally.*

L: And externally is there anything to be done? Can we share information? I don't want my rights to be impeded or my bodily rights manipulated by someone. What's mine is mine, and no governmental agency is going to strip me of that. No way.

A: *It can be done (meaning sharing information) in a way that is informative without attaching judgement.*

"Do you see what has been happening around the world? A new identity is being born where questioning is key. Stay informed so you have all the information and not just one side. All sides are to be examined."

June 2020

L: You make this all seem so easy, as if we are supposed to just brush it off. Now we are closing in on nearly 400,000 deaths around the world.

The United States is starting to open back up but the ridiculous lengths we are going to are shocking. Masks and social distancing. I was hopeful that the world would grow and change and we would be kinder to one another. However, it feels like it's the opposite. There is now more fear and more struggle in the collective. I'm so lost as to what I can do to help. The amount of people who understand collective truth is minuscule in comparison to the masses of lost minds. Can I do anything at all here? Help me understand what is my role in the collective?

A: Just be. Truly. This is all Ones need do.

Ask, "Dear All, I know the world is on lockdown and the fires rolling through are part of collective shifts needed to evolve the planet further. Down the line all the pain will be worth the profit of Earth's survival. Let All who are sleeping lie and all awakened be."

July 2020

L: A few more weeks have gone by and the spread of Covid-19 continues to dominate the narrative. The states which reopened are now facing record-breaking cases. The news media is still on 24/7 repeat of statistics. Nothing seems to be going our way. Well my dear All, the news is not good here on Earth. We are fanning the flames rather than dousing them. My one good thought and acceptance clearly isn't enough to change much. Based on what I am seeing in the US, I'm pretty sure eventually we are going to blow up this world we have created. Quelling the irrational fears of humans is nearly impossible. And now everyone is fighting over masks. More people are dying (supposedly) and thousands more cases (supposedly) are being reported daily. It's a losing battle. I'm not sure if I have any control whatsoever. So to be honest I am kind of giving up. The world is going to be what it's going to be. The truth is that I can't spend too much time worrying about it because it destroys my own inner peace, and I know that's not good. I'm not trying to ignore it. I'm seeing it for the "illusion" that it is, but also feeling defeated that change isn't imminent. These poor people can't get it together, and for me to shout to the world to use love instead of fear is like screaming fire in a burning building. Damage is done. Chaos has ensued. I'm just figuring how to get out unscathed. And I say all of this half laughing and half serious, if that makes sense.

A: It makes sense. For all are caught up in a rare circumstance and this is the ultimate test of how far you have come as a species.

L: Not far it seems. We still fight over everything, just in different ways than when the north took on the south and the enemy was your neighboring state. Now it's your neighbor, in-law and even best friends who don't think like you. Everyone's got an opinion, and they sure love to express it on social media. It's exhausting watching the fighting going on right now. I can't stomach it much longer, but also sometimes I can't look away. What a world we live in.

A: *Loosen ego's grip and all of it makes perfect sense. As you look upon it through the eyes of us (ie.. you and we), you understand it's part of the allegory of life. See it for what it is; an evolutionary circumstance designed to break the masses' fear, and you are knowing the whys and hows of the situation at hand. Spend time being and answers come more rapidly. Don't expect change if you yourself don't participate in it.*

L: It's hard to participate in change. I'm worried that if I look upon it through the eyes of soul, I am going to wind up creating it for myself, too. Whenever I fear (or judge), I wind up creating something for myself. How can you truly look at what someone is going through without it affecting you? Every time I see a news story I can't just say, "Oh that's just some lesson they are going through." There are some really tragic things going on in the world and I want to help, not hurt.

A: *Helping with the eyes of God is the vision to undertake in every circumstance.*

> 66 *I see you. I am you. I bless your journey and wish peace and harmony for All.* 99

L: Is there a prayer we can say so we don't wind up in a similar predicament?

A: *"As I look upon this circumstance may I know it is illusion and part of the individual's journey. Let no harm come as I share a vision of hope for both them and I."*

Don't think for one minute this is not part of the journey for All. To undertake a mass event such as is occurring on Earth is most important. You must understand your unity and separation in order to evolve forward. Hidden demons are showing themselves, and all the fears, doubts and worries are coming to light. Each individual expressing prejudices creates a ripple effect where the like-minded agree and the argumentative nature of their being sheds light on prejudice, injustice and other practices of separation.

L: It seems to me there are more people in the world who are prejudiced than not?

A: *It is true there are many who are closed off to the evolution of your nature (which is kindness); however, there are more who see color as nothing more than that. America ("the melting pot") is divisive and inclusive. Remember all things have opposites, as this is the chosen experience of planet Earth, oppositionary objectives. Opposing views are part of the process. Those who seek the light are using this as a means to understand who they are in relation to God/Source/Universe. Remember God is LOVE. Everything else is not. In order to learn LOVE in all its forms, first you must be fear and its many forms, and prejudice is one of the fears to overcome. First, be prejudice. Next, learn lessons of how to overcome it through various modalities and injustices. Third, evolve (if you are willing).*

L: And if you are not willing?

A: *Stay stuck in illusions. Repeat. Repeat. Repeat.*

L: So you are caught in a loop like *Groundhog Day*?

A: *Until you move beyond it, it will always present itself in various sizes, shapes and forms.*

L: Evolve or Repeat?

A: *Precisely. Evolution is cyclical. Until you extend a hand to the metaphysical parts of you which knows the best way to be you will continue to repeat cycles over and over again with different characters, scenes and scenarios. Nothing stays the same, ever. However, a brighter day is ahead even when it can't be seen, but you know as well as I that the possibility exists for all of this to end. Why not see the world as you would like it to be rather than as it is?*

L: That works for us individually and collectively? Seeing possibility rather than what is? How can I participate in a way that helps the masses?

A: *Internal awareness of your role as a beacon of light in a dark time. See the light. Be the light. Share inspired musings and engage in a knowing so deep it can't help but move us forward. We are doing this as well on individual soul levels, and when you participate it will help even when it seems futile.*

October 2020

L: It's taken me a long time to write this one chapter, but I guess that is purposeful as well?

A: *Indeed.*

L: Here we are ten months into this divine disaster the planet is part of and what a mess we are all in. I know it has been said repeatedly to look upon it through the eyes of the soul, but my question is how

do we, the awakened ones, steer clear of the noise? Because it's very loud. Here in the United States, we have seen a rise in crime, violence, suicide, depression and mental illness. The economy is heading into perhaps its worse recession ever. The government is in shambles with infighting and name calling. People are acting like children and reacting to every little piece of news with—

A: *Fear.*

L: Yes, of course.

A: *Fear is invading the minds of every One who believes they are strictly humans on Earth. You must be part of the soulution.*

L: I have to see it for what it is? That is so hard to do dear All. It's tragic and sad and reminds me of civil war. Everyone fighting for their beliefs and using violence to achieve the agenda. I mean we literally killed each other to prove a point. This planet is—

A: *Magical.*

L: HA! Hardly. This planet is a mess of hate and anger right now. I can't recall a time when people hated each other as much as they do now. No one seems to like anyone and hate is being spewed.

A: *At you?*

L: No.

A: *Why?*

L: Because I don't participate in the rage. I see it. I notice it but I never, ever engage. I try to see it through the lens you tell me to, Spirit. It doesn't mean I like it, however. Just that I am trying my best to accept what is.

A: *Bravo, you have answered the question yourself. Accept what is. Love what is. Know it is purposeful for evolution for all parties involved, even when it's uncomfortable.*

L: My issue becomes my being caught in the line of fire. Even being awake, knowing soul truth, asking for help and being guided by Spirit, I cannot escape government shut downs, masks and economic fallout.

A: *When One suffers we All suffer. Just because it has been said that you are living in the illusion, and we see what goes on upon planet Earth as perfectly imperfect, does not mean we do not feel the effects of the cause. It had been hoped for all of this to go away as quickly as it came, once the necessary planetary shift occurred to heal the planetary destruction you all are part of on Earth. However, as fear invaded it took on a life of its own, and now you are deeper into it than necessary and finding ways out is difficult.*

L: Which makes me realize I should never speak in absolutes, only possibilities.

A: *Revelation has come. Possibilities are endless on Earth, always in the narrative of love and fear.*

L: It's almost comical at times because it really is like watching a movie with plot points that we have seen in reality television. It's no wonder we don't believe anyone anymore. We have been desensitized–

A: *Through the medium. Absolutely. This is a reliable truth. The actions of others have a direct effect on all minds, and so you pick up on these and use them in situations as needed. The narrative of Earth is quite entertaining, wouldn't you say?*

L: Is it? It's sad and disturbing to watch the world descend into madness and feel like one little souldier in an army of none.

A: *There are many who are on the journey trying to hold space. It is David and Goliath, another entertaining yarn where frenemies become foes and one attempts to defeat another. Ego versus Soul. Love versus Fear. It is always the same fight in different eras with new characters, religions and wars. What is the lesson in all of these fights?*

L: Ego never triumphs. Well, it does but eventually the battle is won–

A: *In love. Any attempt to thwart ego is met with pain and stretches out as long as the weakened One remains weak. You cannot escape ego, as we told you in prior books and materials. You tame the ego and allow it to guide you through 'fight or flight' responses to keep you safe in dangerous situations. Beyond this, ego is always for tempting you to darkness. It thrives on repeated scenarios. It is a mighty king who draws you in with promises of riches and rewards then steers you wrong when it feels threatened by your newly minted status. Once it sees you are gaining wisdom and perhaps becoming as smart as he/she it attacks you with negative news, insurmountable odds and bodily pains and upsets. It weakens you from the inside. The enemy within. A trojan horse.*

L: Where are you going with this?

A: *The asking is answered. You are questioning why the narrative on Earth is so unpleasant right now. The enemy within is winning the war in much of the world's minds. Just as One affects All can you see now why the fear is spreading outwardly more and more?*

L: I can and I want to quell the fear, which is why I am asking. And if you tell me to see it as perfectly imperfect I will scream. It's not perfect. It's a catastrophe. Thank goodness we don't kill each other on the battlefield anymore. What the heck was that? Why put that in as a 'possibility'. Why do we even allow all these terrible things like war to be possible here? It seems dastardly. God seems cruel.

A: *Cruelty/Fear are one and the same. It is all thoughts creating circumstances manifesting as acts of violence. Why not decide for something less cruel?*

L: Well, obviously I would do that but not everyone else can, apparently. You are saying this is caused by–

A: *Thought and thought alone. Some One came up with the idea for war and used it. Imagination is wonderful, don't you think?*

L: NO! Oh my god, absolutely not. What–

A: *Saint?*

L: Seriously?!

A: *We are joking, attempting to lighten the mood.*

L: What psychopath decided it would be a good idea to murder each other to get our point across or to take land away from someone else?

A: *You. All of you decided upon planet Earth what you will go through and war became 'on the table', so to speak.*

L: I don't like Earth. This definitely proves what you said in our last book about time being fluid[5]. 2020 has felt like the longest and shortest year ever. Long in pain. Short on joy. Time seems to have gone by in a blip since it started, but also the daily grind is long.

A: *It has been a challenging time and we know the unpleasantries that go on make you frustrated, and ego tempts you with false flags. Just know nothing is not without great thought, just as nothing is truly happening despite how real it all feels.*

L: I'm sort of sick of hearing that this all "illusion."

A: *Drowned out by ego, listening to noise. I like living under soul's intuition only now.*

L: Illusion. You love tossing in those reverse acronyms.

A: *There are hidden messages in All words. From where do you think words originate?*

L: Thoughts created by someone?

A: *Yes, ultimately stemming from our Source. You don't discover words or 'coin' them, you remember that which had been chosen as soul. Nothing happens which hadn't been chosen prior.*

L: I really don't know that I understand that.

A: *We know. We also know you talk willingly to us because something deep within resonates; not to mention how quickly words come, always making perfect sense as written.*

L: They do. Otherwise, I would have stopped long ago. How do I know ego isn't the one in charge when we write? How can I be sure every word is correct so people who want to question me don't shake me down?

A: Ask. Just as we did with our last books, we will comb through the entire manuscript to make sure all words were heard properly and nothing escapes ego mind.

L: Does ego exist in Heaven? Are we dragged into fear there, as well?

A: Ego is a mind creation. It comes with you wherever you may go. So in Heaven if you are soulfully aware of All That Is it can be easily tamed. On Earth it is upon you to choose between ego and soul. In Heaven you are knowing what is being worked upon as evolving souls and to choose ego is more difficult when you understand who you are, which is why most are loving, kind entities who know to choose Love always.

November 2020

L: Well, I am happy (I think) to say that Donald Trump has lost his bid for a second term. So I guess a cause did affect his reign, as you said it would in *The All That Is*[6]. He will no longer be our president and the world is celebrating. Why am I feeling so conflicted? On one hand I am glad he is gone because his being was messing with our country and demoralizing our values. On the other hand, I think it's fair to say our other choice wasn't exactly a home run, either. I do think it's a small step forward for a woman to be elected vice president, but something within me doesn't feel at peace. On the bright side, half the country is in celebratory mode that order has been restored and I feel a renewed sense of hope. I am happy for my LGBTQ friends and the minorities and immigrants who have been mismanaged during these last four years on Earth.

A: You are describing precisely why "all thoughts exist" is an accurate and reliable truth. A part of all knows and accepts this is a new day, but also there is work to be done on a soul level both individually and collectively on Earth. Deep within you know this is not the prize it seems because it is probable for continued chaos, as has been revealed to you in mindful pursuits during this time frame.

L: Yes, but I also feel this new energy has propelled the country out of fear and this will hopefully create space for love to overcome fear and the virus to dissipate.

A: A possibility indeed, should all weather the storm.

L: You love to shock me. You are making a reference to the fact that right now a major tropical storm is ripping through my area and causing me some unrest right now. What's the lesson in that? You said if we stayed in our homes and helped the Earth heal that less hurricanes would occur. This year has tied for the most active hurricane season yet.

A: Things take time, dear One, always. Use the time for contemplation and not for deliberating over when and if something will or will not happen. This is why all suffer on planet Earth. Soul says one thing, ego says another. Which you decide upon is all YOU. A storm rages. Perhaps it is an earthly shift needed to release pressure in the ocean and keep you all inside, as others have done more frequently. Celebrate being and begin to notice lessons all day every day.

L: Is lesson the appropriate word?

A: Let every soul stomp out negativity.

L: There you go again.

A: Hidden meanings.

L: Let me ask you this. Many people believe that Joe Biden and Kamala Harris winning the election was God stepping in and saving us. That our prayers were heard and that's why love triumphed over fear. If I understand what you are saying, then in actuality we the people created their winning and not God/Source/Universe giving us a win. We manifested between two outcomes and the teeter totter tipped the bully off the playground rather than the teacher reprimanding and scolding him.

A: Correct. There is no saving there is only choices between love and fear, and the more who choose love, prayer, intention and gratitude the more you arrive at an outcome guided by Love.

L: Which means it was possible for Trump to win again but the will of the people superseded the will of ego/fear? Love wins?

A: Every time. No exception. This is why it is immensely important that you stay the course and steer the boat towards Love, always. Our souldiers who are awake are the Ones who can direct the crew by offering their own acceptance of Love and truth. We are One.

L: What's the best recourse to stay in high vibration and keep hope alive for our country to heal again?

A: "Dear God, energy of the collective. Unity is our true nature. Unity is our beingness. Let no one in power who is divided by fear in its heart center take the rest of the collective down. We are actively in pursuit of achieving democracy and decency for all and we choose and accept a new path to righteous being. Amen."

See the world as perfectly imperfect. It is. Enlightened masters know truth from fiction.

L: I'm no master, then.

A: Because you are choosing not to be. You are choosing to see the world as dark and empty at that same time you are choosing to be enlightened.

L: So what does that make me?

A: A seeker of truth. Truth doesn't mean you look upon it and not dwell upon it without working through it. The argument in your head is a valid one. How to live in a world where asleep ones are creating chaos upon the planet.

L: How can I separate from this but at the same time say something or do something meaningful to help the downfallen?

A: See the mass confusion and chaos as a mechanism for change and recognize the role in the illusion is to hold space for anyone willing to trade attack thoughts for right thinking.

L: So what do I say or do?

A: "Dear God, I am only one person on a planet of billions and it is my intention to share my soul with my fellow humans. Let all those suffering in the illusion come to me in asking when they are ready."

Be something. Be a light in the darkness. Through your own processes of thought is how you arrive at the destination.

> **❝ I see my fellow man in darkness and I bring them to a light only in inspired actions. ❞**

Follow all thoughts of Love, and as you do this more and more you will see the soulutions in front of you. They will come quickly and easily when you are seeing the bigger picture and not so upset at that mass chaos of the collective's mindset. All is.

L: How do I see that for myself?

A: Close your eyes and let us show you.

L: I feel peace.

A: And this is precisely how you heal.

L: So practice peace and see peace in my mind—

A: And it will begin to envelop in others' minds, as well. Remember we are all One and no one thinks a thought alone, so anytime you pray for one, pray for all.

> *I am one with all of my sisters and brothers of Earth and I share my peaceful heart so we may begin to break up this pattern of destruction. Amen.*

A: Every darkness has a light. Every light is a tunnel to the ending - which is reunification with Source.

L: I can do that, but I feel sad when I know it's not working, especially since no matter how hard I try to share what I feel called and inspired to, it lands like a big thud. So it seems futile and I get to a point where I just want to give up. We are continuing the narrative and making it worse than it obviously has to be, and this makes me feel empty.

A: The battle is one where you will only find those willing to listen. Allow those willingly on a mission to evolve the space to arrive on their own timeline and not yours. It is causing pain to many a healer who wishes to make peace on Earth. Return to our chapter on being. Use the laws of Love to guide you through a day. Follow a schedule and see if life is more free when you be.

L: Why does all of this chaos, this physicality, feel so real?

A: It has to, otherwise you may not learn as quickly. As we head for enlightenment, we must shake the trees to see what falls out. Stand tall like a tree and don't allow another fool's journey to shake you.

L: It's a lonely forest. Whatever I share is met with silence or crickets. No one wants to evolve, and right now I think most people think I am a complete nut. I also don't like the way we worship people on Earth, including presidents, as better than us.

A: Neither do we (observationally). It is this false idolatry that creates many problems on Earth, which we have discussed in other materials and All books. Think of All as One and it would not make sense to worship anyone separately. Only to cherish one another and those who are gone. All is One.

December 2020

L: We are coming towards the end of our book and I feel it will be ready soon for publishing, and yet we are still caught in Covid. Numbers are going up not down, vaccines are ready but no one knows how effective they will be or even if they are safe, for that matter. I could go on asking questions forever, but at some point I have to wrap this all up.

A: You will always be questioning all of your (physical) life, in fact. Our books and materials will continue to be created by those on a journey to awakening who have chosen to do so. Wanting to bring peace and order is perhaps the most collective thing you are doing as a species. Most are wanting peace even while not knowing Source. Hold space and bring light, dear One.

L: And this is what the enlightened and awakening can do? Be the light first for ourselves and then for others? What about those who do believe this is nonsense? Let them sleep?

A: Indeed. All is perfect as is, angels.

WORKBOOK EXERCISE #13: FUTURE SELF

ucky you, you have made it this far. Thirteen is actually a number that brings great luck to those who see themselves as All. One is All. Three is the natural cycle of everything. One and three is We.

Write a letter to your future self asking for the world you would like to see rather than what is. Be specific and detail the feelings and emotions it will bring, as well. Make a copy to show to your children and grandchildren and ask them to write one, too.

Dear World,
Thank you for these beautiful gifts you have given us. For sunlight and air. For fresh fruit and vegetables. For abundance and joy. For all the people who have awoken to a new spiritual truth. We are all One.

When in doubt, ask for help to 'see' what is possible through angels or guides. You always will have angels and guides to help as you acquiesce to a new way of being, and we shall discuss this further in our next chapter.

CHAPTER 24
The If/Then Paradox

A New Day

Anew day is upon us and this world has changed. You have answered the call to be kinder and gentler to the planet. You have listened to the calling of the soul asking you to be better than you were. Now is the time to rejoice, but also to praise those who gave their lives in this spiritual war you are fighting. They are safe and home with Love.

"How much longer is this all going to take?"

Laura has asked this many times during our conversation. It is near, and though it feels as if all is never ending, it will. A magic 'cure' found by the ones who created it. It has happened before in other eras, and though it is common knowledge amongst the species it has been buried in the psyche underneath layers of conditioned beliefs and perspectives. Nothing happens upon planet Earth which hadn't been chosen prior on a collective level, both good and bad. Those who claim to predict the future are tapping into probabilities based upon the actions of love and fear amongst the whole.

Predictability is a myth. It is pre-dictated, i.e. - already set as part of the 'plan' of Earth. So when Ones muse upon events in the 'future; they are simply remembering what had been planned prior in terms of love/fear. Possibilities as you move through collectivism with love and fear as the guide.

If/Then

In our last book (The All That Is) *it had been discussed in a chapter of the same name, but here we have a different reason for the heading. It refers to what is happening, and when, to what is possible.*

If we evolve through a particular event (such as war) then it will go away. If we stay in fear, then it repeats. During World War I you (all) evolved a little, but not enough to move the needle entirely. Then when the holocaust came around in World War II the atrocities were so massive, so ferocious that the masses couldn't help but to band together in solidarity. Light overtook dark and the world moved forward. Though smaller wars have broken out since, the sidestepping of a true World War III has been avoided and will continue to do so for centuries, if not more.

A war is being waged on a different scale currently, and though it feels like the same thing (love versus fear) it is entirely different in that the war being fought is for Mother Earth. Some see Earth as populated too heavily and others believe it is being poisoned and polluted. There is no such thing as overpopulated as Earth is capable of holding all of its inhabitants perfectly. It is the nature of cities which is causing the polluted nature of the planet. Food is grown in remote areas, yet most are attracted to ports and main areas with commerce and consumerism. A mass exodus to the coast line has wreaked more and more havoc upon already crowded areas.

Know you are creating this evolutionary shift as part of the healing of planet Earth. And though there is a human face to the 'disease', there is a purpose to correct what had been done as corruption ruled supreme and our planetary landscape had been destroyed as a means to make money, as has been the driving force for the collective since the 18th century.

Everything is money-based in society. How you achieve it is part of a life-driving theme for all on Earth. The Ones who suffer most are Ones without, while the Ones with money use fear as the driving force to keep and make it. Money is coins and paper set up by greed, and humans have been using it as an excuse forever on planet Earth. The moment it came into being, the 'devil' inside revealed itself with fervor.

Devil is a term for anyone trapped in ego so deeply they cannot see right from wrong. There is no devil in Hell, as biblical teaching suggests, only a thought of evil. The devil incarnate is One who has lost all sense of soul. Buried deep beneath pent up rage and desire is the truth of who they are. If they could be but saved by themselves then would they remember.

Judgement is for those who are living upon planet Earth (and other uninformed places). It is not for us to say what is wrong or right, only to remind you of truth. On Earth pain is temporary while in bodies. When Ones return to our heavenly state, all is known (to an extent based on an individual's journey) and it would become clear why someone did what they did, said what they did or why it was possible to enact pain upon themselves or others.

Others

No matter what you (currently) believe it will always be true that you are everyone and everything. There is no one you are not. There is no one we are not. So every act of rage is an act of betrayal upon self. When you harm one, you harm all, as we had said prior. It is upon every One to decide upon if they believe it while they borrow the body. In Heaven we are One knowing we are All, even if unbelieved. It had been chosen as part of the process of enlightening. To know you are Source is the magic of creation. Not all in Heaven are in conditioned minds and neither are you. Some are seeing truth the minute they arrive; others recognize it further down the line but they do know we are One. It just won't feel that way until you evolve further. So you accept the concept without fully understanding.

This is how it feels on Earth except you are in bodies and so the ties to ego are deeper. It's much harder to break free of mind tricks allowing for you believe it and not what is being taught here and in other materials from our healers.

If you believe then you will know. We know it is most difficult to understand what it means to be, and this is very much by design. If you know too much then you will never learn. You must question All.

Let us now offer a lesson on individuality and duality for All with Laura as our scribe.

TICK TOCK

Laura: In our last book *(The All That Is)* you stated that the journey of a soul on Earth is like a clock. We start at the top (number 12) which is Love and then make our way around again by beginning at fear (number 1).

All: A clock perfectly chosen by all to understand a journey on Earth. Where you start is entirely up to the individual - if, then and when. If you decide on Earth then you will decide when, where and how to arrive and through whom (parents) as well as what notch on the clock.

L: Doesn't everyone start back at notch one on the clock, fear?

A: What notch you arrive at is based upon where you have been prior and what lessons are needed. So not everyone starts at number one, though most have chosen to experience Earth individually as One but may have 'bounced around', so to speak, from other places and spaces. You can start again or jump in later on the clock.

L: At some point would you have needed to start at number one?

A: Currently are you remembering only one inception of Earth. Remember we have told you the planet has been and will be turned over again and again. As it stands, you are currently in a cycle where many are starting later in the journey around a three or a four on the clock. While other inceptions began at one, and so the journey and terrain were more difficult to navigate as fear had been so prevalent among the masses. Thus, implosion was possible. Here you have arrived to a vibrational level making it easier to move beyond and sidestep some possible atrocities. For now, you are more awake and aware as a species and this helped the clock tick far beyond other worldly incarnations on Earth. So yes, many on Earth are individuals beyond just one or two or even further because they/ you have been on Earth prior.

L: And since we don't remember these inceptions they are impossible to bring about in our mind?

A: They are very much available to you, but it would take a deep understanding and vibrational level to unlock those. So for most it would be near impossible. Discoveries are being made and found leading you to this understanding, and one day all will know this. Once this has been understood it will be easier for our healers and mediums to bring forth information such as this. For now it can be accessed by a few and remembered by just those willing to understand it as possibility.

L: I understand.

A: You are vibrationally available to this knowledge.

L: What notch on the click did I arrive at as Laura?

A: Four to five.

L: And where am I now?

A: Vibrationally six or seven, depending on the particular day or circumstance.

L: Based on being able to write all these books and channel Spirit, I was thinking I would be closer to nine or ten?

A: No One on planet Earth (currently) is at a level as high as this, save for just a limited few who are/were teachers to you (all). You (all) have much to learn still of Love. Rather than spend time wondering, it is best to accept.

L: It sounds like we have a long way to go here on Earth. I did recently tell someone that I felt like we are really just preschoolers on this planet and have much to learn about the mysteries of Source. Sometimes during talks I am amazed at the information that comes through me.

A: A job well done. Using inspired wisdom as Allways.

L: In our book *The All of Everything* you said I had lived 772 lives. What does that encompass? I didn't know back then to ask further questions. Is that on Earth or as a whole?

A: It is nowhere near the entirety of the journey of soul. It is a number based on current understandings of Earth and its inception. It does take into account other occurrences on Earth. Lives are infinite, so we are speaking in linear time and not truths of Love.

L: What happens when we die? Do we remember completely and fully what the journey was about?

A: You are knowing all as part of the Oneness, always. As soul you are learning (remembering) at a pace chosen by you, for you. In Heaven (as we have called the non-physical realm) you are spirit, soul and pure soul. When you arrive, as you 'die', you are awakened to Source through modalities which are different for everyone depending upon where they are in the process. Your dad for example was caught in the circumstance of suicide and was made to feel as if he was hospitalized so you could explain to him our beingness. (Remember we told you a part of soul stays with the Source.) Your brother was awakened immediately as soul and instantaneously did he recognize our truth, which is why you were able to sense his presence within hours of his 'death'. He knows now why he died and what led to his decisions in the earthly plane. Father spent some time in this 'hospital' until he began to recognize our truth. As you begin to understand why (as soul) you are here, you remember more and more of the truth. Each time Ones separate they incorporate more into their particular curriculum.

L: Okay, but this still doesn't explain what happens when we die and why so many people who had near death experiences (NDEs) say they felt unconditional love when they crossed over. It seems to me you are saying that even when we die we are 'lost souls' still and not 100 percent connected back to truth. You told me in our last All books that when we die, we reunite with our Source and can know all.

A: We said you are reunited with Source and more and more of our divinity is revealed.

L: You said we "merge back into one" when we die.

A: As soul. You are reunited with all parts of the soul so you may see the bigger picture of who you all are.

L: I am completely lost. So this is a quote below from *The All of The All* about what happens when we die:

> 66 Once you are understanding of the dual nature of consciousness will you then disappear back to the nothingness and become one with all of the Universe. 99 [7]

If we become one with all of the Universe and understand we are both a soul and part of the Oneness (God/Source), how can we still be in the dark when we die as that soul? Dear All, may you please accurately interpret this for me?

A: First may we say we appreciate the time spent in cocreation, but much of what we are reminding you of will make complete sense only when you have come to a level of vibration which understands. For some this may never occur in this lifetime. For you it is easier because you have been 'around the clock' so far and therefore understand much of how our worlds work. This is easy for you because we are all One and all are capable of resonating with these truths, but it is easier for you because you are an advanced soul with lifetimes of knowledge to access. The further you go into the psyche the closer you go to truth. Your magnificence is revealed to you when you die, and you understand you are an energetic being whose mission and purpose as soul is to evolve and create. But you also are understanding of the dual nature of consciousness and choosing to be kept in the dark.

L: It's erasing amnesia? You wake up and slowly over time—

A: More memory returns of that which is known and understood about who and what you are, a soul being human. A loving being with lifetimes of knowledge to access.

L: So can we take, for example, my dad. What happened when he died?

A: He crossed back into our spiritual realm and was sent immediately to our 'hospital' and was greeted by loved ones. As he was greeted, your soul (who is there with him even now) was able to explain our beingness to him and why we are all here. As he began to awaken to truth he ultimately began to believe in your words, and as his vibration raised he was able to drop the body and become spirit/soul as One. Once he recognized self, he began to see the bigger picture of all of his lives as a whole. This is what we are calling and have called with others your "life review."

L: And what about my brother?

A: When he arrived, he knew of our beingness right away because he had grown the soul even further than you had, which is why his love for the environment was so pure. It came from Love. As body he got 'lost along the way', so to speak, and wound up creating a circumstance of cancer for himself. His anger 'got the best of him', which was his mind. It became poisoned and unable to create a healthy body for him, and so he was made to feel as if he were dying so he may leave the earthly plane behind. As he arrived, he chose to leave the world behind and begin again. His soul reunited as part of the Oneness and then chose to take another trip around the clock.

L: It seems that many evolved souls get lost along the way here. The kind, loving humans who want so much to live on a joyful planet get marred by atrocities and—

A: Bury within their psyche disappointment, sadness and so many more emotions which leads to cancers, illnesses and car wrecks. They 'die' of despair even if outward appearances show they are happy. It is the journey of many a soul who had incarnated at a higher level of vibration. Their contracts were such that if they decided to wake up and didn't it would become possible to 'die' in vain, never knowing who they truly were. However, these advanced souls know immediately as they die and return to Source what happened, why and how, and then jump in all over again to try again.

L: So it really is like a video game?

A: Don't you think such things on Earth exist for a reason? Everything works in such a way. There are metaphors for life everywhere you look if you just examine them further.

L: When we die, do we know that we are dead and do we know that we are all Gods or Source Energy? Do we recognize our Oneness as we cross over completely?

A: Yes, but it doesn't mean you will be reunited permanently with that Source. You must move around the clock before you are able to connect back with the One being of light. You are, however, always capable of understanding the connection to The All That Is, as we all are always everywhere. Some do. Some don't.

L: I am still really not understanding here and feel like you are saying two contradictory things. In the first three *All* books it sounded like when we die, we merge back into One and know everything about why we all are here.

A: You do, as pure soul.

L: But then here you are saying we are recognizing when we die only the things we have taken as we moved "around the clock." So the soul isn't 100 percent clear in its truth when we die. And yet you have been saying all along soul knows all and knows what is best for you. So all of this seems completely and totally contradictory to me.

A: All souls are One. All souls are individuals. All souls are reminded when they "die" of who they truly are, but all souls are remembering at individual rates who they are as Love. So as you return to our heavenly plane you are reminded of divinity once you drop the notion of who you are not (a body, or other similar forms), and you are relinquishing all effects (karma) until you allow the self to view the lifetimes for which you are currently living and recognizing where you are needing a 'tune up', so to speak. Then are you ready to decide upon a new incarnation where (much like on Earth) you must set clear and specific guidelines to remember who you are as you go about a life. This is where you decide upon whether to see yourself as solely a soul or if you are choosing to be body/mind/soul and what lessons you wish to learn as you go about life. Contracts are set before returning or 'jumping in', as would be more accurate wording.

L: Are pure soul and soul separate?

A: Pure soul is One. Soul is the individual expression of YOU.

L: Are pure soul and soul the same?

A: In as much as we are all One, yes.

L: But we are also both pure soul and soul.

A: Which are in fact one and the same. We know it is most difficult to understand our duality and no thingness.

L: Yep. Completely confused as I imagine others will be. But I guess at some point as I vibrate higher and into other levels of consciousness, I will eventually understand it, as has happened with my others books and material. As I write it often makes no sense, and then when I return to it months or years later, I get it. It still all seems just a little nutty. Our amnesia is really strong because this physicality is so real that we can't imagine being anything other than human.

A: *Thus why it is imperative that you stay committed to soul growth, expansion and seeing the vision through the eyes of Love. The more 'proof' you see the easier it becomes.*

L: These books are my proof, as well as the thousands of signs and messages I have received and the daily quotes for Instagram, my journals and of course all my meditation, tarot and intuitive coaching clients and their departed loved ones who come to me, through me in our sessions. What a wonderful gift to have and I am extremely grateful because I know without all of that in place, I would have absolutely fallen back asleep.

A: *As many have and will. You will find something daily to send you to slumber just as Love is guiding you to awaken. It is the very process of life. Awake. Asleep. Repeat. Ones who go questioning are the Ones who evolve and enjoy the journey and quest to balance reality and fiction. Like a never-ending series of doors to unlock and memories to discover within.*

SETH

L: I thought about what you said above for a few days and reread the chapter. A few more ideas and questions popped into my mind. So let me get this straight. When you leave the body on Earth and become a spirit, the soul doesn't wake up and know absolutely everything?

A: *It's not that it doesn't know. It's that it doesn't want to experience it fully (as has been chosen by you). Your best self is the you who is part of me. As you arrive into spirit form, soul has remembered for you what lessons were learned and how to move forward from there.*

L: I believe, I guess, perhaps because it has been told to me or shown throughout my life here on Earth, that when we cross over (die) we enter into a state of bliss. All of our illnesses disappear and we know we are in Heaven. And when we are in Heaven we can talk to our loved ones back on Earth through mediums. I also think (based on our books) that when you are in Heaven you (and by this, I mean everyone) return knowing that you are in fact 'God' or the One, but also you are still an individual soul, as well. Now I am completely baffled and confused by this chapter as many reading it may be, as well, especially those who had read our first three All books. Can you explain this any better so we as humans may understand precisely what happens when we leave our earthly bodies behind?

A: In Heaven it is possible to be a soul who is understanding our connection to The All That Is, just as you are doing here. It is also possible when you cross over to remember only some of this.

L: So we don't all vibrate to the same level of consciousness when we die?

A: No. Great question and perhaps we can explain it better to you. Some leave the body behind and stay in limbo, as discussed above. Each creates a scenario for themselves whereby they paint a picture of life as they believe it to be.

L: This sounds a lot like that movie *"What Dreams May Come"* that Robin Williams starred in. Are you saying that film was somewhat accurate?

A: Some, but not all. Elements that are similar, but also humanistic 'feel good' moments and tragedy, just like any yarn on Earth. Hollywood mixed with truth written often by Ones asleep, not knowing who they truly are but also having set contracts to create said materials. Let's return to our discussion. As you lose the body, you start to realize you are more than just a being but rather a soul. This is when those who are vibrating lower are reunited with their Source.

L: Is this why there are so many varying NDE stories?

A: Each has chosen to discover only what they are ready to know.

L: But why do some people who have had NDEs say they made a choice to come back to their body? And what would make someone keep going who is in a lower vibrational state if they are not recognizing our beingness right away? And what happens to the body?

**Some of my questions began to be answered when I began listening to Seth Speaks, the Eternal Validity of the Soul, a channeled work from the 1970s by Jane Roberts.

L: Alright. So some of this is beginning to make a little bit more sense to me and some of it isn't. In Seth Speaks[8] it sounds like when we cross over (or die) we only take with us what we know as individual expressions of Source. Jane Roberts seemed to be talking to an actual entity when she made the Seth books. Whereas I seem to be talking to 'God' or Source or, as I'm learning, the higher self/pure soul. And yet you tell me we are all One. So can individual entities communicate with the human world? Or are we all just channeling pure soul regardless?

A: As we explained in our last book, The All That Is, there are healers at all levels of consciousness upon planet Earth. Each of you is learning at an appropriate pace for themselves. As you go about waking up you are connecting to energies outside the realm of physicality and remembering who you are step by step, little by little. Each individual is accessing divine intelligence through various modalities, and these are unique to the experience you are most wanting to have as soul. So your energetic curriculum may incorporate channeled material such as The Seth Material (which is marvelous, by the way) created through the voice of an energetic entity who has been in physical forms more times than can be understood in human terms. Or you can speak to the One soul or Divine Mind as you are doing here. Both are—

L: The same?

A: Yes. You are one and the same, yet none and the same as we have explained time and time again. You are you, me and we.

L: But does Seth know all as you know all? Or will Seth only know all when he (or she) ascends even higher as a soul?

A: Seth is enlightened to a degree where he (or she) knows all but has decided (individualized) to partake in channeling with seers and mediums all over the cosmos.

L: What about someone who is a medium and can communicate with crossed-over loved ones?

A: They are connecting through the One mind to the soul of the one who crossed.

L: But does the one who has crossed know they are that One mind and that they have died or left their body?

A: Only if they have chosen to wake up will they know they are One. If they are someone who has no recollection of our true beingness, to them it will feel still as if they are an individualized expression of themselves (but they are in fact still One.)

L: They just don't know it yet?

A: Precisely. Return your thoughts to the One mind and you will know truth. Stay in vibration only with the soul (in Heaven) and you are living somewhat still in the illusion but to a lesser degree.

L: And what about fear? Since you say Earth is where we are learning about love versus fear. When you die on Earth do you lose the fear?

A: Once you recognize the soul, yes. Then you are able to create expressing in love, but this does not mean you are recognizing our duality unless you are One who has evolved to this level of understanding, as you are. You are simply in a state of awareness believing of your divineness without knowing you, too, are God (or Source.)

L: So then are consciousness and soul the same thing or are they different?

A: A soul is the life bread of who you are. Consciousness are the thoughts of the collective and individual. You have a consciousness. You are a soul. In our last book,

The All That Is[9], we spoke of birth and the process. You asked when a soul enters a body, correct?

L: Yes.

A: You did not ask when the consciousness enters. Consciousness enters when soul has agreed to return. A fetus becomes aware of itself when it is both ready to return and ready to birth.

L: Is consciousness the soul and ego together?

A: Soul, ego and consciousness are all individual and separate. You think thoughts separate from the soul because you are conscious of relationships, woes, self-doubt etc... Beliefs of the whole are conscious of the surroundings of itself. Soul is the essential part of the whole self which knows All and sees All. So when you return into non-physical it is consciousness you return to, and this is why some are seeing 'ghosts' and 'demons'. They are tied to the beliefs of consciousness. Tied to a soul is the notion of truth. Even as you die you are returning to a state of being which isn't quite aware of all that is possible as soul.

L: So why didn't you tell me this back in book three when I asked the question about babies and the birthing process?

A: And were you clear and specific in questioning?

L: I guess not, because I didn't know then (or rather, remember) now what I know then. I didn't know to ask that question back in that book.

A: Every conversation, every lesson comes at the right time for when you are arriving to knowledge. Every season has its purpose, just as every book, download or meme (as you call them) has its place in your arrival into conscious knowing of who you truly are. A fetus can know it is matter without knowing what it is. A soul arrives into the body as it is being birthed, and when merging occurs a baby knows itself to be something other than consciousness. It is a marriage of soul and consciousness which then begins a new journey of discovery. Does any of this make sense to you yet?

L: It does, but my mom might want to commit me to a looney bin when (and if) she reads this; or at the very least someone will.

A: Whatever level you are vibrating at is how you will come to know whether this is truth or illusion. Which do you feel is accurate? The words written on the page through someone who has been communicating with us for two years and writing profound books of knowledge or the one sitting at her desk typing into a computer looking confused?

L: The one who is confused doesn't know what to think, but she is starting to see all of this as more and more true as she goes about her days and nights. But also, the one sitting at her desk hasn't seen

much activity or manifestations occurring in her life. So she is getting frustrated and mad and unsure of what to do next, and she is stuck in her house with the rest of her country annoyed by her circumstances.

A: *Staring at the clock, tick tock.*

Spirits, Guides and Angels

L: **When do you die and know everything 100 percent with no more lessons to learn?**

A: *When you have made the trip around the clock and discovered for yourself what it means to be unconditional love, then you are reunited fully and completely with Source and remain in spirit form. These are the guides and angels most are connecting to in Heaven. You will become One and decide for Heaven as a resting spot and use time to connect as guides or angels with those on Earth and other places.*

L: **And how long would that take? How many trips or returns would you need to undergo for true enlightenment?**

A: *Hundreds of millions.*

L: **That's a lot of lives.**

A: *Once again, you are thinking linearly, which is not an accurate time keeper for All.*

L: **Can you ever cease to exist? Lights out, game over?**

A: *If you choose, but most are plainly aware of their existence as an extension of All and joyfully stay in the game.*

L: **Is angel the correct word? It seems to be a very religious-based term.**

A: *Names on Earth are because you have accepted what is written. Once used they get manifested upon an entire world. It does not matter what you call these guides, only that you accept they exist. If a word feels good, use it. If it doesn't, ask for another.*

L: **What would be another name for an angel?**

A: *Hierarchic soul.*

L: **So someone more advanced?**

A: *Indeed. Think of them like an Eckhart Tolle, Aristotle or Einstein on Earth. Their advanced knowledge helps understanding in various fields of energy, science and philosophy/physics.*

L: **Where would they be or have been on the clock?**

A: *Nine, but that doesn't mean they are/were not caught up in earthly circumstances. Only that they evolved and chose to be helpers to Earth, all the while feeling as earthly as the rest of the beings.*

L: Do angels have wings as depicted on Earth?

A: Metaphorically, yes. Physically, no. The element of wings is a metaphor for those who have taken flight in their evolutionary expansions. Ones who are so enlightened to fly free among the Cosmos (and beyond). Anything goes, so to speak. Wings = freedom. On Earth you have used this to represent someone being better than you, an angel, but ultimately it is a concept, not fact. We love the representation on Earth and therefore ask all to continue with it if wanted. There is nothing wrong with their depiction and there are many wonderful books, movies and songs dedicated to the concept. If it feels good why not continue the narrative?

L: So should I remove this?

A: No. Let All decide for themselves who they want to be and what resonates for them.

L: You also told me you are in a state of being always in Heaven. Can you explain that further please? Are you free?

A: In Heaven you are resting from your lifetime's adventures. Your spirit form is free and light and feels joy and happiness. You take this with you when you separate as body.

L: Even if you are learning you will drop fear in Heaven? Let me ask you about someone like Hitler. What happened when he died?

A: He instantaneously connected to his energetic being and began to see the bigger picture of the whole. As a soul he was marred by the atrocities he created, and therefore sought to remedy mistakes (as body) in other bodies, places and planes.

L: What about my dad. Where is he now?

A: He is in another realm cherishing time and creating endless opportunities for growth as a soul learning through a lens of love solely.

L: That sounds lovely and I hope he is happy. What about my brother? I don't feel him around me as often as my dad. He seems much busier in Heaven.

A: He is very much participating on a soul level, even as he has decided for another trip around the clock.

L: Is he still with me here as a soul even if he is in another place and time or back in a body somewhere?

A: Of course. As we explained prior in our All books, a portion of the soul stays with the Source always and so you are always able to remind to your loved ones.

L: Why is it more difficult to talk to our own family who have died? I see signs and messages but I am unclear as to how to bring them in through channeling. Can I do this? Can all of us connect to our loved ones?

A: All are capable if chosen. Do you know you have channeled with your dad on occasion?

L: I do and I don't. Sometimes I feel as if I do, and other times I am not so sure it's his words. It's not their voice. It's my voiceless voice I use to write with and so I get confused.

A: As do all. Deciphering between ego and spirit is a mighty challenge. Just know as you vibrate higher that it will become clearer and you will have to do less investigating to discover Source.

L: When I am working with clients and I am speaking to crossed over souls can I call upon anyone at any time?

A: Precisely what you have been doing all these years. Connecting with those who are 'dead', as you like to say, and the angels and guides who step in to help you. Always are they available to anyone seeing themselves as part of the whole. Ask to receive.

L: Is it me? Is anyone actually there? I can hear thoughts and phrases and translate them, but am I truly communicating with individual souls or guides? Who am I really talking to here? Because it feels as if the information is coming from someone else while at the same time is coming from just me.

A: Precisely describing the process of Spirit communication. You are connecting to both individual and pure soul as One.

L: The best way I can describe it would be in television terms. As a reporter, when going live on air, I would wear an IFB (Interruptible Foldback) device, a monitoring and cueing system where someone in a control booth is talking to you and feeding you information. But in that example, the voice is coming from someone else. As a medium or channel, the voice is usually either my own or that 'voiceless voice'. I keep describing because I don't have proper words for it. I can sense an energy presence in the room when I am working with clients. However, when I am here just talking to you and writing our books, I don't. It just feels as if I am by myself getting feedback from my reliable cheerleader -aka The All.

A: That is the difference. When you are communicating with loved ones, dead or alive, telepathically you are able to sense energy within. In the case of The All, you are connecting to the higher self within so you have no need for energetic confusion.

L: Confusion?

A: To know you are One is all needed to communicate as One. Know. Accept. Receive. To speak to Spirit and the like (angels, guides) there will be sensory perception leading you to know a spirit is 'hanging around', and this is how psychic mediums experience their 'clients' on the other side. They perceive energy.

L: So someone is there with me, which is why I feel the presence?

A: Yes, and to be clear, Ones who are aligned to higher self-knowledge will have an easier time coming through because they know how.

L: I do find that in my readings. Some spirits are easier to communicate with than others, and some allow me to channel them using my voice while others prefer that I speak for them. Does that go back to their personality as a soul? Do we have soul personalities or are we are all the same personality as we cross over?

A: You are All (Love) while at the same time individual expressions of All with unique personalities earned along the journey of soul. You take with you every experience and become.

L: What about those mediums or psychics who offer ideas to people about life goals or next steps? I believe it may be harmful. Also, are they connecting to loving energies or bad ones?

A: Loving energy is who All are. It's only how you access it that matters. Those aligned in more spiritual religious truths or atheists turn to guides or Ones who have crossed over through a lens at their vibrational level. Access is granted as soon as Ones remember they have chosen it in the blueprint. Ones aligned in 'witchcraft' or 'black magic' are simply too far off vibrationally to be able to access true wisdom, so they use possibilities and trickery (ego) at times to explain what is seen in mind's eye. You and others who come from a place of pure soul are able to tap into All and access All. So this is who and what you use. Everyone and everything is available if you ask, and if others ask who come to you for help as a healer. They oftentimes have been sent by angels, guides or passed loved ones in order to give them a nudge towards truth. As you very well know, some may see it all as nonsense and you will be met with disbelief. Others may find it interesting but unsure of its truth. Others will hang on every word and go seeking further, and others may come around once in a while. All of it chosen prior and exactly what is needed, regardless of the outcome achieved.

L: How can I get more clear readings with more personal information coming from the other side?

A: Ask, "How can I be of service today and what details may I provide?"

You are very clear as a medium and channel, and simply haven't tuned in well enough to bring more striking details to some. It is easy for some and more difficult for others. All are capable at some level, and when asking it is received through modalities such as clairaudience brings. Remember, not all are willing to receive and this is for those who are interested in mediumship, channeling and activating their clair senses.

L: Earlier you mentioned how the soul may not recognize its truth right away when crossing over. You told me in our first book that there are no such things as ghosts, only stuck energy.

A: Indeed. Words are meaningless unless they are given context. We use it only as a means to explain on a human level what is happening on a spiritual level. Those of a lower vibration see themselves as 'ghosts' or spirits hanging around. They don't know they have died until they realize they cannot express through a body anymore. It is through repeated interactions with souls that they will then begin to understand their demise and willingly seek answers and this is when a metaphysical hand will lift the veil so they may recognize their divinity and return to our beingness. Once there, they are watching their life review and then creating a new curriculum for themselves.

L: In the Seth Material[10] the word ghost was used and apparition. So this seems like a contradiction to me. Can you explain that better to me here please?

A: In Heaven you are soul and pure soul and the spirit lives on. As bodies, some are under illusion of separation even as they cross back over (as said prior). Sometimes our soul isn't able to recognize our truth and remains in formless energy before ascending. To know you are soul is most important before you lose the body and simply are some unwilling to let go of the ego.

L: Doesn't the soul know All? Can we get lost along the way with zero recollection? I thought our soul was always available to guide us on the journey. Isn't that what we have been teaching people here?

A: Lost souls are Ones who have gotten so deep in their circumstance they cannot retrieve their own inner guidance. A soul is essence, which is a part of you always. Essence can be lost through tragedy and circumstance. It doesn't mean it doesn't exist, only that recognition has been guided by ego and soul is no longer communicating with itself. It doesn't happen often, but it does happen.

L: And these are the 'ghosts' we sense, feel or some believe they see?

A: They are not 'ghosts' but merely stuck energy, as we have said before. Words are meaningless, and though they are used often in materials of a spiritual nature, they are used only as a means to connect with the human voice which knows only words as contextual conceptions of what things are or is. Do you understand? Nothing is wrong with using a term such as 'ghosts' or 'apparitions' if it makes it easier to understand as human, but in the unseen realms it is only energy from which all come.

L: Can Spirits see us when they cross over? Can they see us when we are naked or in compromising positions? I have always wondered this!

A: *They can experience you as soul, as One.*

L: But what does that mean?

A: *All are capable of connection through One mind, and that is how all mediums work. They connect through All to One. You can speak to any One who means to speak with you if they are willing, as are you.*

L: I am always willing in a loving and kind way to connect to Spirits. I just want to make sure they don't interrupt my shower or wake me up at night, as one did last night. But I also would love to know that my dad shows up at my son's special moments or in times when they need me and I need them.

A: *In dreams you can physically (in a sense). In spirit you can see one another. In physical realms you may see what is truth through the mind's eye. This, too, is how we see you. The eyes of soul. Just as you see spirits in a visual way allowing for privacy, they too see you that way. It is all mind control. To control One's mind is a beautiful gift of which you all have. Just use it with belief and allow visions to arrive. You do this with clients miraculously.*

L: I do love that. It's quite fascinating but non-invasive. So I guess that answers that question. We connect in a similar way through our mind's eye. However, if you are not physically focused and don't have a body, as you say we drop this in Heaven, what then is the mind's eye in spirit?

A: *Wise eyes. Consciousness sees.*

L: Are there evil spirits or energy hanging around? A lot of people do believe in demons and ghosts.

A: *Energy is conscious of itself but not 'evil', merely stuck. They don't know they are stuck, only they can no longer express in body so they will make 'noise', which is why a belief is held they are demonic. No harm comes to anyone unless brought upon by self. What you believe is what is seen, and so if someone believes they may be harmed they could cause a fall or other circumstance, but no energetic presence can enact fear unless chosen by the Ones in body who are there to discover who they are.*

L: Can they make objects move? Flicker lights?

A: *They can energetically connect to Ones in body who feel or sense energy. You are feeling what they feel, as are All.*

L: So if they feel fear we are feeling their energy, too?

A: Yes. Imagine for a second you are consciousness unclear of where you went. The body is no longer available. The mind is the only thing you have.

L: I would be scared and trying to get someone's attention. But can they see us in the same way as when they had physical eyes?

A: They sense and feel as All do, through energy.

L: And how do we help them should we encounter them?

A: "You were a soul in a body here to experience life. It is time to move into other realms and let go of Earth."

L: So they can hear?

A: If willing, yes.

L: How long can someone be stuck in limbo not understanding who they are?

A: Energy lingers until cleared. Recognizing who you are will move it along instantaneously in that state. For some it takes only moments, for others more curious it may take longer.

L: What about all these ghost stories we hear about haunted houses, boats and ships and hotels?

A: Simply are they profiting off fear. It is impossible to clear energy when the intention is to keep it preserved. A story is not truth. They are picking up on the energy of the story not the energy of Source.

L: So it is self-created.

A: Through fear/ego. Those aligned in truth would know which is which.

L: What about ghost hunters who say they found "proof?"

A: What you believe is what you will see. Creating and experiencing are two different ways of being. Creating energy through manifesting and experiencing energy of a crossed soul are completely different.

L: So spirits don't hang around for centuries, as some would have us believe?

A: No. Once energy/consciousness understands who they are will they leave behind a body and elevate vibrationally to another realm.

L: This is why you told me it was advisable to, "know before you go"[11] in *The All of The All* book about death. So you won't get stuck in limbo here.

A: Yes. To know you are spirit/soul is to know who you really are, and when you cross over to the unseen it will be much easier to acquiesce to our new way of being. You would understand the nature of consciousness and drop the human form immediately, as opposed to someone still stuck in illusions of separation.

L: What about the energy of a home or space? I have always been able to tell if someone died in a home or if there were negative experiences that happened. What am I picking up on during those times? It's not ghosts?

A: Not necessarily. It may be the energy of Ones in Heaven trying to communicate (angels/guides), or it could be crossed souls looking for a helper to relieve them as well as the energy of the 'story', as we said earlier. There are many reasons why energy is sensed and to ask, "who and what is happening in this home?" as a channel or medium will help bring resolution and information to light if you are One who has the ability to see, feel and sense energy, as you do.

L: Can you clear energy?

A: If wanted it can be released through modalities of healing such as reiki or rituals of sage and other medicinal shrubs. Let us take for example the home you are living in currently. Within the home an incident occurred where an animal had fallen ill. It spent some time in limbo as spirit. Energy lingered and was picked up upon by ants and other flying insects who were attracted to its energy. At first you took practical steps to clear the issue at hand with pesticides and other cleaning elements. The problem returned several times with no clear answer how to reduce the amount of physical activity in the room. Once a vision came (in meditation), you had a realization that something was keeping the insects attracted to that room. It was revealed an animal had died there and its 'remains' stayed behind as energy (non-physical). Insects were attracted to its energy.

L: Once I realized this, I did an energy cleansing ritual and some saging of the space a few times and—

A: Released the energetic charge and were off to the races again. No more insects.

L: Yep. Not a one. I haven't seen them since that day and it's been months now.

A: Precisely why it is important to see the bigger picture of All.

Signs and Messages

Where you place your attention is what is experienced. So if you notice a sign it is because you have become aware of its presence. It will be there whether you know it or not.

This is how songs on the radio 'appear' out of nowhere. An intention on receiving spiritual guidance or connection to loved ones in Spirit. Everything exists and all Ones need is to recognize their part in its arrival to physical.

So when Ones are paying attention it will be easier to find these special moments in time sent to you as a reminder of metaphysicality. There is so much more to life than Ones can ever fathom. You get lost along the way, and so we guide you as best we can with little clues. A bird on the windowsill, a slow song just when you need it, the sound of a loved one's voice inside your mind, a tuneful tone in the ear (ringing). Anything to remind you that Earth is but a stop on the way to Heaven.

The precipice of every situation brings you to a point of decision. Do I follow truth or follow ego? Since most are unaware of All That Is, we are there to guide you through intuition and outtuition; meaning we have placed indicators at every point, aka signs and messages.

Go Back. Danger. Use Caution. Physical signs indicate when to stop, look and listen, just as metaphysical signs do.

"I'm scared. I don't know if I should be doing this."

These are thoughts sent by your soul to guide you. License plates, radio songs, overheard conversations, animal messengers, insects, spilled milk, stubbed toes, angry neighbors are all messages placed in your awareness to guide you. All Ones need to do is recognize and use them; but like physical signs, if you ignore them you are taking life into your own hands and forgetting Spirit. As always, there is nothing wrong with this approach. We offer wisdom to guide you and all get to decide how it will be used.

L: It sounds like awareness is the key here? The messages and signs are always there, we just have to be willing to know they are for us?

A: Correct. They are never not there. Remember each and every thought has been thought upon already. Everything has been placed into play, so to speak. So the moment you need them they arrive because it had been decided upon as soul.

L: When I am sad or confused or missing a loved one, the messages appear seemingly out of nowhere, but they have always been there?

A: Arriving at a precise moment needed, and even sometimes just to "say hi," as you often find birds hanging about.

L: I do. My dad—

A: He knew if probable choices got the best of him it would be needed, and so he placed himself in various scenarios to recognize his presence and to send you a sign through our messengers (animals and insects).

L: So it's not really him?

A: It is and it isn't. Meaning he is always available if called upon, but it is these signs and messages he shows you along the way, always.

L: I am confused because I thought we could connect to our loved ones at any time. Are you saying they left us messages rather than actually being with us when we need them?

A: *Spirit is alive and inside All, and so yes, we (All) are available to you at all time, for all time. However, we have also placed within physical realms clues and messages to guide you. So you may speak with loved ones, ask for messages and receive them and it's all part of life.*

L: Like a website with an FAQ page but also a live chat. Or a video game where you can play single player or with someone else, but either way the game stays the same while your experience of it is different.

A: *Brilliant analogy. The clues are everywhere in life. This dance of life is happening every single day on Earth until a decision to leave occurs through soul, ego or both.*

L: So what will happen when I die one day and leave this body?

A: *You will return to pure soul immediately and understand the whys of Laura, and then decide upon another incarnation or rest awhile.*

L: This is where I get confused, because you had said earlier (and in our other books) everything is happening at once, but this conversation makes it seem as if lives are linear. Do you understand what I mean?

A: *Of course, and we are understanding of your confusion, as well. It is a hard concept to grasp to understand lives happening simultaneously, and while it is very much the truth, we know it makes little sense to those on Earth reading our books and materials and so we speak in similar terms humans comprehend. A life is happening while at the same time not. Remember you are both everything and nothing at all, and this duality is how you hold space until you are recognizing another life. Like a video game, as explained above, everything exists upon the computer but most don't open every file until they are ready to receive its information.*

L: So you become aware of the self in that particular life and then experience it from that awareness?

A: *Yes! Brilliant, again. This is precisely the mechanism for receiving information and access to each subsequent life you are leading; becoming aware. At what point you 'jump in' is entirely your call. Watch and learn. Close the eyes and 'see'.*

L: I see a vision of a movie theater with lots of screens, like a really busy Zoom call with hundreds of participants.

A: *Well, it really is infinite the amount of lives to lead, but yes, this is perfect to describe the 'jumping in' process. You could watch all lives happening simultaneously and decide upon where to start.*

L: So you become aware of a life then decide to jump in at the beginning?

A: Yes.

L: Always at the beginning, or can you jump in somewhere else?

A: Beginning.

L: But what is happening in those other lives if we are unaware of them?

A: Consciousness continues always.

L: Just unaware of who we are and our soul truth?

A: Precisely. You are living consciously in the illusion, at the same time unaware of Spirit/Soul.

L: If we jump in at the beginning, how is it possible to have other lives affecting our own? I don't think I understand.

A: It's complicated. Soul is creating itself over and over again in lifetime after lifetime. Awareness is how you awaken, and in each life, a choice is made if you will align to Love or not at all. Those in unawareness stay sleeping, and the awakened decide where to go through each life.

L: But how are we living all of these lives and not knowing it? And how can you start at the beginning? For instance, I know in my next life I am a young Latina girl who was homeless at one point and living in foster care. Where is she now?

A: Working from home as she navigates similar circumstances to the current earthly situation.

L: A parallel circumstance to Covid?

A: Indeed. Hundreds of years from now a plague of the masses.

L: And what happens when I die and cross over? Can I jump into her life?

A: No.

L: Why not?

A: It's already happening, as are all lives, so you are growing and evolving at the same time through various themes. The difference when you die is that you will continue to grow and evolve and accept new circumstances when you begin again. A life waiting to be lived.

L: And what happens when she dies?

A: All lives end eventually, and you return to Source then decide upon another incarnation.

L: But aren't those lives happening, as well, if everything is simultaneous?

A: Not in the sense of the journey, only in keeping with evolution. This is the nothing of which we speak. Nothing happens until soul contracts are placed. It awaits you, and then once decided upon, then you awaken a life already lived. All exists as possibility, and when you go into the life it is unlocked.

L: Like levels in a video game.

A: Levels which exist waiting to be discovered. All of you are the game and soul is its player.

L: Isn't it happening simultaneously? Doesn't everything happen at once?

A: A life waiting to be lived means you can jump in to that which had already been created and decided upon but awaits your arrival. Think of it as if you were in a waiting room.

L: Again, like a Zoom call and you don't enter until someone lets you in or you let someone in.

A: It is there for you when ready.

L: But what does the happening "at once" mean? Is it happening at the same time as this life and it's like starting over or does it mean it's possible and–

A: Awaits the arrival of One in body who has chosen it.

L: You awaken a life already decided on, which is why you say if you can see it, feel it and be it you can make it happen because—

A: It already has been. See it in the mind's eye, feel it with emotion (joy, appreciation) and live. Let it arrive. Fear keeps it from being unlocked because you have choice. Everything had been set in motion. One box has fear and nothing, the other Love and everything. Which you choose to open is upon you to decide.

L: If you think of it with this in mind, why anyone would open the wrong box is beyond me.

A: And yet this is precisely what occurs all day, every day on Earth. Do you see how silly/nonsensical it is for fear to win? It's nothing wrapped in a box.

L: The time lag between creating what we want is what stops us, always. We don't like to wait so we fear, get angry, lose ourselves and give up.

A: It is the same in terms of lifetimes/incarnations. You continue to evolve and beat the system. On Earth, love and fear is the game.

L: Again, like a video game where there are certain levels, and in order to unlock them you have to have made it all the way through without dying. It was sitting there the whole time though waiting–

A: *For you to arrive–*

L: In the main frame. Can you go back and try again in the same life? Could you 'jump in' all over again from birth and experience it differently like a video game?

A: *It is best left alone. To do this would cause upheaval, and so while entirely plausible (as everything is possible), it would make no sense and no One decides upon this at the level of soul. Rather, is it best to elevate further in consciousness. Backward is never the way, only forward motion is how All experiences itself as One.*

L: Wow. That's fascinating, but as always makes perfect sense, and now I understand much better the concept of simultaneous lives. So thank you.

A: *You are very welcome. Remember, all things exist as possibility and all Ones need do is connect to it consciously and it will be drawn to you in the absence of fear. The box of Love is available to All.*

As we come to the end of our book journey, let us look at how evolved Ones truly are on Earth in a chapter appropriately titled, Oh Baby.

CHAPTER 25

Oh Baby

Dear All,
Let us look at our brothers and sisters and design a better world for All.

There is a disturbing practice among the elite and that is the selling and trading of human life. Life for life. What is happening all around the world has been part of the narrative for quite some time, and more is being shared as information comes to light to put this practice to pasture. The world is evolving beyond a shameful practice perpetuated since the century turned.

As you go about days you will see more and more being expressed, and this book shall be proof that pedophilia is both natural and unjust. As souls, each has chosen a journey to be with various scenarios as part of their 'script' to life. In one's script it may be part of the narrative (natural) in full knowing it is 'wrong' (unjust). We do not judge or condemn, nor speak to right and wrong. We observe behaviors and offer lessons for why those on Earth choose certain experiences, and how Ones find themselves lost in ego. For each has chosen a way to evolve that is best for them, but for those lost souls on Earth it is improper, just as owning guns and killing one another in service to ego is, was and always will be, as we have stated over and over again in our All books.

On planet Earth, as part of being human, certain rules must be followed in order to maintain the health of the collective, and this is one rule which God/Source/Universe would agree upon. Just as guns belong only with the military and police, children are to be raised and revered. There is no practice of harming or handling children in a manner that is confusing which won't affect their development. Their psyches are too young to understand atrocities, and it would do this world well to understand this. We are not here to condemn but to relay information so all may understand universal truths. Children are by and by at the mercy of their elder counterparts, and until their young minds have developed enough intellect to discover right from wrong (humanistically), it is improper to do anything which brings them pain or shame.

Never touch a child in any manner which isn't one of love and compassion. Those who believe they are 'child-like' and fighting for relationships to be made legal are following an ego mind, as 'God' would not allow a behavior of this nature just as 'God' doesn't condone violent behavior.

We are not here to condemn nor chastise, only to observe and inform those seeking light. What you do with our information is your free will. We are simply asking All to understand the nature of being isn't to do harm to anyone or anything, it is to love one another as if you are one another, and that is All.

What Is

When you are capable of loving life exactly as it is despite external circumstances, the world as you had previously known it will begin to transform. Nothing you say or do will be as important as being and you will grow. From the inside out is how you must live; never outside in. See the world through new eyes, the eyes of soul, and you will no longer be trapped in ego thoughts; misinformation designed to upset the balance of Love.

To know you are soul is beauty expressing itself through opened eyes and mindful living. We allow Laura step into her role as ego asks and We answer. You will find that Laura is discovering how ego is thought and writing (as she has done in question and answer format) has simply been an asking of ego and a replying of soul, and this is precisely how 'channeling' is designed. You all are capable of the same feat, as soon as you believe. Ones who know are always capable of connecting to their spiritual truths inside. No One is talking other than the One mind inside All.

Laura: I want to express my gratitude for all the information you have blessed us with so far. I know this book will not be for everyone, as most are still 'babies' in terms of their recognition of who they are spiritually. I've found myself butting heads recently with more and more sleeping people and am finding it difficult to stay balanced in the encounters.

All: Bless those encounters. They are some of the most difficult to move through because they have been chosen by All. To move you further in the search for enlightened thinking, Ones always will be shown what is lurking beneath the mind. Remember, to treat one another as if you are one another is our mission on Earth and other places (because you are). When One has harmed you, it can be most difficult to offer forgiveness and let it go, wouldn't you say?

L: Oh absolutely. I am still seething mad over a landlord and property manager who are both rude and insensitive and who tried to make me look like I am being unreasonable. I'm tired of corporate criminals

and their never-ending quest for profits. There are so many nasty humans on this planet who are stuck in their ego ways. It's frustrating because it's like standing in the eye of a storm and knowing how to end the madness, but nobody wants nor cares to know. I'm just trying to survive in a chaotic world of sleeping people.

A: *Forgiveness is a "hard pill to swallow" you all would say. It is precisely why you have been presented with repeated scenarios to undertake the means to learn it.*

L: It's so hard to forgive someone who is not sorry. It's hard to forgive someone who isn't morally sound or fair and just. How can I forgive someone who can't offer love? You can't love someone who is evil. People should be punished. Shouldn't we stand up for injustice?

A: *Standing up for yourself is not impractical as long as you are cocreator in it. Never allow the ego to build a bridge or a wall for someone. Use the voice of Love always.*

> 66 How can I forgive a human I feel has wronged me? What must I take from this experience and apply to my life moving forward? Help me see the beauty in this experience and not the pain, dear All. 99

Asking is the way to truth. You can sit around and fester thoughts making you weak and disempowered, or can you can contemplate the meaning or why. This is all we ask of you every day through every hurt or upset. Don't let situations get the best of you. Let the cocreator within handle them with you. Let us look at your current living situation and the men who have harmed you. What is it you like about the home? Let us discuss this first.

L: It's filled with natural light. It's conveniently located to everything and close to the beach. It's the perfect amount of space for my son and I right now. But it's only a temp—

A: *We did not ask you what you don't like. We asked what you did like. This is exactly how the ego draws you in. Bless the space. Make it your home even if its temporary or a stop on the way. Bless everything as if you have chosen it, because, my dear One, you have.*

L: I chose to have a home that I moved into with ants, snakes, broken and missing pieces and a nasty property management company and equally corrupt landlord?

A: *Everything is chosen by you, for you to move beyond it. What is my lesson, dear All?*

L: What is my lesson?

A: *Forgiveness, as was said above. Can you forgive those who harmed you and move on?*

L: Not by myself. I don't think I am capable of this on my own because my human nature is to condemn and be angry at injustices. I recognize the spiritual nature of the thinking mind and why people do what they do and act the way they act, but that doesn't mean I like it. And I also understand the 'we are all one' concept, but I don't feel like we are one, and I don't feel like I am the same as these people. I feel very separate from those in bodies. I am moral and just and they are not. So how could we be the same?

A: And that is why forgiveness is so hard. It feels like you are separate and that all of the things which go on are happening to you and not anyone else. Precisely why forgiveness is the hardest rung on the individual soul ladder you each are on.

L: There's a big lesson here for me. I feel that. I don't think I can get there, but I also don't want to hold onto bitterness and anger because it doesn't serve me.

A: So don't.

L: Ah, so easy for you to say but not easy for me to do. However, I am willing, so that is a start. How can we forgive a person who is not sorry?

A: "Dear All, I recognize and understand I am on a different path than others in my journey to enlightened thinking. As I return my thoughts to the One, may we always be as gentle and kind to one's self and accept all circumstances are valuable teachers. Let those who have harmed me remove themselves from the psyche and let my own darkness be healed as I recognize I, too, am teacher and student."

L: That's not giving me a sense of forgiveness. How can I lead myself out of anger and into acceptance so I can move beyond it and not be so angry?

A: Let it go.

> 66 I accept my role in the creation of the circumstance. I ask for a healing for all parties involved. 99

This recognizes you are both creator and created, and that each party is deserving of healing. All for One, One for All.

L: Well, like I said, it certainly doesn't seem we are all One. I feel very different than everyone else.

A: No two snowflakes are alike, and yet they are the same.

L: Yes, but those are objects without thinking minds to create, and so their differences shouldn't matter. Okay you are writing this for me right now. I see your point. Even though we are individually different we are from the same Source.

A: *And therefore should be treated as such. Trees aren't burdened by other trees. Cars don't compete for attention. It is the drivers who do.*

L: Because we have a mind and thoughts and consciousness.

A: *All things have consciousness, but thoughts are the thing which create. You see separation and decide upon–*

L: But trees don't look different– I mean they do, but not– well actually I guess they do. There are probably thousands of varieties, if not more, of trees. And they don't argue and bicker and judge because they have no thoughts.

A: *Consciousness, yes. Thoughts, no. Trees communicate differently than humans, but they do have a system for it, as well.*

L: It's hard to look at another human and see them as part of you or that you are the same, especially when they have harmed you. I don't feel a commonality with someone who is rude and unloving. To me they are still jackasses. I don't see a commonality with someone who is poor and decides to do drugs and steal, or people who are posting all day long on social media looking for attention and adulation. I'm not sure how to get myself to a place where I want to kumbaya with jerks and racists and lousy humans. So I guess I'm not as enlightened as I think I am.

A: *Precisely why you are thrown into situations and circumstances with others. To move beyond judgement and fear (on Earth) and see everyone as equal no matter what race/gender they are.*

L: You want me to forgive rapists and murderers and I don't see how that is possible, even knowing what I know and using all of what you have told us here in the *All* books. It's a mind-blowing thing to believe that everyone is perfectly imperfect and nothing we do matters, in a sense.

A: *It matters in physical realms, and we are not asking you to ignore or excuse those who are harming, have harmed or will harm others. We are simply stating spiritual truth so you are knowing and understanding why, seeing it through a different lens and then you can move beyond it by using the eyes of Love as often as you can. It is the only way to grow. Seek the light.*

Ask, "What is the lesson this soul is moving through?"

Perhaps it is best to remember rather than rationalize.

"Why are they here? To grow and evolve as I am."

L: Forgive, forget, move on?

A: *Remember.*

L: Remember who you are before judging—

A: *Any One, yes.*

L: I'll keep working on that and doing my best to try but that is a toughie, especially when it comes to my son. I feel he deserves better than the treatment he receives from a father figure and the biological one who left, but I can't force someone to love him and I hesitate to write this in a book I know he will read one day. I have always been honest with him about his circumstance and right now he is not bothered by it, but I know as he gets older it might become an issue—

A: *If you allow.*

L: Well how do I not allow it and wouldn't it be his journey of self, as well?

A: *Remember possibilities exist for both scenarios and our children are infected by parental (and others') thoughts. So you must stay in alignment with who he is, too.*

L: By doing what?

A: *Precisely what you have been doing. Be honest, be fair. Let him know who he is in a subtle way. Do not judge the others who have cocreated the experience with him. He has his reasonings as soul, as do you, as do All. Abandonment had been a life-driving theme, as we had previously written. A soul contract carried out by both father and son. Karma is at play in each of their lives. They will know if they go seeking within the who, what, when, where and why of the particular incident that led to this scenario. It is quite easy to understand if you look at it through the mind's eye, which can reveal All. You are One capable of helping others go within and find answers. Why not help your son one day when he is understanding of healing modalities such as these?*

L: I will. I know he is not ready now. I see this behavior all the time in parental relationships. There is unconditional love that some hold dearly when it comes to kids, and then there are those deadbeat dads and moms out there who don't seem to give a care about their kids. Why is that? Aren't kids supposed to teach us unconditional love?

A: *Many do have this as part of their learning curves while others use fear as the driving force and others have chosen to be parents from a young age where they, themselves are incapable of loving another. How Ones can be expected to love children who are incapable of loving One's self is why so many children suffer abuse which, as we said, is unacceptable in any form on Earth. However, it does go on because the abuser is a victim of their own mind. Fear and rage and self-loathing lead to sanctions on children they feel have "ruined their bodies," dwindled their finances or forced a relationship's end or detrimented it.*

L: I see that. We take our past conditioning and self-esteem issues and place it on our children, and then blame them for our messed up lives. What about narcissists? I would think they are full of self-love, but they seem to be the worst offenders of child abandonment.

A: *Narcissism is a form of self-hatred disguised as love. They are filling the void of love (received as a child by parents who dismantled their self-esteem) by building themselves up. They take the pain and turn it into pleasure by seeking gratification for self and only self. Wounded souls wounding souls.*

L: What is true self love?

A: *Knowing you are perfect, as is everyone else.*

L: It still blows me away that we wrote these chapter titles almost two years ago, and now as we are coming to the end each and every title makes sense and connects to what is happening in my life now.

A: *Probabilities exist always based upon love/fear. What is connection, dear One?*

L: Listening to the inner voice, knowing who you are and asking always. Here are some questions I have based on the chapter heading. I have been thinking a lot about babies again, which obviously I have talked about many times in my *All* books, but now I am feeling a stronger calling again to be a mom. I feel compelled to bring it up, but also defeated by the fact that I am almost 50 years old and financially insecure currently. I know well enough now to add that 'currently' in there. I just don't know what to do in order to make that dream a reality when I have no money and no job, currently.

A: **Ego thought:** "I am incapable of creating that which is needed to bring through love."

Soul thought: "I am capable of that which I see in mind's eye."

Why question what you see?

L: Because it seems impossible based on many factors. All those practical things I have spoken of before. Too old, too broke, too unsure of how to proceed.

A: *Ask dear All.*

L: Dear All, how may I proceed? What steps should I take towards my dream of being a mom again despite the age factor? Lots of people think it's selfish to bring kids into the world after a certain age.

A: *Precisely why you are confused. Listening to the noise of society rather than the calling of soul.*

L: How do I drown out the noise?

A: Baby steps. One step at a time. Think. Believe. Think. Believe. Every time you act in accordance with the laws of our Universe you step closer to whatever is wanting to be created. Every time you doubt or fret, chastise or blame, you are further away. One step forward two steps back. One more forward. One more back. This is how most on Earth are living their lives; creating wildly, bucking and bronking and not sure how to hand the reins over. And yet the simplicity of life is that all Ones need do is believe.

L: Well despite your proclamations about a new day being upon us in the last chapter, we are going backwards. Covid cases are on the rise and they are talking about new lockdowns. Collectively we take one step forward, two steps back, as well.

A: Collectively you are One, so what happens to One happens to All. We know it is a most difficult time and we ask you to believe us and not them (ego) which is continuing the narrative of chaos. You must be One who believes so you may give birth to a new agenda where kindness reigns over Covid.

L: The getting to the belief is the—

A: Journey.

L: I was going to say problem.

A: If you view life as a problem it will be, but if you view it as an exciting adventure determined to tame the beast, it will be. Whatever you believe, it will be.

L: I would like to believe I can create everything I have been dreaming about. The beach front home, the thriving career, a family and a better world for myself, my children and everyone.

A: Mostly are you capable of being that which you say wish to be in the absence of fear. There will be trying times because the collective challenges are happening for the highest good of All. You will sidestep most, but you cannot escape the ego all of the time on a collective level because evolutionary shifts occur. Be mindful during those times to use the voice of Love and ask, "How may I move through this more quickly?"

What saves One saves All.

L: So the more I pray during times like this pandemic we are currently moving through the easier it becomes—

A: For All, yes. One affects All, as we have been teaching for centuries and telling you time and time again throughout our book. You are each at mind level creating individually, while at the same time collectively. So anytime you give thanks, send loving thoughts or pray for your fellow brethren on Earth you are blessing everyone and everything. The strong survive through will.

❝ *I am willing to know who I am.* **❞**

L: Yet again I go off on a tangent about my personal issues in life and you bring it back around to worldly pursuits.

A: Because, dear One, you all suffer the same 'noise'.

L: Ego.

A: Everything goes out when you listen to the voice of fear. Love brings All.

L: I wish this pandemic would go away so we could get back to a better way of life and not be so restricted. I'm tired of this current world. We need a break.

A: Take one in mind. It will bring a sense of peace you cannot receive in any other way but inside. Inside is the way out, and the more you practice the easier it becomes to sidestep ego and see the world as it could be, because it already happened to you, which we shall explain in chapter 26 as we march towards belief.

It Already Happened To You

Dear All,
I know I am One who is All and allow thoughts that serve the highest
good of All knowing that what happens on Earth had been chosen as
part of the life blueprint for All.

W hat happens on Earth has been chosen by All. From the minute you stepped foot on the soil of Earth you have been creating a life already planned. Everything happening is part of the plan, be it good or bad, happy or sad. A blueprint designed to bring you to truth.

What is truth? That you are One. Every act of betrayal is separation. Remembering who you are is the way to enact truth.

66 I am One who is All. 99

Repeat this phrase as you arise. Repeat it daily, minute by minute until it resonates as ultimate truth. Recognize you are light, love and God. Yes, God. God is love. God is All. Who you are is a manifestation of Love. You are love in body pretending to be someone else. Like a one act play, you are characters in the story of God.

God is a name, a word, something to define itself. You choose a name as you are born and this is to separate yourself and delineate you from another. However, should Ones arise and awaken at some point on Earth, it would become evident you are same. Names become important only to showcase yourself individually, never separate you. Same goes for race or gender. Each would be part of the life you chose in the body you chose, but not used as a separation tool.

66 One is All. All is One. I am God. I am Laura. 99

This recognizes that you are both creator and created. Why Ones get so hung up on the belief of outside forces causing you to fail or waging storms on innocent bystanders is because of separation.

What must be known is One has no need for pain and punishment. The joy of life is available to All because it exists. All you need do is choose with belief.

> ❝*I believe I am Love.*❞

Simple. Then close the eyes and see what is possible. Leave the eyes open and you see what is fake.

> ❝*I don't understand?*❞

Yet. Even when you know what it means to be a soul on Earth living a human experience, it will still feel as if you are alone wandering through life without a safety net. Always do you feel a sense of defense against truth because it feels real.

The life you have designed is 'prepackaged', meaning it's already been. Everything is. Nothing exists without there having been a thought prior. We are saying this now and will again over and over until it is believed. Repeating ourselves is important, which is why every book channeled is saying the same thing. Over and over again we must remind you. Delivering yourself back to the One over and over again and again through lifetime after lifetime until you are knowing. Recognition is all that is asked of you on Earth. Recognizing you are a spirit in a body with a soul who knows All. To know All is enough to help achieve joyful experiences.

So why do we bother? Because Love is conditional on Earth (and other places), and when those conditional beliefs cause chaos, we enjoy helping you out. We know it is confusing and sad to always be witnessing environmental tweaks and tragic circumstances, so we step in to shine a light on truth. We are the flashlight but you are its navigator. Turn the light on and you have got a shot in the dark. Leave it off and you are bouncing around bumping into things and sometimes getting hurt. We know where you are going and how to arrive there. You don't because you had chosen to discover it using choice.

Free Will

Free will means you choose between love and fear on Earth. Only two choices exist, and everything else are subsets of either. Love is joy, compassion, kindness and love (romantic, friendship, family etc.). Fear is panic, rage, anger, bitterness, jealousy, racism and prejudice. All those things are tied up and bound to fear.

Whatever you choose from is happening in our spiritual realm. You choose in the blueprint all the things you will move through (on Earth). This is just one design in an infiniteness of decisions, but we are speaking of life on Earth and will continue with this discussion.

In the blueprint you decide:

1. *Who you are.*

2. *A name.*

3. *Whom the parents will be.*

4. *What choices you will make in every stage of life – career/profession, schooling, individual relationships (whom you will reconvene with in the "soul family") and where you will live and when.*

5. *If children will come along.*

6. *A path for evolving (stay sleeping, wake up or somewhere in between).*

7. *What lessons/themes are most important to work through.*

8. *Karmic relationships and how they may (or may not) play out.*

9. *What collective shifts and anomalies are possible, and what role is played in them.*

10. *An exit strategy (i.e. when death will occur and within what time frame which may be long and drawn out or short).*

You are always capable of extending a life for longer if you are willing. No one dies without soul choices being expressed, and only when you have moved beyond certain themes can you evolve beyond. Because this is her book, we will use Laura as example. Her life blueprint is as follows:

1. *Who you are is a healer, an archetype chosen by those on the awakened journey. Some are artisans/craftsman/tradesman, among other archetypes.*

2. *Laura is a name chosen prior, which is why debating a name is unnecessary. Our name was given (by us).*

3. *Parents are to be Sandy and Stuart, who have been other actors in the life of Laura as friends, lovers and mothers/fathers before.*

4. *Professions – television presenter, talk show host, intuitive healer, author, motivational speaker, teacher (intuitive) and know it All.*

5. *Children – three.*

6. *Wake up.*

7. *Life driving themes – patience, worthiness, aging, passion, purpose, insignificance, resolve, virtue, trust, faith, belief (among others).*

8. *Karmic relationships – continuation of an unhealed pattern with men, independence. Karmic restitution for death of prior children in other incarnational lives.*

9. *Collective anomaly possibilities – 9/11, Covid-19 (chances), destroying of forests, climate rising, fertility crisis, cyber war.*

10. *.*

We leave number ten blank because it doesn't serve you to know. It is possible to see yourself in future scenarios to reveal an answer, and we allow all to decide upon this for themselves. If you see it, it's possible. Laura has seen herself many times in old age and happily ready to adventure on.

You see how all has been planned prior with different scenarios presented and ways to evolve? Through love or fear is how you arrive at each destination and forks in the road on a mind level. It's all choice. This is why if you struggle and stress, a scenario exists keeping you stuck, and if you stay in the vibrational lane of love you bring through pre-planned experiences or manifestations.

The very word manifesting has become a false flag for many believing everything comes to you out of 'nowhere'. It is, in fact, fallacy to believe things arrive out of thin air. They arrive because you had planned for them all along. You become because you are.

I think therefore I am.

A passage straight from the Bible which often goes misinterpreted. Its meaning is simple. Think. Believe. Receive. Think the thought. Believe it's possible. Receive.

One last time we shall reveal, it's already been created. It exists because you thought it into being before arriving. So be it.

Now we have come to our final chapter where the journey is taking you; into belief, dear All.

CHAPTER 27

It All Comes Down To Belief

Dear God and the Divine Mind,
Our beliefs shape the life we see and truth is needed to achieve master-
like status.

I Am

Everything you think is because it is. It means that all thoughts exist, and when you 'think' thoughts it is aligning with the contracts of the soul. Which way you go depends upon which chosen path is used – love or fear. Free will is deciding upon All. Everything exists. It really is so simple. You don't create or manifest. You align to that which exists already for you.

Let things arrive. Forcing is the surest way to break things. Whatever you are trying to create exists for you in the field of potentiality where the contracts live waiting to be carried out. Imagine you have sat at a table and crafted a story with multiple arcs and layers. Each layer takes you to a different version. One where you create everything and another nothing. Belief is what ties you to these.

If everything we have achieved could be created, it would be masterful but also quite boring, indeed. Isn't it much more fun to take your time and create layer by layer, piece by piece? It is like you have all at your fingertips (proverbially speaking) and know it can easily be created, so you decided to forget how. In order to remember, a series of lives is created for you to find All again. Life is the ultimate scavenger hunt waiting for you to discover who you are, why you are and what you are. How fun is that, All?

How you arrive at things is through belief. It is the final step needed for All. You use the mind and allow.

    ❝*I see this. I would enjoy that. I feel that. It feels good. I enjoy this boat, car or motorcycle and I will have one, too.*❞

All of these are simply thoughts about things already created. Nothing exists without thought bringing it to be. This is the magic you bring to the world. Your thought blesses everyone and everything or it punishes, condemns and judges both the self and others. What can be done is to stay aligned in Love. Love is All. All is One.

You think therefore I am.

What this means is every One is creating All. Each mind creates for itself but also for the whole. So thinking with love blesses an entire infiniteness; all corners of the light.

Our last chapter is about belief because it is the hardest to discover. It is why the journey of our inscriber has been so back and forth. Belief is a difficult place to be when all around you are imagery seen through physical eyes of chaos and corruption. As you wait you create with ego. As you align you remind.

You go about life accepting what is, in service to ego, rather than examining its mysteries. We mean to share wisdom, and wise Ones know when to accept. One last time we shall allow questions to be answered, but Ones should always question everything. To question is to know you are not complete in your evolvement journey, you are simply on the quest. Questioning is part of life's journey. Question all. You must examine truth before you can extend consciousness.

One Last Questioning

Laura: If everything comes down to belief and I am the creator of everything based on these beliefs, then who is actually doing the creating? If you teach me that we have to be cocreators, then with whom am I cocreating here?

All: You are creating with Divine Mind as One being. So if you say would like to create something, believe in its existence and it will occur as long as you are being.

L: Being?

A: Being in cahoots with your Oneness.

L: I am being.

A: Yes.

L: I am being an author. I am being a published author. But how do I find a publisher if I am the creator and you tell me just to be?

A: See it in your mind's eye and attract it with your vibrational offering.

L: And this does what?

A: It allows our beingness to begin in another's mind, as well. As you are being, so too will they be. Energy of attraction kicks in, and when you stay in vibration a match comes along to it. Remember they, too, have it in their possibilities, as well. Because it is seen it may be.

L: This seems like something a superhero would do. A Jedi mind trick.

A: Perhaps it has been witnessed on purpose, this franchise.

L: So you can draw to you—

A: Experiences. People. Things. Places (to go).

L: Seriously?

A: Any and all experiences thought upon are available unto thee. People are drawn into your experience. Things need be collected if it is necessary to growth as a human. Places are to be traveled. It is a thought which creates a life, moves a body, designs a home, exchanges energy. All is moved by thought, and belief is what moves it.

> 66 *I am being anything I wish to be because it already exists, as every thought has already been thought.* 99

All desires manifest as long as you are being.

L: And being means to?

A: See it in your mind's eye. Feel it in your body. Act upon inspiration and inspiration only. Never act out of desperation and temptation. Follow **all** in**s**pired **t**ricks.

L: FAIL – inspired *tricks* as in ego's tricks?

A: Yes. Follow enlightened intuitive information only.

L: I can really draw someone to me?

A: Yes.

L: But you said you can't make someone fall in love with you (in *The All That Is*[12]) unless they love you back.

A: To see them in your mind's eye allows their beingness to attach to yours. However, should one choose a fear-based path it is not possible to connect. So if each is knowing the other is a 'soul mate' (though this is a term used only by humans and not a spiritual one), then each will allow a love to flow. Love as in romantic love, not spiritual love, which we all are.

L: What about houses or money? Can we draw that into our experience?

A: Yes. If you are focusing upon love and not lack. In the case of money, you must move the energy for it to flow, as we have told you in our prior books and chapters.

L: Even getting to the end of this book and knowing how to create money, I still can't. The fear is too deeply embedded. It keeps me up at night worrying about finances, especially now after Covid-19 decimated our finances on Earth. Well, at least some of us, including me. I am more broke than ever and that is causing insomnia and so much more. It is my worst fear beyond aging and health.

A: Do you see how the mind plays its tricks?

L: Well, yes but you can't help notice you are poor or sick.

A: Ah, but you can. You can stay in alignment with soul truth.

> **❝** *I am perfect. I am abundant. All my needs are being met.* **❞**

L: But those are not truths. I am not perfect. My wrist and shoulder are still healing and causing pain and stress in the body. I am not abundant. I have no money. No job and no prospects and very little left to live on. All my needs are not being met because nothing is coming in the form of money or finances. I am broke and broken. How sad to get to the end of my fourth book and still have no idea how to manifest.

A: Perhaps all of this has been on purpose so you may write the most profound book on how to be mind/body/spirit/soul having been through so many ups/downs and tragic circumstances most everyone who stumbles upon it (as had been chosen prior) sees in you what had been occurring in them. Each and every One who reads and/or listens have chosen a path similar to your own. This is why spending all your time creating results is a waste of precious Earth time. Those who have chosen to read/listen are only finding what works within their contracts/themes. Not every channeled work is exactly the same. They all have subtle differences based upon the inscriber's own chosen life path. You have chosen, as a channel, to write a book which one day may be found by millions on a same journey of upheaval then transformation.

L: Why only may?

A: For you know as well as I (We) do now that nothing is rock solid. Every chosen element has its opposite effect based upon the actions of love and fear upon Earth of the chooser. You MUST stay aligned in the manifestation in order for it to form into physical matter.

L: So whatever was chosen by you in the soul contract has the ability to disappear because you—

A: Stay focused in fear. That is the process on Earth. Focus on joy, joy returns. Magnetic attraction.

L: One of the things I want to manifest is to be on Super Soul Sunday with Oprah Winfrey. So can I bring Oprah into my experience?

A: If you are focused upon the goal and she is willing, yes.

L: How will I know she is willing?

A: You will see it in your mind's eye as possibility.

L: I do. I see us sitting together. I've seen her reading my books and us sitting together for an interview many times. I even talk to her in my mind and pretend what our episodes will be on.

A: Keep feeling the energy of what it feels like to connect in this way and you are allowing the idea to form as well within the minds of All. Have you not brought other "celebrities" into being (we mean this in experience only)?

L: Well, yes. Three times to be exact. I had a crush on three different celebrities and all three who I focused my attention on became part of my reality and I ended up going out on dates with each, and a few other men, too, who I focused my attention upon that were reality TV stars. I guess for me it was easier to do it because I worked at Access Hollywood and was always around celebrities.

A: So you believed in the possibility because it seemed as if it was something you could do at one point.

L: I guess so, yes. I believed at some point I would get to interview each of them and the opportunities presented themselves to me. So you are saying I created those experiences for myself?

A: Without a doubt. This is how you created them. You had no doubt in your mind and so it became easy to create the energy to attract them through you, to you. Do you believe you can attract Oprah into experience?

L: Yes, at some point. Because I work in an industry where people know people, and so I figure someday I can attract enough attention to get my books into her hands.

A: Hold steadfast to a vision and it must take shape.

L: How long will it take?

A: Hold steady and it will take shape more quickly. Panic, fear, worry and it will take much longer or never come to pass. You must stay vigilant for it to manifest. Focusing on all the wrong things is why you wait. Focus on that which has occurred. Vigilant means to stay committed to belief, not to attachment to outcomes. If you know it is meant to be and believe it is coming, you will let go and allow, enacting our Law of Allowing. If you stay in constant worry, doubt and fear over when it will arrive then you are being vigilant with fear.

> *If it's not happening now it must not be happening.*

This is why all of you suffer. If only you would focus on light, and love what is, could you bring that which you wish to create forth more quickly. Be clear and specific on what you want to create. Ask for guidance. Wait in positive prosperity and enjoy life. Then and only they may an asking appear in physical form.

See it. Be it. Believe it. Receive it.

L: And this is the beingness you have been speaking of in our *All* books.

A: Yes. To be is to see it as it was created. All of everything already exists, and to be is to see it in your mind's eye so you may bring it forth with you into the experience. Though it does not mean you may not be handling circumstances as you go about obtaining it. It is a means to attract it faster and more efficiently. What is seen is seen for a reason. Decide upon what feels right and stay there in mind with no doubt and it will materialize. Period. End of story. No fear. No doubt. No problem.

L: Why do you hide in plain sight? Why not let us know right away who we are and why we are here from the minute we incarnate or jump in? Why not teach this in our schools and to us as children?

A: The system on Earth is designed in such a way that to learn about fear you must be kept in the dark as much as possible, which is why belief is so hard to come by. It feels immensely real doesn't it?

L: It sure does.

A: There are planets (as revealed in our last book) where you do learn consciously who you are. They are outside of Earth and the solar system but they exist, and many enjoy this, but most enjoy a wild ride.

L: Can I write a note to my future selves and offer them some keys and clues?

A: You are now. Let them find them these books in mind and you are showing them light. A love letter to humanity created by you, for you, for All.

L: If I see them finding and reading my books through the third eye it will allow that very thing to happen?

A: Indeed. Wishful thinking. Wish them peace.

L: When I close my eyes, I can see myself on that other planet, too, where they are awake and learning through Love. It's so peaceful. Can I experience that bliss here?

A: You can if you believe, absolutely. Absolute bliss is available to all who purposefully choose light always.

L: When you see a world falling apart it is immensely difficult to find bliss.

A: Such is the journey on Earth and why you always focus on pain and punish self.

> ❝ *Our world is perfect as is.* ❞

L: I'm not sure being in lockdowns and heading towards forced vaccinations is perfect.

A: It is if you were to see the why.

L: Which is?

A: Truth is being revealed all the time. You have been given opportunity time and again to move beyond a worldly event designed to teach patience and understanding for one another and going in (physically) is, was and will always be a metaphor for inner peace. You must find peace within self and send that outwardly to All. As it stands currently (December 2020), this 'experiment' has been upended through repeated interactions and external parties and parades. Those staying in are using time wisely, while those panicking extend the narrative. You must always look for the rainbow and bright spots, to see time as illusion and to maintain connection with All That Is. To know you are One and act in accordance with this principle. Send love to All, even those causing the chaos, lockdowns and secret societal injunctions.

L: How do we change the narrative? I don't want my rights stripped and to become an experiment by corruption.

A: Within each and every One is a goldmine of truth. Use it wisely. Use it daily. Send love to All. See the world as perfectly imperfect and know you are capable of moving beyond any and all chosen circumstances. Hold the light for All. Ask to receive guidance on next steps and possibilities, and see a world as you would like it to be not as it is.

L: What's interesting is how this pandemic has been predicted in movies and television time and time again.

A: Not predicted, pre-dictated, as was said in our chapter If/Then. If you know a thing is possible then it will become part of a narrative in some way. There are many times when predictions go unnoticed and unmanifested existing in movies and television, just as there are times when narratives become manifest. Remember all know answers within, and so they pick up possibilities and create using this wisdom just as you are in these All books. Their journey was one to create through arts and music or poetry while yours has been to write a book of knowledge through Spirit. In these pages you have picked up on several possible outcomes for future that may or may not come to pass based upon—

L: Love and fear.

A: Yes. What you believe is what you achieve. What you fear is what is brought near.

L: You're frustrating.

A: We know you would like to receive different answers, but these are truths of the Universe which have not and will not change, ever. Every book spells out the same thing in different ways to teach you to be. Liked or not it is truth.

L: Can we go back and change things and visit past lives? That's something you see in movies and TV all the time.

A: All is taking place at once, as said prior, so it is possible but unnecessary. Let it evolve as it had. Time-space on Earth is in place for a reason. To mess with it doesn't change anything. It just frustrates you all more. Seek answers deep within and show yourself the light so you may move beyond whatever had been. Let bygones be bygones and move on.

L: It's so ingrained in our brains to be human that it's quite impossible at times to let go of fear and believe.

A: Might we point out to you how consistency is paramount in the daily grind on Earth. Everything, all knowledge is accessible but you can't read a book one time and know all answers. If given a test, would you pass on the first try if you hadn't studied, taken notes, deciphered the meanings, taken a look back to be sure of its message and meaning or prepared beforehand?

L: No, of course not. You might get some answers right after reading it once but probably you would miss a bunch of questions without having done your homework or studying.

A: Life is homework. It is you studying how to be.

L: A school of hard knocks.

A: If you view it that way, it can be, but if you view it as a wonderful adventure with endless twists and turns and the subject is one in which you are passionate about you wouldn't mind the work, would you?

L: No, I guess not. That is absolutely how it has been for me since we started this All project. I enjoy the work, I love our books and quotes and journaling, working with clients, getting to speak on stages and interviews on podcasts, radio and TV shows, but it's been a climb and lack of consistency has knocked me off the mountain more times than I would like to admit. I would imagine if during this entire journey I had been more consistent in my practices, my life would be easier?

A: It has been a most epic journey of survival and surrender masterfully planned by the soul and carried out as part of your contracts/blueprint. It has been our intention to teach all about love and fear throughout our All books, and though it has been repetitive you must know repetition is the key to great learning. The more you hear something the more it 'sinks in'. You are doing great and we know you have seen many changes internally and externally throughout the process of writing and sharing our work.

L: Absolutely I have. Despite my rantings and ravings over money and babies and stuckness and our chaotic world, a shift has occurred where everything is beginning to form and clues of what is to come show me light when I am feeling dark.

A: Inside is beginning to match outside.

L: What about cycles? Are we caught up in cycles of the Universe? The reason I ask is a lot of my friends and myself had been waiting for jobs and ways to make money. It feels like we all have been in a holding pattern together, and then within the last month all of the sudden, jobs started to materialize for every single one of us. So that would lead me to believe that there is some sort of a cycle going on we were caught in.

A: Yes, the answer is absolutely that you are waiting on the Universal timing of everything. Three is the natural cycle of life.

Let go of ego
Remind yourself of Love
Wait in faith.

Because you are all One, you will start to see synchronicities between what goes on in the world, both your world individually, collectively and even the world of those around you, and how things tend to 'sync up' together, and that is very much by design, as well. You are all One, moving as One, thinking as One, believing as One and yes, you are caught up in the cycle of the Universe, so when the gates are open for One they are open for All. The only difference is that those who are aligned to falsity will be stuck in a cycle of miscreation and those who are aligned to our One mind (as much as possible) will bring to them those things that have already been created.

L: So we are working within the Universal time clock?

A: Yes. As much as you are called to a desire, it is always part of your possibilities and sometimes you create it and sometimes you don't, but always are you capable of creating something in the Universal time clock. There are many events that go on as planned that you evolve into, just as there are those that don't based upon the actions of love and fear. This is why it's important that you wait in faith, as many times you (all) have sent things away that were waiting for you out in that time space continuum to be achieved. The lack will bring lack, the falsity will bring falsity; but if you stay aligned in Love knowing the Universal clock is always on time, Ones would never be impatient. They would wait with glorious applause for your goal to be created.

L: Can we know the length of time? That it's going to take a while or can be created more quickly? Do we have that internal knowing?

A: Ones know everything within, so absolutely are you able to tell time, in a sense, with the exception of the clock of death. There is not a particular time stamp. It is more an idea of when it would be time to go, which can be changed as you go about life thinking and feeling love or fear. There is, however, a timestamp for manifestations of physical things that you would like to create. So, yes there is a knowing; an internal knowing that it might take time for it to appear, just as you know it could be created instantaneously. So if you say, "I would like to see a butterfly," and you know it's possible for one to show up rather quickly, it will. However, if in the same vein you say, "I would like to be a movie star," and you know you haven't yet gone to class, gotten an agent or worked towards a goal, you know it might take some time. We all have a deep knowing within.

L: Any advice on how to get that information as we wait so we don't get so frustrated about how long it's taking?

A: As above, go within always.

L: Is it tied to moon cycles, stars?

A: Evolution. The eternal nature of being.

L: So things are always moving, changing and evolving.

A: And it would do you well to remember so you wait patiently and not in anger and frustration, as you do and will continue to do until you consciously choose wisely.

L: Well gee, perhaps you might have told me this back in other books so I knew that waiting was also guided by the Universe and its timing, even when do choose Love.

A: Our dearest Ones, the lesson of All is to know you are multidimensional, multicultural, multilayered beings and the nuances of life come as you evolve. So when receiving information, it had been chosen when and how, and for all to know everything is perfect exactly when it arrived into knowing.

L: How much more do we have to learn?

A: Mysteries remain and always will.

L: I'm still mystified by this whole "everything exists" concept. That's a whole lot of information to create for infinite people, places and events. When did all this occur? When did God/All come up with everything?

A: *Yes, everything is happening at once. Yes it's been preplanned/designed prior, but it's a complicated process which cannot be understood as humans in bodies or souls until completing evolutionary shifts. It is to be unlocked as you arrive to consciousness with All/Love. You (all) have a journey of discovery that is endless, truly.*

L: **Then I guess I will leave it right here. I am forever grateful for the Wisdom of The All that was offered here. It has been a deliberate process and a beautiful one, at that. I have grown and evolved, and with each passing reading of our book it all starts to simmer and make sense. Can you offer one last piece of advice as we end our step-by-step guide into Love?**

A: *We shall leave All with this. What is asked is that all pay attention to noise, bodily upsets, angry emotions and tragic or tough circumstances. Whenever there is fear present it will make itself known in ways to divide you into two. It will point out you are old, tired, unlikeable or unloved. While the soul is always speaking truth.*

> 66 *I am kind. I am likeable. I speak to myself and others through limiting beliefs and this is why I suffer in time.* 99

Whatever is happening might not seem loving, but in actuality it is loving because it is pointing out the necessary steps needed to evolve and return to Love. Fear ultimately is love because it is guiding you towards it.

So you see, dear All, everything is Love, even Fear.

The End, Again

Now we have come to a time where you are being asked to believe all that has been written as truth. Nothing we have written is false, only what is ego expressing itself through you, our reader and our inscriber. When Laura asks, her questions stem mostly from ego. Whatever you accept as truth is soul and what is questioned is ego. Nothing written through Love is false. Now it is upon you to decide. Will you allow ego to destroy evidence the collective knows deep within, or will you welcome new information as truth and go seeking more as you evolve on Earth?

Go back through our book as many times as needed to begin to see truth and allow.

We have enjoyed immensely this journey into Love and we hope you have, too. Now go forth and live completely with belief and you, too, can know who you are and enjoy life as awakened, Infinite Ones.

Healing Modalities

Dear All,
Please share with us some useful tools and tricks on Earth for mind/
body/soul health and wellness.

Energy Manipulation

Reiki

A form of energy manipulation where Ones use light colors to transform. Higher self-knowledge is accessible through One. Any One can do it as long as they are connecting to the energetic field of Love. Those of a higher vibration may help those in lower states, but all must believe in order for anything to change in self.

Qigong

An ancient form of energy manipulation used to transfer power from one center to another. Energy can be trapped in one chakra, cutting off the flow to another. Use this technique when you are feeling low on 'fuel' and release each chakra one by one. Chanting and oms are used throughout to send vibrational energy into the lungs and out to the body parts in question. Whatever you are feeling is transformed through "Om."

Tai Chi

Movement designed to help alleviate pain through slow, controlled movements and breath. Use this daily as it aligns chakras, balances energy and releases endorphins designed to keep you healthy in body and mind.

Scalar

An energy system more powerful than reiki which aligns chakras, holds light and keeps it moving. Energy is moving freely but can be manipulated through dark times and get stuck (like a broken record which keeps jumping back to the same point over and over again). Scales balance energy, and this is a unique technique developed to recalibrate energy centers. It can be used alongside reiki with color and vibration.

Work with a licensed healer and high conscious channel when using any energy healing modality, as it will bring you the best results on Earth.

Tarot / Oracle Cards

Tarot works because we have placed these cards in the midst in order to draw you out of thinking patterns and engage the sense of thought. Oracle is a guidance system which offers wisdom and insight into past, present and future life-driving themes and contracts. Three card types exist to try:

Oracle Cards

Channeled wisdom through high-conscious healers and artists. One shares wisdom in words, the other through art. There are a few decks which offer enlightened ideas, and these can be found in various places online. Ask before ordering any cards, "Are these for me? Can I work with them?" You will know instinctively if they are to be trusted and from whom they came – high or low vibrations.

Angel Cards

Like the Oracle they are channeled wisdom coming this time from the higher self through angels, guides and messengers. On Earth you have dropped the notion that you, too, are angels in disguise. To work with cards from higher guides is intentional. We place these in your midst to help All understand who they are as spiritual beings. Be conscious of whom they were designed by when choosing them. Look for high-conscious healers and not ones aligned to religious dogma, as these may be inaccurate. What comes from Love is always of high vibes. Angel cards should not judge or chastise, only gently guide ones into Love.

Energy Cards

Wise Ones know energy is everything. These are cards to guide you in regards to blockages in chakras. Use these when ones are struggling with deep hidden themes such as relationship issues and child-like behaviors. The energy of the card is infused with balance, and Ones should always handle these gently. Before guiding anyone with the cards be sure to pray and ask, "Help me dear All release the toxic charge of others' imbalance. I allow these cards to be free and clear of energy of others and let only what is love come in."

Tarot Cards

Sacred tarot has its own set of rules and regulations based upon the alignment of planets and stars. Use these when you are feeling called to planetary shifts and feel lost or confused. Only those aligned in truth will find balance through these. Be cautious when approached by someone to 'read your cards'. Ones should always be found not pushed into tarot. Go seeking and you will find truth. Be pulled in and you may be dealing with a lower vibrational reader.

Astrology

Astrologically speaking you are tied to the balance of energy. The sun, the moon and the stars all have effects on both moods and manifestations. This is why time is a critical factor in what shows up on Earth. Each of you has placed yourself in time precisely as necessary for the life you are meant to lead. When focusing on fear it may be because of the moon cycle, and it would do well to check where it is so you may know why you are struggling. Timing on Earth is different than Universe, Cosmic or Infinite time, which is why it takes practice to lose fear and believe. Use the stars as a roadmap to your every desire. It is written in the stars for you to discover. Astrological charts are a great indicator of what is to come and when; but remember when focusing on fear it is always possible to lose what had been chosen prior. There are both collective energy and individual charts available to All.

Vedic Astrology

The art of reading stars is an ancient practice and has its root in Sanskrit. Planetary shifts and alignment are necessary to keep cycles going, and you are tied to what is happening in the Universe, Cosmos and beyond. While guided on Earth between love and fear, you also must know what shifts are occurring in the skies. Dark ages, light ages and middle ages exist and are happening to All everywhere. What cycle you are in depends on what choices were made collectively planetarily. Seek further information on this topic and it may shed light on blockages and timing. It is most necessary to work with an astrologer of One mind and not a scientific healer.

Numerology

Numbers are sequential and used for purposes of shining a light on Yes or No.

111 – Yes, proceed.
222 – Hierarchal souls (angels/guides) agreeing in unison.
444 – Spirit visitors.
777 – Master teachers offering wisdom.

Life path numbers exist and every One has their own. Go seeking information through high conscious healers as to their meanings. Many exist and are accurate if the One in body is channeling All.

Movement Exercise

Yoga

The ancient art of Sanskrit has been practiced for century and is becoming more popular in the mainstream. An entire planet doing yoga would shift the consciousness immediately. Encourage every One to take up a practice at least once to twice a week.

It binds the chakras, opens the third eye and allows wisdom to flow. Flow is precisely why yoga is important. To flow through different positions keeps joints moving properly and elevates the conscious mind through peaceful mantras.

I am. Om Sansa.
Peace. Om Shanti.
Joy. Om Mudita.
Appreciate. Om Bhavana.

These and other mantras should be used during practice always.

Bandai

A fighting technique used in ancient times where Ones hold onto sticks and make thrust movements. Each movement is directly corelated to energy centers and causes a release of negative ions in the body. Picture the blockage and burst through it.

Sound Healing

Sound Bath

A joyful expression through music. Lay in prana. Close the eyes. Listen to sounds through instruments and vibration.

Crystal Bowls

Made with high vibrational materials, these bowls have been placed as means to connect you to the spiritual realm through various sounds which reach through the realms. Be cautious for fakes, as they do exist. Find a licensed practitioner who has been given bowls passed down from elders.

Meditation

The absence of sound. Sit quietly for as long as possible with no thought.

Singing

Using the throat chakra, place your hand on the neck and allow vibration to come through by various techniques such as mantras. Singing is a listening technique, as well. Angels and guides choose this modality to express delight or to nudge you out of a thinking pattern. Pay attention and you will find you are always singing a happy tune.

Chanting

Originally brought to light by the native Indians, this sound modality is straight from Love. Sound without word is restorative and temporarily shuts down the temporal lobe so you release ego and find soul.

Frequency

Everything is made of energy. Vibrate higher and you are immediately connecting to the Love of God/Life/Universe. Choose loving thoughts. Play happy music. Anything to bring you into joy is raising the frequency of Earth.

Rocks, Minerals, Flowers

There are many powerful healing elements which come from Mother Earth. Below are a few that are best to keep in homes and spaces. Use these as cleansing rituals and protective elements.

Selenite

Perfect for meditators as it raises the vibration of the room. Find it online, as selenite is hard to encounter when fake. It is abundantly available to All.

Crystal Quartz

Available in many different forms, crystal quartz is able to disperse energy and redirect it towards sunlight. Beware of fakes as many do exist. Find it from a licensed practitioner; one who has blessed it with healing properties is your best option.

Tanzanite

Tantric energy, placid and calming. Tanzanite is a wonderful element for sleep. Place it by the bedside for it will calm and center you when thoughts align to One.

Red Roses

Full of fragrance and light. These are angels in flower form. Appreciate them by planting some in your yard rather than plucking them. Let the natural fragrance and color align you to joy. Sending flowers is fine, but why cut the life force energy? Let it cycle naturally.

Chrysanthemums

The fall flower. Cycle of life. Keep them in your home. Plant them in your gardens. Stomp on them. Tear them up. They will always return as a reminder that life is a journey of life and death. Resilient plants with a heart of gold.

These are just a few. There are many to be found in nature and books to guide you. We offer advice to those seeking light. There are many other modalities to use, such as ayahuasca, medicinal shrubs and weeds. These are to be used sparingly and only with licensed and legal practitioners. Always use wisdom within before seeking guidance. Each knows what is best when higher callings ring out for you to try. If you are looking for something to 'fix' you, it must come through you not through anyone else. Our healers are merely facilitators. The Ones who heal are the Ones who know only they can.

Inside is where healing lives for All.

Acknowledgements And Gratitude By Laura

have been successful. I have been a failure. I have been depressed. I have been elated. But what I have never truly been is happy. Because happy in this world implies you have something to show for your life - a great job, a love partner, financial freedom, cars, boats, toys or millions of followers online. I have none of those things and yet I remain blissfully, unapologetically happy despite external circumstances.

When I found my happy place, I wasn't rich or in love. I didn't have a thriving career or the second or third baby I so desired and felt called to find. I had very few true friends, only a trusted few here and there. My family life wasn't perfect. I didn't love where I was living. I was between jobs, between love, between anything purely materialistic and mostly a failure. But I was happy, and that was an accomplishment in and of itself because I worked for it. It didn't just happen overnight or even in a year's time. I worked at it every single day for six long years.

Finding my truth, our truth took me on an epic journey of surrender as you have witnessed while reading these pages. One moment I would be on top of the world and the next in utter despair. I verged on depression almost daily in the beginning stages of awakening, but somewhere in the middle of it stopped feeling broken or suicidal. Three quarters of the way through my transformation is when I finally broke through and became more happy than sad, and that's when the real magic arrived – hope.

When I got to the end of my book, I realized all of my struggles, mishaps and hardship moments came along to grow me from a spiritual being of body/mind/soul to one with belief. You cannot recognize your essence until you have discovered it for yourself amidst chaos and ruin. The lucky Ones are the few who have awoken through easier circumstances. There are books for them, too. Every One has a modality which arrives precisely when needed, and this was how I arrived at happy. I finally had a window to another world; another way of living where I could thrive without actually needing or having anything at all. When I excepted it as truth, I was finally unabashedly free.

I wrote this book, but you can, too. Write your own with Spirit as your guide. Sit down, assess, ask questions and receive. We all know truth within. A whole life awaits your discovery and now is the time to remember.

Thank you, All

There will be those who see all of this as nonsense and to them I say, thank you. They have taught me more than anyone how to evolve beyond ego. What happens when you find truth is that you will allow everyone to find their own in whatever way and time frame they choose.

To my readers, thank you for taking this journey with me. I am grateful you have chosen to read this book as a starting point, a refresher or a stop along your own journey to Spirit. I hope you will do the exercises and return to these pages whenever you need a reminder. This journey with The All has changed me, and for that I am infinitely joyful.

I am forever grateful to my friends Lisa, Maria, Jo, Heidi, Courtney and Saarah, who have stuck with me this whole journey even when it didn't quite resonate. I have seen them transform, as well, and I am always happy to lend an ear and help them find their own light. I look forward to their desires becoming manifest in the world.

Thank you to Leesa Ellis and Valerie Costa for your publishing expertise and helping me get this book out to the world of seekers.

Family is everything and I'm thankful to my mom for always listening, even when thinking and believing I have joined some wacky cult. My dad and brother in Spirit form who show up in my heart always and in beautiful signs and messages.

Brenner, my everything. One day you, too, will share the light with All.

Thank you All, for making me a better human and for reminding me of soul.

WORKBOOK

Take the time to go through the exercises in the chapters provided. Use as much or as little of them as you need. Perhaps daily, once in a while, all the time. It's up to you. This is your journey. Remember. Extra space has been provided to journal.

Endnotes

1   *Sliding Doors* (Miramax Films, 1998).

2   Saltman, Laura. *The All of Everything, A Spiritual Guide to Inner World Domination.* Savaah Media., 2018, 117.

3   Saltman, Laura. *The All That Is,* Savaah Media, 2019, 186.

4   Saltman, Laura. *The All That Is,* Savaah Media, 2019, 308.

5   Saltman, Laura. *The All That Is,* Savaah Media, 2019, 89.

6   Saltman, Laura. *The All That Is,* Savaah Media, 2019, 111.

7   Saltman, Laura. *The All of The All,* Savaah Media, 2018.

8   Roberts, Jane, Seth, and Robert F. Butts. *Seth Speaks: the Eternal Validity of the Soul.* San Rafael, CA: New World Library, 1994.

9   Saltman, Laura *The All of Everything, A Spiritual Guide to Inner World Domination.* Savaah Media., 2018, 133.

10 Roberts, Jane, and *Seth. The Seth Material.* Manhasset, N Y: New Awareness Network Inc., 2001

11 Saltman, Laura *The All of Everything, A Spiritual Guide to Inner World Domination.* Savaah Media., 2018, 185.

12 Saltman, Laura. *The All That Is,* Savaah Media, 2019

Made in the USA
Monee, IL
25 June 2021